EXPLORING BLACK AMERICA

A History and Guide

EXPLORING BLACK AMERICA

A History and Guide

MARCELLA THUM

ATHENEUM   1975   NEW YORK

The author wishes to thank the many librarians,
archivists, curators, historians—and friends—for
their assistance in collecting the material
for this book. And a special thanks to my sister,
Gladys Thum, for her never-ending moral support.
My gratitude is great, but the errors
in the book—hopefully few—are my own.

Library of Congress Cataloging in Publication Data

Thum, Marcella.   Exploring Black America.
SUMMARY: A guidebook to museums, monuments, and
historic sites commemorating the achievements of
black Americans and discussions of the aspects of
black history and culture the sites represent.
1. Historic sites—United States—Guidebooks—
Juvenile literature.   2. Negroes—History—Juvenile
literature.   3. United States—Description and travel
—1960-   —Guidebooks—Juvenile literature.
[1. Negroes—History.   2. United States—Description
and travel]   I. Title.   E159.T45   917.3′04′92
74-19428   ISBN 0-689-30462-5

To Gladys

Contents

EXPLORING BLACK AMERICA

A History and Guide

Introduction

For many years there were missing pages in history books about America. These were the pages that told of the part that black Americans played in the development of our country. Today historians are filling in those missing pages, but information about black historic sites and landmarks is still lacking in most guidebooks of the United States.

Young—and not so young—visitors to Washington, D.C., rush from the Lincoln Memorial to the Washington Monument. Most of them are not aware of the fact that only a few miles from the Washington Monument is a National Historic Site dedicated to another great American—Cedar Hill, the home of Frederick Douglass, who has been called the George Washington of black America. Or how many visitors to the National Gallery of Art realize that only a short distance away is the elegant Museum of African Art, the first museum in the country to exhibit only African and Afro-American art.

Most tourists to historic Boston are sure to visit the Old Granary Burying Ground, where three signers of the Declaration of Independence are buried. How many of them know that in the same cemetery is also buried Crispus Attucks, a black man and the first man to be killed in the Boston Massacre—or that a monument to Crispus Attucks and the men killed with him stands in the nearby Boston Common?

How many sightseers to fascinating old Charleston, South Carolina, ever learn from their guidebooks that one of the most unique museums in the country, The Old Slave Mart Museum, is located not far from the center of town?

Admittedly, during the days of slavery and the long, hard years afterward, black men and women had neither the wealth nor leisure to look back upon their heritage and try to preserve what they could for their children and their children's children. In recent years, however, a small but growing number of museums have been formed—or already established landmarks have been refurbished—honoring black Americans and the role they played in the shaping of this nation.

It is impossible, naturally, in one short book to cover the 400-year-long cultural, political and military history of black Americans. Instead, each chapter in this book is intended to serve as a brief introduction to some aspect of black life in America. Also, each chapter provides background material for young tourists visiting or planning to visit the sites described at the end of each chapter.

Many black landmarks have long been erased by

time. Often only a plaque remains to mark the spot where an historic event took place. Inasmuch as possible, the sites included at the end of each chapter are not a listing of such plaques but are actual homes, museums, parks, battlefields, forts, colleges, churches and monuments of all kinds directly related to black history. All the sites listed may be visited and viewed by the public for only a small fee or no fee at all.

Although visits to these landmarks should be of special interest to young black people, such visits would be of equal, if not more, benefit to all young—and old—Americans. As the United States celebrates its two-hundredth birthday, it is important that the nation acknowledge its debt to all its people. For only by learning as much as possible about each other, sharing the mutual experiences and heritage of all our many peoples, can America one day be truly indivisible, with liberty and justice for all.

DAYS
OF
SLAVERY

In 1756, in a small African village in the present-day country of Nigeria, eleven-year-old Olaudah Equiano was playing near his home with his young sister. His parents and brothers, along with the other adults in the village, were off working in the fields. There was a protective wooden barricade around the Equiano home, but two men and a woman managed to scale the wall. They overpowered both of the children before they had time to cry out for help. The intruders placed gags over the children's mouths and, tying their wrists, carried them off into the woods.

Olaudah was never to see his parents or family again. Within a few days his sister was taken from his side and sold by the kidnappers to a slave trader. The separation so grieved Olaudah that he had to be force-fed to be kept alive. Olaudah himself was sold and resold but always watched closely so that he could not escape, and always taken further and further away into strange new country. Finally he realized that even if he could escape, he was not sure he could find his way back home.

At the end of seven months he arrived, still a captive, at the western seacoast of Africa. Here a huge ship rode at anchor, the largest Olaudah had ever seen. Aboard the ship were strange men with white faces and long hair who spoke an odd language. Olaudah was terrified of the men and even more frightened when he saw the cargo of the ship—row upon row of black men, women and children, their faces filled with despair, all chained together.

Olaudah was chained with the rest, and the sufferings he had already endured were nothing to what he was now to encounter. The human cargo was placed below deck, so packed together that there was scarcely room for them to turn; the air so hot and foul-smelling that Olaudah felt sure he would suffocate. He and his fellow victims were given just enough food and water to keep them alive. Those who refused to eat were flogged until they submitted; but then Olaudah, on one of the times he was taken above deck for exercise, also saw one of the white men flog another white sailor to death, then toss his body overboard. Watching, Olaudah trembled. What manner of men were these? And he envied the two black men who, during an exercise period, jumped overboard and drowned, and the other slaves who died from disease and ill treatment on the voyage.

When the slave ship finally reached an island called Barbados, merchants and planters came aboard to examine the cargo. The frightening rumor spread among the captives that these men were cannibals. Olaudah was much relieved when he was told he would be put to work, not eaten alive.

Olaudah, however, did not stay in Barbados. He was shipped to the colony of Virginia, where he was resold again to a Lieutenant in the British Navy. Olaudah served as a seaman for several years, changing his name to Gustavus Vassa. More fortunate than most, he was able to buy his freedom in 1766. Afterward he traveled extensively and even managed in 1789 to write and have published the story of his life (which may still be read today), entitled *The Interesting Narrative of the Life of Olaudah Equiano, or Gustavus Vassa.*

The story of Olaudah's adventurous life makes fascinating reading; but the kidnapping of young children, like Olaudah and his sister, was not an unusual occurrence in eighteenth-century Africa. For more than a century Africa had been a profitable hunting ground for European slave dealers. These men made fortunes, either buying kidnapped men, women and children from unscrupulous Africans or encouraging warfare among neighboring tribes. Then the dealers bought the defeated warriors, as well as their families, from the victorious tribal chief, although some African tribes insisted upon keeping the slaves for their own use.

It was on August 20, 1619, that slavery reached America. On that date a Dutch ship sailed into the harbor of Jamestown, Virginia. The ship's arrival was little noted except for a brief mention by John Rolfe in his Journal: ". . . there came in a Dutch man-of-warre that sold us 20 Negars." Yet no other cargo ever shipped to the colonies was to prove so explosive an influence in shaping the future of America—for good and for evil.

No one knows exactly what happened to those first twenty African people to reach America. Some histo-

9

rians believe they were treated much like the white indentured servants who were sent to the colonies. They worked on the tobacco plantations, and after serving their "time," bought their freedom and some land of their own, married and had children.

Tobacco plantations—and tobacco was the most important product of these early Southern colonies in America—needed a great deal of cheap labor. Mostly they used indentured servants shipped to the colonies from England. In those days, a man or woman could be "indentured" or forced into bondage for not paying debts, or a son or daughter might be indentured for a father's debts. Molly Welsh, the white English mother of the black inventor Benjamin Banneker, was shipped to Maryland and indentured for seven years because she was accused of stealing a pail of milk!

The planters, though, had a problem. They could not depend upon a constant supply of indentured servants. And these servants, once their indenture was up, left the plantations to find easier work—or set up, as some black men did, their own plantations with indentured labor. The planters discovered they needed to own permanently the labor of the men and women who worked the tobacco fields if they were to make a profit.

Under British common law that governed the early American colonies, it was unthinkable, if not illegal, for a white indentured servant to be permanently enslaved. On the other hand, enslavement of black people was commonplace in the world of the seventeenth century. The Spanish and French used black people as slaves in their colonies, as did the English in the West Indies. And most important, by 1672 the Royal African Company, chartered by the British government, dominated the world slave trade. It was in the royal interest, therefore, that her American colonies be the consumer for her human cargo.

By 1669 the law had already changed in the Virginia colony. The early Africans might have been lucky enough to serve their time and secure their freedom, but the black people who arrived later were not so fortunate. Under the law they—and their children—were forced to serve in bondage for life. Most of the other Southern colonies also believed they needed such slave laws, securing their black labor, in order to survive.

In New England the situation was different. While the first slave was sold in New England in 1638, and slavery was by no means restricted to southern colonies, farms in the North were small. The use of slaves as field hands never became the custom in the New England colonies. Instead of being a plantation owner, the wealthy man in Massachusetts or New York made his fortune by becoming a merchant or shipowner. Most of the American ships used to transport slaves from Africa and the West Indies sailed from New England ports and were mastered by Yankee sea captains. Although there were those shipowners and captains who refused to carry slaves as cargo, nevertheless, slave trading became one of America's earliest and best paying businesses.

What was life like for those African-Americans who were slaves? A man like Gustavus Vassa was the exception. Very few slaves ever learned to read, much less write, so written records telling the true story are difficult to find. There are, however, journals kept by plantation owners and diaries and letters written by visitors to the South. There are court records and newspapers, too. In the nineteenth century there were also a great many autobiographies written and published by escaped slaves

11

or free black men and women with the assistance of white and black abolition societies.

Also, in 1934, under a government Federal Works Project, thousands of former slaves still living throughout the United States were interviewed. Their firsthand stories of how life actually was during slave days, including photographs of the former slaves and documents about slavery, were finally printed in seventeen volumes, which are kept in the Rare Book Room of the Library of Congress. The more than 2,000 stories contained in these volumes are a tribute to the indestructible human spirit of these men and women.

Most of the people interviewed were born in the United States and had not endured the cruelty of the voyage from Africa aboard a slave ship. We can be sure that only the strongest man, woman and child survived that three-week to three-month trip. The records that do exist indicate that thirty percent of the slaves died en route.

Once he reached the new world and was sold upon the auction block, how well a slave lived depended completely on the financial circumstances and character of his owner. House servants on a wealthy plantation might have quarters above the kitchen or live on a street of wooden plank cottages near the "big house." Women servants often slept on a pallet outside their mistress' bedroom door. At Boone Hall Plantation in South Carolina, which had 1,000 slaves, the cottages of the house servants were built of brick with tile roofs. On the Kingsley Plantation in Florida, each individual cottage housing two slave families was built of tabby, a mixture of oyster shells and lime, and had its own fireplace.

Field hands, however, seldom fared as well. They lived near the fields in little more than hovels, with often

12

a dozen slaves huddled together in one small room, the only furniture a bed of straw, and no fireplace, only the wind whistling through cracks in the walls.

Booker T. Washington, writing of his quarters as a slave for the Burroughs family, said that, "The log cabin had a fireplace and a 'potatoe hole' but no wooden floor or glass windows. John, my older brother, Amanda, my sister, and myself, had a pallet on the dirt floor, or, to be more correct, we slept in and on a bundle of filthy rags laid upon the dirt floor."

Washington pointed out, though, that his owners, James and Elizabeth Burroughs and their fourteen children, lived little better than their slaves. When a family owned only a few acres of land and one or two slaves, the slaves lived in much the same fashion as the family, sharing their hardships as well as their few luxuries. The food for the slave in a poor family was, as Washington recalled, "a piece of bread here and a scrap of meat there."

Josiah Henson, an escaped slave who had worked on a large plantation, remembers that his principal food consisted of cornmeal and salt herrings. "We had two regular meals in a day, breakfast at twelve o'clock after laboring from daylight, and supper when the work of the remainder of the day was over. Our dress was a tow-cloth . . . and a pair of coarse shoes once a year."

The day's work on a tobacco, cotton, hemp, indigo or sugarcane plantation was long and backbreaking, or as one former-slave said, "from can to can't." Punishment was severe for those workers who shirked their jobs. Yet despite the penalties, the slaves devised many methods of outsmarting their overseers or, as Josiah Henson said, "first-rate tricks to dodge work."

Hoe and ax handles would unaccountably break—so

many, in fact, that unusually thick handles were constructed especially for use by slaves. A slave would develop an incurable ailment or pretend clumsiness or stupidity to get out of work. Crops would be mysteriously destroyed. A barn or stable would burn. There were so many fires on southern plantations that for a while the American Fire Insurance Company refused to insure property in the South.

The extreme cruelty in the punishment of slaves who shirked work, ran away or simply, according to their master, acted in an insolent fashion, has been well documented. The floggings, brandings, mutilations are mentioned too often in journals, diaries, court cases and newspaper accounts to be considered unusual. But there were also those slave owners who realized it was more sensible, as well as more profitable, to feed, clothe and treat their slaves in a reasonably humane fashion. After all, an adult field hand in 1860 was worth $1,000 in Virginia and $1,500 in New Orleans. In Louisiana one rice planter hired Irish immigrants to clear his fields—a difficult job that often caused injuries—rather than risk the valuable investment he had in his slaves.

Even the kindest of slave owners, though, always had the nagging fear of a slave uprising. Despite the history books, which have made it appear that the slave was a passive, docile creature who loved his chains, from the very beginning of slavery in America, there were slave revolts.

Undoubtedly the most publicized slave uprising took place near Jerusalem, Southampton County, Virginia, in 1831. Even as a boy, the young slave Nat Turner was convinced by his parents that he was "intended for some great purpose." As he grew older, he quickly learned to read and was looked up to by the other slaves for his leadership and wisdom.

Becoming religious, he devoted his time to fasting and prayer. Eventually he saw visions that made him believe he was chosen to inflict the wrath of the Lord upon the planters. He gathered twenty to thirty followers to help him carry out his mission; they were other young rebellious slaves like himself, pledged to secrecy.

The night of August 20, Nat Turner and six of his lieutenants met to make final plans, vowing that "neither age nor sex was to be spared." They began their bloody trail of vengeance at the home of Nat Turner's master, Joseph Travis. In almost military fashion, the troop of slaves moved along from house to house, ransacking and murdering, increasing their forces until there were sixty men with Turner.

The trail ended after the death of fifty whites and the final capture and hanging of Nat Turner on November 11, 1831. Forty other blacks, some in no way connected with the uprising, were either murdered or executed in connection with the revolt.

Nat Turner's Rebellion was by no means the only slave revolt nor the first. The records show that there were dozens of small slave uprisings and at least nine large-scale slave revolts in America between 1691 and 1865. In New York City in 1712 more than thirty slaves revolted and attempted to burn down the city. In Louisiana in 1811 Charles Deslondes and hundreds of slaves marched on New Orleans and were only stopped by U.S. troops who killed sixty-six of the slaves in open battle. Even before Nat Turner's revolt, Gabriel Prosser had led a slave insurrection in Virginia in 1800, and Denmark Vesey another in South Carolina in 1822.

Few of the revolts succeeded. Some of the rebellions

15

57694

were betrayed by fellow slaves, but in any case the slaves involved in the conflict were always greatly outnumbered, had few weapons and no hope of escaping and blending in among the white population.

Yet the planters still feared slave uprisings. News of an insurrection in even a faraway state could turn plantations into armed camps. Patrols searched the roads nightly for slaves out without passes; women slept with guns or axes beside their beds for protection. It was this never-ending dread of slaves turning upon their masters that brought about the most stringent and cruelest laws restricting the life of a slave.

A slave could not own property or legally marry. He could not leave a plantation without a pass. He had no control over the lives of his own children. He could not testify in court against a white man or have any legal rights except those the white man chose to give him. He could not strike back at a white man even in self-defense.

To be sure, there were those men and women who adjusted as much as possible to the chains placed upon them. The slave who played his role with a cheerful subservience was often rewarded. The slave, however, who resisted such a role was an affront and a danger to his owner. For slavery to exist at all, it was vital that the slave consider himself or herself inferior to his or her master. Only through such repression of all pride and dignity could the slave owner hope to completely control "his property."

If a slave owner died and his property was to be distributed, or if he had a bad year in growing crops, or if a slave proved too surly and difficult to train, then the slave could be sold at public auction.

Mother was separated from child; husband from wife.

16

Often slave auctions were held in the most prominent section of a city, in public squares, city halls and marketplaces. European visitors to Washington, D.C., were shocked to discover that a wealthy slave trader had his slave pens in a house across the square from the White House (in what is now called the Decatur House).

To settle estates, slave auctions were held at the eastern door of the St. Louis Courthouse, in the center of the business district. Before an auction, the slaves would be spruced up, the women given new calico frocks, the men new suits and shoes. A visitor watching one such auction in St. Louis reported the auctioneer's words on a sale, "How much is offered for this woman? She is a good cook, good washer, a good obedient servant. She has got religion!"

Although slavery was commonly accepted in America by the time of the Revolutionary War, not everyone approved of the institution. Even Southern political leaders like George Washington, Thomas Jefferson and Patrick Henry, although they owned slaves, realized the injustice of the system. Patrick Henry wrote, "Every thinking honest man rejects it [slavery] in speculation, how few in practice . . . I am drawn along by the general inconvenience of living without them; I will not, I cannot justify it." Patrick Henry's sister, Elizabeth, however, was able to adjust to the "inconvenience" and freed all the slaves she owned.

Thomas Jefferson, who tried and failed to have the abolition of slavery written into the Constitution, wrote prophetically, "Indeed I tremble for my country when I reflect that God is just; that his justice cannot sleep forever. . . ."

In the North the Quakers were among the first to speak out against the evil of one human being owning

17

another. Colonial patriots Benjamin Franklin, Dr. Benjamin Rush, James Otis, Thomas Paine and others vigorously denounced slavery. Samuel Adams, the firebrand of the Revolution, when his admirers gave his wife a slave girl as a gift, refused to allow the girl into the house until she was a free woman.

Then in 1793 Eli Whitney invented the cotton gin. Whitney has been called the savior of the South, but for slaves, his invention was the knell of doom. Before the invention of the gin, it took a worker a whole day to gin a pound of cotton lint by hand; cotton was a small industry, producing only 6,000 bales a year. After the invention of the gin, production of cotton grew to over 6,000,000 bales a year. Naturally more and more slaves were needed to work the cotton fields upon which finally most of the economy of the South depended.

The same situation held true in the deep South of Louisiana. There sugarcane had been grown without a great deal of success, although in 1795 Etienne de Bore, a Creole planter, had succeeded in granulating the syrup from the cane into sugar. Ironically, in 1843, it was a Creole Negro, Norbert Rillieux, who invented a process of boiling the cane juice in vacuum pans to make sugar crystal. Thereupon, sugarcane, like cotton, became extremely profitable to grow. Also, like cotton plantations, sugarcane plantations required a large labor force, and more and more slaves were imported or "sold south" to meet this demand.

Although working the cane fields was hard, brutal labor, with slaves dying of malaria and cholera (as did many white residents of Louisiana of the time), there was some difference between the American and the Creole ownership of slaves. The Creoles were of French and Spanish stock with a more tolerant Latin-American

18

attitude toward the institution of slavery. In many ways the Catholic church controlled the lives of the Creole planters, and the priests frowned upon excessive cruelty toward slaves. In the eyes of the Catholic Church, black men and women were considered to have souls the same as whites, which was considered by some slave owners in other parts of the South as an outlandish idea. Slaves in Louisiana were encouraged to become Christians and allowed to marry. For a while marriages were also allowed between whites and blacks.

Along the Cane River area of Louisiana in the 1800s, there grew up a settlement of Afro-Creole planters. A deeply religious people with a great pride of race, they built their own large sugarcane plantations and often owned slaves themselves. One of the oldest of these families was the Metoyer family, founded by Marie Thérèse, a freed slave who married Thomas Metoyer from Paris. The Metoyer family owned the lovely plantation house called Yucca, still standing today, overlooking the Cane River.

Not all slaves in the South worked as house servants or field hands. Some were trained to be blacksmiths, carpenters, wheelwrights, brickmasons and in other occupations necessary to keep the largely self-sufficient plantations running. Such skilled craftsmen were often hired out profitably by their owners. Occasionally a slave was allowed to keep a small portion of his "hire" money and use it to buy his freedom. Also, through the years, a growing number of slaves in the South worked in factories, such as the Bell Factory in Alabama, a textile mill whose 100 looms were operated by slave labor.

The actual number of slave owners in the South was relatively small. Three-fourths of the Southern whites

19

managed to live without slaves. And 50 percent of those who did own slaves owned less than five. But the big planters ruled the South politically and economically, and even those who didn't own slaves had a vested interest in maintaining the belief that slavery was a necessary if "peculiar" institution.

What of the blacks who were not slaves? In 1840 there were over 400,000 free black men and women in the country. Some of these, like Amos Fortune, had scrimped and saved long years to buy their freedom and that of their families. Others had been given freedom, or been manumitted, as it was called, as a reward for military service. Some were freed by will at the death of a master; this was true of George Washington's slaves. Some had been born of free parents. A few slaves sued for their freedom in a court of law, like Elizabeth Freeman, who won her case in Massachusetts in 1781, and Dred Scott, who lost his in Missouri in 1857.

Most of the free blacks lived in the cities. A check of the city directories before the Civil War shows that FMC (free men of color) engaged in many different and varied occupations. They were photographers, teachers, dentists, carpenters, tavern keepers, ministers. In New Orleans the majority of skilled artisans were blacks.

Over half of the American seamen before the Civil War were black, many serving on whaling ships. There were even a few free blacks who managed to amass small fortunes, such as Thomy Lafon of New Orleans and James Forten of Philadelphia.

Whatever free blacks managed to achieve took talent, industry and persistence, for they often met the same prejudice as slaves, whether they lived in the North or South. In many states a black man, although free, couldn't appear as a witness in a court case or have his children attend public schools, even though his taxes helped pay for the school. In the South the position of a free black could be precarious. Some Southern states did not allow free blacks to live within their borders, and any who came into the state were automatically considered slaves. It was understandable why the slave owner was not happy to see a free black man or woman achieve any measure of success. He secured his hold over his slaves partly by convincing them that a black man was too inferior to possibly make a living outside of slavery.

Free blacks were only a small portion of the blacks in America before the Civil War (never more than 13 percent were free), but they were an important group. They formed a hard core of agitators, holding meetings, lecturing, writing pamphlets, presenting petitions to legislators, constantly pressing for the abolishment of slavery. They were, in effect, in the forefront of the abolition movement before there was such a movement.

The Constitution provided that importation of slaves into the United States was forbidden after 1808. Unfortunately, the young navy that America possessed at that time had neither the men nor the ships to enforce the law. Slaves continued to be smuggled in illegally by unscrupulous Yankee ship captains and bought by equally unscrupulous Southern slaveholders.

The last slave ship to arrive illegally in the United States was the *Clotilde,* arriving in Mobile, Alabama, in August of 1857. Captain Mohear purchased his cargo of slaves from a Dahomey Prince of West Africa who had raided a peaceful Tarkar village further inland and sold 130 of his captives to the captain. One of the captives, Ka Zoola, could have escaped but went with the

21

slave ship so that he could be with his wife. In order to avoid capture by the authorities when he reached Mobile, Captain Mohear set the slaves ashore, hiding them in a canebrake, and burned his ship. Because he could not find buyers for his illegal shipment, the captain was forced to keep the slaves himself and finally to free them when the Civil War started.

As it turned out, the group of slaves that arrived aboard the *Clotilde* was unique in black history. Most slaves reaching America were sold apart and seldom saw people from their own native village again. Under the leadership of Ka Zoola (in English pronunciation, Cud-Joe Lewis) and his wife, Celia, the Tarkars managed to stay together, and after the war formed a village called "Affriky Town." A proud people, they retained the customs they had brought with them from Africa. They ruled and judged themselves, kept their Tarkar names and spoke the Tarkar language among themselves. Although they never gave up yearning and hoping to return to their homeland, they built a good life for themselves, farming, living frugally, and at last converted to Christianity, building their own church. Descendants of the Tarkars still alive in and around the settlement of Plateau, Alabama, as African Town is called today.

It took a Civil War, which almost split the nation in two, to end the infamous system of slavery in America. Today one can travel throughout the United States without seeing any physical evidence that, in fact, slavery ever existed. There are those who feel it should be that way: that slavery was an unfortunate stain on the history of America and should best be forgotten. Yet the history of a country is not only its triumphs but its failures as well, its flaws as well as its virtues. To blot

22

out the history of slavery is to demean the memory of those thousands of men and women who, although brought to this country in chains, helped beat back the wilderness and forge a nation. Their lives are woven into the very warp and woof of America.

If one searches hard enough, landmarks from the days of slavery can be found. The lovely plantation homes that still dot the southland are, in a way, a monument to slavery—although the debt is seldom acknowledged. One such restored ante-bellum plantation home in Georgia proudly proclaims that "plantation life depended to a large degree on the self-sustaining efforts, ingenuity and management of owner and family." The statement is not accurate. The gracious lives of the Southern planters, the beautiful ante-bellum homes themselves, could never have come into being, much less been maintained, without the constant labor of hundreds of slaves.

The slave quarter or "the street," that was once an inevitable part of such plantations, has disappeared on most that remain. Some cottages, built of brick, still stand in some places, although they are now used for far different purposes than their original reasons for being. The pens that once housed slaves in the Decatur Mansion are today used as offices; the slave quarters behind the Beauregard Mansion in New Orleans were made into a study where the famous novelist Frances Parkinson Keyes wrote many of her books. At the University of Virginia botanical gardens in Boyce, Virginia, a part of the Orland E. White Research Arboretum is housed in slave quarters built in 1825.

There are a few surviving slave quarters that are open to the public, some in picturesque, crumbled ruins, some restored much as they were during slave days. And there are other landmarks, too, which help tell the almost forgotten story of this period of American history.

They are more than landmarks. They are a reminder of the many black men and women who died, fighting for freedom, and of the thousands of others who endured the years of bondage and oppression, somehow managing to maintain their self-respect, pride and dignity against overwhelming odds. They tell the story of a remarkable people and their indomitable will to survive.

Like all other immigrants to America, the Afro-American's roots reach back across the ocean to a culture and lifestyle uniquely his own. For many years little was known of African culture and history. Today, however, there are several outstanding collections in American museums that give a good introduction to how the African lived—his technical skills, handicrafts, weapons, religion and tribal life.

MUSEUM OF THE PHILADELPHIA CIVIC CENTER

This museum houses one of the largest and oldest African collections in the country with many rare artifacts that cannot be duplicated elsewhere in America. The great bulk of the collection comes from the west coast of Africa, which has contributed the most to the black population and Afro-American culture of the United States.

Location: Museum of the Philadelphia Civic Center, Civic Center Boulevard at 34th Street, Philadelphia, Pennsylyania.

No admission charge. Guided tours and gallery talks and demonstrations by artists and craftsmen.

AMERICAN MUSEUM OF NATURAL HISTORY

One of the most interesting collections on African culture in the United States is housed in this museum. The exhibit areas are built to resemble African round houses with green carpeting

24

underfoot, the sound of African music and even the scent of grass and forest air!

The many exhibits in the Hall of Man in Africa cover the wide diversity of peoples and social systems in Africa—at least 1,000 culturally different groups, each of which may have a language and way of life very much different from its nearest neighbor.

All the exhibits in the Hall are fully labeled for easy reading, and trained guides are available to assist visitors.

Location: American Museum of Natural History, Central Park West at 79th Street, New York, New York.

No admission fee. Donations accepted.

NATIONAL MUSEUM OF NATURAL HISTORY
(THE SMITHSONIAN INSTITUTION)

The Africa Hall in the National Museum of Natural History has a broad collection of exhibits that explain the lifestyle of the traditional African, who still may be found in rural Africa.

Artifacts displayed include African art, household implements, dance costumes, musical instruments, religious ritual equipment and weapons.

Location: National Museum of Natural History, The Smithsonian Institution, 10th and Constitution Avenue, N.W., Washington, D.C.

No admission charge.

NATIONAL MUSEUM OF HISTORY AND TECHNOLOGY
(THE SMITHSONIAN INSTITUTION)

Of particular interest in this museum is an exhibit entitled "African Backgrounds and the Beginning of Slavery." The materials included—wood carvings, metalwork, textiles, ivory—are of African origin. Other items, such as face jugs and hand-woven baskets, were made in early America by slaves and show their African heritage.

Location: National Museum of History and Technology, Hall of Everyday Life in the American Past, Constitution Avenue between 12th and 14th streets, N.W., Washington, D.C.

No admission charge.

25

Other museums also have good to excellent African collections from which a visitor can learn a great deal about African history, social life and customs. A select list of such museums, follows:

Dartmouth College Museum, East Wheelock, Hanover, New Hampshire. No admission charge.

Everhart Museum of Natural History, Science and Art, Nay Aug Park, Scranton, Pennsylvania. No admission charge.

Field Museum of Natural History, Roosevelt Road at Lake Shore Drive, Chicago, Illinois. Small admission charge.

Haffenreffer Museum of Anthropology, Mt. Hope Grant, Bristol, Rhode Island. No admission charge.

Martin and Osa Johnson Safari Museum, Inc., 16 South Grant Street, Chanute, Kansas. Admission charge.

Milwaukee Public Museum, 800 West Wells Street, Milwaukee, Wisconsin. No admission charge.

University Museum, 33rd and Spruce streets, Philadelphia, Pennsylvania. No admission charge.

JAMESTOWN HISTORIC SITE

It was at Jamestown colony, Virginia, that African slaves first landed in 1619 and the first black child was born. His name was William Tucker.

Over the years the original Jamestown settlement fell into ruins and few of the original buildings are still standing. However, today historic Jamestown is being restored and is part of the Colonial National Historic Park.

At the Visitor Center is a museum displaying artifacts from the early days of Jamestown. One of the exhibits describes the important role that black Americans played in the everyday life of this early settlement.

Adjacent to the historic Jamestown site is Jamestown Festival Park, with many interesting exhibits from colonial Virginia, including a reconstructed James Fort, Chief Powhatan's Lodge and replicas of the ships that first brought settlers to Virginia.

Location: Jamestown Visitor Center is at the Jamestown terminus of the Colonial Parkway, a road that runs from Yorktown battlefield to Williamsburg to Jamestown, Virginia.

26

Admission charge to both Jamestown Historic Site and to Jamestown Festival Park.

SLAVE BLOCKS

In many communities slaves were sold on the steps of a courthouse or in open-air auctions, where black men, women and children mounted blocks so that they could be better seen by the audience of prospective purchasers. At least two such slave auction blocks have survived.

One is located at Charles and Williams Street, Fredericksburg, Virginia. The other auction block is on the Courthouse green in Washington, Kentucky.

It was at Washington, Kentucky, that Harriet Beecher Stowe watched slaves being bought and sold. The horror of the experience stayed with her, and later she used the scene when she wrote her famous novel, *Uncle Tom's Cabin.*

THE OLD SLAVE MART MUSEUM

Some communities, such as Charleston, South Carolina, did not approve of slaves being sold out in the street, and an ordinance was passed that slaves must be sold inside licensed markets. One such building in Charleston was called Ryan's Mart, and there real estate, slaves and other property were sold.

Today The Old Slave Mart, as it called, has been turned into a museum of the cultural history of the black American.

Displayed in the museum are documents and handbills from slave days, examples of African art, as well as one of the largest collections of slave-made handicraft in the United States—cane-back chairs, baskets, trunks, farm tools, delicately woven bedcovers and lace, furniture, toys and household implements of all kinds. In some cases the influence of the African heritage may be seen clearly in the slave-made product.

Location: The Old Slave Mart, 6 Chalmers Street, Charleston, South Carolina.

Small admission charge. Special arrangements for groups.

CHICAGO PUBLIC LIBRARY

The G.A.R. Memorial Hall of the Chicago Public Library contains exhibits relating to slavery, the abolition movement and the Civil War. Included in the exhibits on slavery are copper slave tags, a slave whip, notices posted for runaway slaves, bills of sale for slaves and antislavery tracts.

Location: G.A.R. Memorial Hall, Chicago Public Library, 78 East Washington Street, Chicago, Illinois.

No admission charge.

MELROSE HOUSE

The first Melrose House (originally called Yucca) was built about 1750 for Marie Thérèse Metoyer, a freed slave. Her grandson, Louis, built the present lovely main house in 1833.

Also on the plantation is an unusual "Africa House" of brick and cypress from which Marie and Thomas Metoyer controlled the more than fifty slaves who worked their 2,000-acre sugarcane plantation on the Cane River.

By the time of the Civil War, Melrose House had passed into the hands of white plantation owners, but many of the Metoyer possessions and furniture may still be seen in the house.

The buildings at Melrose are open for annual tours by the public the second weekend in October each year. At other times there is a committee whose members will set up tours upon request.

Location: Melrose House is located near Natchitoches, Louisiana, on Louisiana 119, 6 miles north of Derry, Louisiana.

Admission charge.

COLONIAL WILLIAMSBURG

When the capital of Virginia was moved from Williamsburg to Richmond in 1780, Williamsburg became a small, sleepy college town with many of its historic buildings falling into ruin.

The town was restored, beginning in 1926, so that today for a visitor to walk down the brick paved streets of Williamsburg is to step back into the eighteenth century.

There is little written record of what life was like for the free blacks and slaves who lived in Williamsburg in the eighteenth century. Most of them were undoubtedly house servants or worked as skilled craftsmen in the many shops of the town— their contributions anonymous and forgotten but essential to the colonial economy.

28

There are, however, several examples of living quarters of slaves in Williamsburg, as well as the homes of famous and not so famous men and women who lived, worked and made history in colonial days.

Wythe House. One of the loveliest of the many restored homes in Williamsburg belonged to George Wythe. Mr. Wythe was Thomas Jefferson's law professor and one of the most influential Americans of his day. Although many outstanding men in colonial Virginia disliked slavery, George Wythe was one of the few who acted upon his principles. He firmly believed that "the birthright of every human being is freedom" and that black Americans should have the same rights as white Americans. He freed his slaves while he was still alive.

Despite Wythe's efforts on behalf of black people, the black man was still regarded as property rather than a person. He could not, for example, appear in court as a witness against a white man. Ironically, in 1806 when George Wythe was poisoned with arsensic by his grand nephew, the black servant who witnessed the deed was not allowed to appear in court to testify against the murderer, and the grand nephew was acquitted.

The Wythe house and outbuildings, including the servant quarters, are open to the public.

Location: Wythe House, Palace Green, south of Prince George Street.

Brush-Everard House. More modest than the Wythe house, this frame house has been carefully restored to its former elegance, complete with brick kitchen, wooden smokehouse, delightful gardens and slave quarters in the scullery or kitchen.

Location: Brush-Everard House, east side of Palace Green.

Governor's Palace. It is probably at the Governor's Palace that the talented black musician Sy Gilliat played his fiddle in the beautifully decorated ballroom. Outside the palace are elaborately landscaped gardens, as well as a smokehouse, laundry, scullery and a black groom's quarters in the stables.

Concerts are still given for visitors in the evening by candlelight at the Governor's Palace. The musicians are dressed in eighteenth-century style, with wigs and satin vests, much the same clothes as Sy Gilliat might have worn.

Location: Governor's Palace, north end of the Palace Green.

Bruton Parish Church. The records of this church, erected in 1711, show that George Washington was godfather to fourteen slave children baptized here. This church is a strong link between the past and the present, since it has been in continuous use as a church from the day it was consecrated.

Location: Bruton Parish Church, the corner of Duke of Gloucester Street and Palace Green.

Raleigh's Tavern. Today Raleigh's Tavern is a restaurant, but in the eighteenth century it was the center of Williamsburg's social life and also a favorite place for slave auctions.

Location: Raleigh's Tavern is located at Duke of Gloucester Street near the capitol.

Location: The colonial town of Williamsburg is located at the junction of Interstate 64 and Virginia 143, 50 miles southeast of Richmond, Virginia.

Admission charge to Williamsburg.

MOUNT VERNON

The home of George Washington, like many other plantations, was a self-sufficient little empire. There were about ninety slaves in residence at Mount Vernon Farm in 1786. Many of them lived in small neat houses along service lanes. Some of them lived in the same building where they worked. The ten or more women slaves constantly employed spinning and knitting (the wool, flax and cotton were grown on the farm) lived in the Spinning House Quarters.

Mount Vernon and its outbuildings are today open to the public. Two of the interiors, in addition to many others that have been restored, have been furnished and equipped as they were when they were living quarters for the Mount Vernon servant-slaves. The two interiors are the Spinning House Quarters and the West Quarters.

Location: Mount Vernon is 16 miles south of Alexandria, Virginia, via the George Washington Memorial Parkway.

Admission charge.

30

DAYS OF SLAVERY

MONTICELLO

Although it was the genius of Thomas Jefferson that designed
his home, Monticello, it was largely slave labor that did the
actual building. In some ways Jefferson was a contradictory
man. He called slavery "the most unremitting despotism" and
yet he never gave up his own slaves. He was considered a kind
master but, like other slave owners, he turned to the sale of his
slaves to raise money when he was in financial difficulties.

Today Monticello is one of the most fascinating historic
homes in America due, in part, to the many unusual inventions
of Jefferson that may be seen in the house. One of these inventions is a special kind of music stand. Jefferson had a high regard for the musical talent of the black man, and black musicians often performed for guests at Monticello.

There are no restored slave or servant quarters, but visitors
to the mansion are reminded by the guides of the important role
black servants played in the life of Monticello.

Location: Monticello, 3 miles southeast of Charlottesville,
Virginia, on State 53.

Admission charge.

THE HERMITAGE

President Andrew Jackson inspired great devotion in the soldiers
who served under him as well as in the slaves who worked the
fields around his home, called The Hermitage. Perhaps one of
the reasons for this devotion was that Andrew Jackson insisted
that his workers be treated humanely. Once he fired an overseer
when he heard the man had mistreated a slave.

Not too long after Jackson's death in 1845, The Hermitage
became a shrine, visited by thousands of tourists each year.
One of the guides who proudly showed visitors around the
house and grounds during those years was Uncle Alfred, who
had been President Jackson's personal servant.

The Hermitage and farm are preserved today much as they
were in Jackson's time. Uncle Alfred's log cabin, with furnishings, where he lived as slave and free man, may also be seen by
visitors.

31

Location: The Hermitage is 13 miles east of Nashville off U.S. 70N.

Admission charge.

BELLE MEADE MANSION

The double log cabin on the grounds of the Belle Meade plantation was the original home of the Harding family, who first came to Tennessee in 1807. When the family moved out of the log cabin into a white-pillared Greek-style mansion, the log cabin became quarters for the household slaves.

In addition to working in the fields, some of the black servants at the Belle Meade plantation were employed in the stables, which were noted for raising fine thoroughbred horses. During slave days, the black man's skill in handling horses was well known. It was not at all unusual to have black stableboys, trainers and jockeys in the horse races that were held before the Civil War.

Today the mansion, log cabin and stables have been restored and are open to visitors.

Location: Belle Meade Mansion, 7 miles west of Nashville, Tennessee, on U.S. 70 (Harding Road at Leake Avenue).

Small admission charge.

KINGSLEY PLANTATION

After the importation of slaves was prohibited by law in America in 1808, slave trader Zephaniah Kingsley moved to Fort George Island in Spanish-owned Florida. On his plantation black men and women imported from Africa were taught to be craftsmen and farmers, then smuggled for sale into Georgia, where they brought 50 percent more than the regular market price for slaves.

Kingsley's African wife, Anna Jai, lived in a separate house on the plantation and assisted her husband in running the plantation.

Kingsley's paradoxical attitude toward slavery, from which he made a fortune, was revealed in his will. He made sure that Anna Jai was well provided for, and warned her and their children to "remove themselves to some land of liberty and equal rights where the conditions of society are governed by some laws less absurd than that of color."

The Kingsley Plantation has been restored and is now a state historic site. The remains of the original slave quarters can be seen at the Palmetto Street entrance, as well as the plantation homes and a small museum. The island of Fort George, in addition to its historic interest, is also a wildlife sanctuary with well-marked nature trails.

Location: Kingsley Plantation, Fort George Island, Florida. The island may be reached by traveling from Jacksonville on State Route 105 (Heckscher Drive) or crossing by ferry at Maport to State Route A1A, then turning north at the village of Fort George.

Admission charge.

BOONE HALL PLANTATION

Boone Hall Plantation was one of the largest cotton plantations in the South before the Civil War. The plantation spread over 17,000 acres and required more than a thousand slaves for its operation.

Handmade bricks and tiles produced by slaves were used to construct the present buildings on the plantation—the white-columned mansion, the gin house, smokehouse, garden walls—and the street of small brick cottages near the mansion for the house slaves.

Nine of the original tile-roofed slave cabins are still standing today, constituting the only intact "slave street" in the southeast. Boone Hall was one of the first plantations to provide education for its slaves.

Boone Hall Plantation has remained a working, productive farm since its establishment in 1676, although today it grows pecans, beef cattle and vegetables. The mansion, the crumbling "slave street" and the picturesque avenue of moss-draped live oaks leading to the house have been used many times in motion-picture films and television documentaries.

Privately owned, the plantation and mansion house are open to the public.

33

Location: Boone Hall Plantation, 8 miles north of Charleston, South Carolina, on U.S. 17.

Admission charge.

MAGNOLIA PLANTATION

Built in 1784, Magnolia Plantation was burned during the Civil War and rebuilt after the war on the old foundations. The original owners raised thoroughbred horses noted throughout the South.

The plantation includes the old slave houses, a row of brick cottages with tin roofs, built like tiny forts. The stocks in which slaves were punished can also still be seen.

Location: Magnolia Plantation, 1 mile north of Derry, Louisiana, on Louisiana 119.

Admission charge.

THE ANTE-BELLUM PLANTATION
IN STONE MOUNTAIN MEMORIAL PARK

This exact replica of a working plantation was created to give visitors an idea of what plantation life was like in Georgia before the Civil War. The buildings on the plantation were brought here from various points throughout the state, including the traditional Big House where the owner of the plantation would have lived, an overseer's house, slave homes, smokehouse, cookhouse, barn and coach house, all complete with authentic furnishings and enclosed within beautifully landscaped gardens.

The two slave houses shown are again those used by the more favored house slaves, with furnishings which were handmade by the slaves or cast-offs from the Big House. The field slaves lived in much more primitive housing closer to the fields where they worked.

Stone Mountain Memorial Park is a recreational and historic park of 3,200 acres including Stone Mountain itself, a massive dome of granite, several lakes for swimming and boating, a scenic railroad and skylift, game ranch, Civil War museum and many other attractions.

Location: Stone Mountain Memorial Park, just east of At-lanta, Georgia, on U.S. 78.

Admission charge to both the park and the plantation.

STRATFORD HALL AND PLANTATION

Stratford Hall began as a tobacco plantation in the 1720s and was the home of four generations of the famous Lee family of Virginia. The original Georgian mansion still stands, along with a schoolhouse, smokehouse, stables and other outbuildings.

In its day Stratford was called a "town in itself," but its self-sufficiency, as with other colonial plantations, was largely due to the countless number of slaves who lived and worked on the plantation.

Today Stratford is still a working plantation, but it is open to the public. Two of the original slave cottages have been reconstructed and furnished as they might have been in the eighteenth century.

Location: Stratford Hall and Plantation off County 214, Stratford, Virginia.

Admission charge.

THE BURROUGHS PLANTATION
(BOOKER T. WASHINGTON NATIONAL MONUMENT)

The Burroughs Plantation of only 207 acres was more typical of the average Southern farm before the Civil War. The Burroughs home was a simple five-room log house with several outbuildings and not more than three slave cabins.

Booker T. Washington spent his boyhood as a slave on the Burroughs Plantation, and today the Burroughs farm and restored farm buildings are part of the Booker T. Washington National Monument.

For more information about the Burroughs Plantation and the Booker T. Washington National Monument, see historic sites, Chapter Nine.

THE ORDEMAN-SHAW HOUSE

Many slaves worked and lived in cities rather than on rural farms and plantations. The Ordeman-Shaw House was typical

35

of the more affluent town houses of the 1850s. Built in the Italian style of architecture, the courtyard of the house is surrounded by service buildings, including the kitchen, wash house, slave quarters and other outbuildings. Such care has been taken with the restoration of all the buildings that a visitor could almost move into the Ordeman-Shaw house and live as one would have lived in the 1850s.

The slave quarters above the kitchen are furnished with simple but sturdy furniture, constructed by the slaves themselves.

Location: The Ordeman-Shaw House is at the corner of Jefferson and Hull streets, Montgomery, Alabama.

Admission charge. Guided tours.

THE 1850 HISTORIC HOUSE

Freed blacks and slaves were commonplace in the city of New Orleans. Most of the houses in the old French Quarter contained a unit known as the slave quarters. One of the distinctive "row houses" fronting on Jackson Square has been restored in the style of the 1850s. On the third floor of the house one can glimpse the slave or servant quarters, decorated as they might have been before the Civil War.

Five blocks from the 1850 house is Beauregard Square, formerly called Congo Square, where slaves and free blacks danced and socialized.

Location: The 1850 Historic House, 523 St. Ann Street on Jackson Square, New Orleans, Louisiana.

Small admission charge.

CAPTAIN DAVID JUDSON HOUSE

Slavery, of course, was not restricted to the South. Slave holding in the North, however, was on a much smaller scale, so slave quarters still standing are few and far between. In many cases household slaves in the North did not have separate quarters but lived in the house.

The Captain David Judson House, built in 1723, had its slave quarters in the cellar. Here also is an enormous fireplace ten feet long and seven feet high, containing two brick ovens where food was cooked for the household. In the inventory of the Judson estate in 1775 are listed seven slaves valued at 267 pounds, along with other household goods.

The house itself is an excellent example of eighteenth-century New England architecture and furnishings.

Location: Captain David Judson House, 967 Academy Hill (between Main and Elm streets), Stratford, Connecticut.

Small admission charge.

WHALING MUSEUM

Whaling was one of the most important industries of early New England, and New Bedford, Massachusetts, was the largest whaling port. Many black seamen worked on whaling ships, and one black seaman, Paul Cuffee, who lived near New Bedford, made his fortune as a shipowner in the whaling industry.

A black metalsmith, Lewis Temple, settled in New Bedford and modified the design of the whalers' harpoon in the 1840s so that lines could be securely fastened to the whale. This new type of harpoon, called a "toggle harpoon," more than doubled the catch of whales and the profits of the whalers. Temple, however, never patented his harpoon and died in poverty.

The Whaling Museum contains a fascinating collection of whaling relics, including examples of Lewis Temple's toggle harpoon, a compass used by Paul Cuffee, as well as a full-rigged model of a whaling ship.

Location: Whaling Museum, 18 Johnny Cake Hill, New Bedford, Massachusetts.

Small admission charge.

THE WITCH HOUSE

Slaves could be found in some unusual occupations in colonial America. There was even one slave who was accused of witchcraft.

In 1692 in the small village of Salem, Massachusetts, a group of young girls began acting strangely and accused Tituba, a slave, and several elderly women, of having bewitched them. Tituba and the other women were tried as witches in the colonial courts and sentenced to death. Before the witch hysteria ended, nineteen men and women in all were convicted of being witches and hanged on Gallows Hill.

Tituba had confessed to being a witch but later admitted that her master, the Reverend Parris, had beaten her until she agreed to confess. Although she was saved from execution, Tituba stayed in jail for more than a year and finally was sold to pay her jail fees.

The Witch House, now open to the public, was the home of Jonathan Corwin, one of the witchcraft judges.

Location: The Witch House, 310½ Essex Street, Salem, Massachusetts.

SALEM WITCH MUSEUM

This museum offers a twenty-two minute history of witchcraft depicted in thirteen bloodcurdling scenes. One of the scenes includes Tituba, the accused witch who managed to escape the hangman.

Location: Salem Witch Museum, Main Square, Salem, Massachusetts.

Admission charge.

FRAUNCES TAVERN

During slave days there were many free black men and women who successfully engaged in all sorts of occupations. Samuel Fraunces, a free black man, operated a tavern in New York City that is still in use today. Before the Revolutionary War the Sons of Liberty used to meet at Fraunces Tavern and plot revolution.

Legend has it that "black Sam's" daughter, Phoebe, saved the life of George Washington. She stopped him from eating a dinner poisoned by one of his bodyguards, Thomas Hickey. Hickey was later hanged.

When Washington was elected president, Sam Fraunces was steward of the first presidential mansion, in New York.

Today there is still a restaurant on the first floor of Fraunces Tavern. A museum of Revolutionary War history occupies the second and third floors.

Location: Fraunces Tavern, 54 Pearl Street at Broad, New York, New York.

No admission charge to museum.

AMOS FORTUNE GRAVE

Amos Fortune may not have been the most famous black American but he certainly was one of the most determined. He bought his freedom from slavery in 1770 when he was sixty years old. At the age of seventy, when most men have retired, he started a tannery business in Jaffrey, New Hampshire. A highly respected citizen of the town, he left his small fortune to the local Quaker church and school district when he died. Each summer on Friday evenings in July and August, the Amos Fortune Forum is held at the Old Meeting House where he attended church.

There were many like Amos Fortune in America's history, men and women who by sheer grit, courage and determination rose from slavery to respected citizenship. Most of their names are unknown, but on the headstone of the grave of Amos Fortune can still be read:

"Sacred to the memory of Amos Fortune, who was born free in Africa, a slave in America, he purchased liberty, professed Christianity, lived reputably, and died hopefully."

Location: Amos Fortune grave, Old Burying Ground in Jaffrey Center next to the Old Meeting House, Jaffrey, New Hampshire.

CHURCHILL DOWNS MUSEUM

In the first Kentucky Derby run at Churchill Downs Race Track, fourteen of the fifteen horses were ridden by black jockeys. Black riders guided fifteen of the winning horses in the first twenty-eight runnings of the Derby. Black jockeys continued racing successfully in the Kentucky Derby until 1911.

At the Churchill Downs Museum, visitors may see photographs of early, as well as present-day, winning jockeys and many interesting mementos of Kentucky Derby Day highlights. Free tours may also be taken of the famous Churchill Downs grounds and gardens.

39

Location: Churchill Downs, Louisville, Kentucky.
No admission charge.

MAN O' WAR PARK

One of the greatest jockeys of all times was Isaac Murphy, a
black man and the first jockey to win three Kentucky Derbies,
in 1884, 1890 and 1891. This record was not broken until Eddie
Arcaro won his fourth Derby in 1948. In 1882 Murphy won 49
out of his 51 starts at the Saratoga Race Track, and in all his
career rode 628 winners in 1,412 races. At one time he owned
his own racehorse, an unusual feat for a black man of his day.

In 1967 Isaac Murphy's almost forgotten grave was moved
to Man O' War Park, where it was placed not far from the
grave of that great racing horse for whom the park is named,
Man O' War. Engraved on the stone marker of the jockey's
grave is a picture of Isaac Murphy and a list of the many outstanding races he won.

Location: Man O' War Park, Lexington, Kentucky.

NATIONAL MUSEUM OF RACING

Isaac Murphy was the first jockey voted into the Jockey Hall
of Fame at the National Museum of Racing.

The museum contains an interesting array of racing silks,
mementos and paintings of early jockeys, horses and racetracks.

Location: National Museum of Racing, Union Avenue and
Ludlow streets, Saratoga Springs, New York.

No admission charge.

MADISON SQUARE GARDEN CENTER (HALL OF FAME)

In addition to successful black jockeys before and after the
Civil War, there were also black prizefighters. One of the earliest of these prizefighters in America was Tom Molineaux, a
young slave in Virginia who won his freedom by defeating the
champion fighter on a neighboring plantation.

In time Tom Molineaux became the self-styled first heavyweight boxing champion of America. In 1810 in London, England, he was defeated after a forty-round bout with Tom Crib,
a white man who held the English prizefighting crown.

40

It wasn't until the 1890s that interracial prizefighting once again took place in America. Early white American boxing champions like John L. Sullivan refused to face black boxing challengers. Then in 1892 black George Dixon won the world featherweight boxing championship; Joe Walcott the welterweight in 1901; Joe Gans the lightweight in 1901; and Jack Johnson the heavyweight in 1908.

Many of the early famous black prizefighters won their matches at Madison Square Garden. The present Garden contains a theater, bowling center, convention space, facilities for handling seven major events simultaneously—as well as an art gallery and hall of fame of white and black sports heroes.

Location: Madison Square Garden Center is above Pennsylvania Station, between Seventh and Eighth avenues and 31st and 33rd streets, New York, New York.

Admission charge.

STATUE OF CUD-JOE-LEWIS, LAST SLAVE TO ARRIVE IN AMERICA

The small statue of Cud-Joe-Lewis, the last slave to arrive in America aboard the slave ship *Clotilde,* stands in front of the modest church he helped to build in "Affriky-Town," Alabama. The town is now the settlement of Plateau.

Location: The community of Plateau is near the town of Prichard, Alabama, which is just north of the city limits of Mobile, Alabama.

PRINCE HALL MONUMENT

A veteran of the Revolutionary War, Prince Hall was inducted into the Masonic Lodge by a group of British soldiers stationed in Boston, when no American lodge would accept him. In 1787 Hall received permission from the Mother Grand Lodge in England to start African Lodge No. 459 in America. Thus Prince Hall became the founder of the oldest social organization among blacks in the United States.

In addition, Prince Hall fought for the establishment of schools for black children and petitioned the Massachusetts legislature to abolish slavery.

Prince Hall is buried in the Copp's Hill Burying Ground,

41

Boston, Massachusetts. There is an imposing monument as a gravemarker erected by the Prince Hall Grand Lodge, which was named in his honor.

Location: Prince Hall Monument, Copp's Hill Burying Ground, Boston, Massachusetts.

In the 1960s several new and unusual museums were established in the United States—museums that specialize in Afro-American history. The following museums and their exhibits are not limited to the slave period of black American history, but they are placed with this section because a visit to these museums serves as a good introduction to the contributions black men and women have made to America.

DU SABLE MUSEUM OF AFRICAN-AMERICAN HISTORY

One of the oldest black history museums is the Du Sable Museum, begun in the early 1940s by Margaret Burroughs. In 1961 the museum moved to an old gray stone mansion, and plans are being made to move eventually to even larger quarters.

Among the many exhibits at the museum are paintings, sculpture, photographs, mementos of black families, broadsides and posters. One of the museum's most cherished possessions is the powder horn carried during the Revolutionary War by a black fifer, Barzillai Lew. From Africa have come masks, drums, pictures and even dolls.

In the lower level of the museum are murals telling of black history from slave days to the present.

Location: The Du Sable Museum of African-American History, 3806 South Michigan Avenue, Chicago, Illinois.

Small admission charge. Guided tours available for groups.

THE FRANK LONDON BROWN HISTORICAL ASSOCIATION

The Association's Afro-American Pictorial Exhibit covers African history, slavery, black military heroes and the Civil Rights Movement. Since its formation in 1962, the exhibit has been on display at 100 schools, libraries, universities and other institutions. Lecturers accompany the exhibit.

The exhibit may be borrowed directly from the Association

or may be seen at the Hall Library at 4801 Michigan Avenue, Chicago, Illinois.

Location: The Frank London Brown Historical Association, Chatham YMCA, 1021 East 83rd Street, Chicago, Illinois.

MUSEUM OF AFRO-AMERICAN HISTORY

One of the newest and also one of the most important museums on black history and art is the Museum of Afro-American History in Boston.

The museum, organized in 1964, was built around an extensive collection of documents and artifacts and mementos, gathered from all parts of the United States and covering three centuries of Afro-American life. A portion of the exhibit tells of the free black's role in the abolition movement in New England.

The museum recently moved its collection to the restored Old African Meeting House on Beacon Hill. The Old African Meeting House, built in 1804 as a Baptist church, is the earliest building in the United States built by free black Americans for use by other black Americans.

The Meeting House was a center for abolitionist activities and was where the famous all-black 54th Regiment was organized during the Civil War. Frederick Douglass and Harriet Tubman, as well as other noted black leaders, spoke from the pulpit.

The Black Heritage Tour of Boston, sponsored by the museum, begins at this building. The trail includes the Old Granary Burying Ground, the site of the Boston Massacre, Old South Meeting House, Crispus Attucks Monument and other sites relating to black American history in Boston.

Arrangements for visits to the museum and the guided walking tour must be made in advance with the curator of the museum. The museum also sponsors traveling exhibits.

Location: Museum of Afro-American History, Smith Court, Beacon Hill, Boston, Massachusetts.

Admission charge. Group rate for Black Heritage Tour.

STORE FRONT MUSEUM

Established in 1971, this combination museum, cultural center and Paul Robeson theater has a permanent collection of works of art, relics, memorabilia, photographs, souvenirs, artifacts and documents relating to black history, past and present. The museum's exhibits, workshops and performances all reaffirm pride in being black.

Location: Store Front Museum, 162–02 Liberty Avenue, Jamaica, New York.

Exhibits and workshops are free.

FREDERICK DOUGLASS INSTITUTE

The Frederick Douglass Institute is operated jointly with the Museum of African Art in Washington, D.C. The Institute deals with Afro-Americans' contributions to the United States and presents exhibits on black American history. For full information about this institute, see the Museum of African Art in Chapter Six.

Location: Frederick Douglass Institute and Museum of African Art, 316–318 A Street, N.E., Washington, D.C.

Admission charge.

ANACOSTIA NEIGHBORHOOD MUSEUM

Opened in 1967 in an abandoned movie house, the Anacostia Neighborhood Museum is a combination historical museum, cultural arts center and meeting place for neighborhood groups. Some of its constantly changing exhibits had the following titles: "The Douglass Years"; "This Thing Called Jazz"; "Black Patriots of the American Revolution"; "This Is Africa"; and "Science, Man's Greatest Adventure," among many, many more.

Partly supported by The Smithsonian Institution and through private donations, the museum also sponsors traveling historical and art exhibits, as well as film programs and handicraft classes for children of all ages.

Location: Anacostia Neighborhood Museum, 2405 Martin Luther King, Jr., Avenue, S.E., Washington, D.C. (The Anacostia community is also where the Frederick Douglass Home, Cedar Hill, is located.)

No admission charge.

INTERNATIONAL AFRO-AMERICAN MUSEUM, INC.

Founded in 1965, this museum seeks to give through its visual displays an understanding of the true role of the black man and woman in the building of this country, and to correct the distortion of the black man's rich cultural heritage in Africa.

The museum has had exhibits on the black inventor Garrett Morgan, singer Paul Robeson, and the Underground Railroad, among others. One of its newest exhibit areas is a mobile unit, which travels from place to place and is called "History on Wheels."

Location: International Afro-American Museum, Inc., 1549–53 West Grand Boulevard, Detroit, Michigan.

Advance reservations required for groups of ten or more.

Small admission charge.

BLACK HISTORY EXHIBIT CENTER

Blacks were among the first settlers of colonial Long Island, New York. Today there is a Black History Exhibit Center, which tells of the accomplishments of these black Americans as well as other black residents of Long Island, living and dead. The center features objects from original bills of sale for slaves to photographs of the great professional football player Jimmy Brown, who once lived on Long Island. Booker T. Washington had a home on Long Island, and for a time tried to create a black Tuskegee on the island. Alexander Bell created his telephone, and Edison the first electric light, with the assistance of Lewis H. Latimer, another black resident of Long Island.

The center also displays works of local black artists.

Location: The Black History Exhibit Center, under the sponsorship of the Nassau County Museum, is located at 106 North Main Street, Hempstead, Long Island, New York.

No admission charge.

The importation of slaves was
forbidden in the United States after 1808.
Slaves, however, continued to be imported
illegally and the selling of slaves at
domestic auctions, as shown above, increased
rapidly. In 1860 a prime field hand sold
for $1,500, roughly equivalent to $6,000 today.
By the time of the Civil War, the larger
plantations had millions of dollars invested
in slaves. COURTESY LIBRARY OF CONGRESS

This gracious planta-
tion home was typical
of a weathly planter's
home in the ante-bel-
lum South. Boone Hall
Plantation was estab-
lished near Charleston,
South Carolina, in
1676. Black labor built
the Hall and even
made the bricks and
tiles, as part of the
work performed by
plantation slaves.
COURTESY CHARLESTON
POST CARD COMPANY,
CHARLESTON, SOUTH
CAROLINA

Nine tile-roofed brick cottages are all that remain of the original "slave street" for house servants at Boone Hall, South Carolina. The almost 1,000 field slaves lived elsewhere on the plantation.

A completely reconstructed plantation complex has been built at Stone Mountain Park, Georgia, including a "big house," stable, overseer's home, cookhouse, smokehouse and gardens. To show the type of cabins occupied by black people employed as slaves on the plantation, two log cabins, homes of former slaves, were brought to the park from a plantation near Covington, Georgia. A plantation of this size would, of course, have had more than two slave cabins. COURTESY STONE MOUNTAIN PARK, STONE MOUNTAIN, GEORGIA

The interiors of the slave cabins at Stone Mountain Park, Georgia, have been simply furnished as they might have been when they were quarters for house servants on a Southern plantation. COURTESY STONE MOUNTAIN PARK, STONE MOUNTAIN, GEORGIA

On the Kingsley Plantation, Ft. George Island, Florida, lived Anna Jai, the African wife of Zephaniah Kingsley, a successful slave dealer. Anna Jai's home may be seen in the foreground; in the background is the house in which Kingsley lived. Although Kingsley was devoted to his African wife and children, he made his fortune importing slaves, training them on his plantation and smuggling them across the border for sale in Georgia. COURTESY FLORIDA DIVISION OF RECREATION AND PARKS

While being trained in a variety of crafts, black people brought as slaves to Kingsley Plantation, Florida, lived in these rows of cabins, two families sharing a cabin. Made of tabby, a mixture of oyster shells and lime, the ruins of these cabins still stand.

These old wooden stocks, similar to those used in colonial days to punish lesser offenders, were used to punish disobedient slaves. These can be seen in the museum on the Kingsley Plantation, Florida.

There were a few black people who also owned plantations and slaves. Melrose House (originally called Yucca House) was owned by the Metoyers, a black family who owned a sugarcane plantation along the Cane River near Natchitoches, Louisiana. COURTESY THE PELICAN GUIDE TO PLANTATION HOMES OF LOUISIANA, PELICAN PUBLISHING CO.

The oldest building on the Metoyer Plantation was called Africa House and was built for Marie Thérèse Metoyer, a free black woman and the original owner of the plantation. Africa House was used partly as a prison for slaves and partly as a store. COURTESY THE PELICAN GUIDE TO PLANTATION HOMES OF LOUISIANA, PELICAN PUBLISHING CO.

An exhibit from the African collection at the Museum of the
Philadelphia Civic Center, showing types of metal implements
made by African blacksmiths in iron, brass and copper. Within
each African tribe there were also skilled gold- and silversmiths,
weavers, woodcarvers, potters and basketmakers. Many free blacks
and slaves in colonial America became master craftsmen, using the
knowledge they brought with them from Africa or the training
they received on plantations. COURTESY MUSEUM OF THE
PHILADELPHIA CIVIC CENTER

This graceful wrought-iron balcony railing found in the Vieux Carré section of New Orleans is an early example of skilled craftsmanship by black ironworkers. The majority of blacksmiths in early eighteenth-century New Orleans were either slaves or free blacks. COURTESY NEGRO IRONWORKERS OF LOUISIANA, PELICAN PUBLISHERS

An exhibit of Yoruba textiles and clothing at the National Museum of Natural History, The Smithsonian Institution. Status and class distinctions in Africa were often indicated by the quantity and quality of the fabric worn by a man or woman. The knowledge of weaving that black people brought with them from Africa was put to good work on the largely self-sufficient plantations, where wool, flax and cotton were grown and spun, and woven into cloth by the women slaves. COURTESY NATIONAL MUSEUM OF NATURAL HISTORY, THE SMITHSONIAN INSTITUTION, WASHINGTON, D.C.

An example of early slave woodcarving by Henry Gudgell of Ohio that still shows African influence in the symbolic animal figures—the snake, turtle and lizard—on the base of the cane. In Africa such carved canes were called "juju" and were considered to hold magic. COURTESY NATIONAL GALLERY OF ART, WASHINGTON, D.C.

Slaves often made much of the furniture used in plantation homes. The plantation clock, at right, was made by slaves in St. James Parish. The Index of American Design, National Gallery of Art, Washington, D.C., has a collection of paintings of slave handicrafts from Southern plantations. COURTESY NATIONAL GALLERY OF ART, WASHINGTON, D.C.

A display of some of the articles made by black craftsmen in the South before the Civil War is on view at The Old Slave Mart Museum, Charleston, South Carolina. Basketry and weaving were highly developed arts in Africa. Many of the same weaving techniques used in African villages may still be seen in the baskets that are made and sold around Charleston today.

Slaves and free blacks were involved in almost every occupation in colonial America. One black woman, the slave Tituba, was even arrested and convicted of witchcraft in eighteenth-century Salem, Massachusetts. This scene in the Salem Witch Museum, Salem, Massachusetts, shows Tituba reading the fortunes of the young girls who were later to accuse her of being a witch. COURTESY SALEM WITCH MUSEUM, SALEM, MASSACHUSETTS

Very early in American history, black men entered the
American sporting scene. Shown above is Tom Molineaux, an
ex-slave and the first American heavyweight contender, in his
fight against Tom Crib, heavyweight champion of England, in
1810. Many later-day black prizefighters are honored in the
Hall of Fame, Madison Square Garden Center, New York City.

Shown above is a picture of The First Futurity Race, which may be seen at the National Museum of Racing, Saratoga Springs, New York. The two jockeys in the lead positions in this race at Saratoga Springs were both black. FROM THE COLLECTION OF THE NATIONAL MUSEUM OF RACING, INC., SARATOGA SPRINGS, NEW YORK

The Old Slave Mart Museum of Charleston, South Carolina, contains exhibits from slave days and examples of handicraft made by black people who were slaves. The museum is housed in a building that was formerly a slave auction house. Slaves were sold from the second-floor balcony. COURTESY CHARLESTON POST CARD COMPANY, CHARLESTON, SOUTH CAROLINA

One of the finest museums of black art and history is the Du Sable Museum of African-American History in Chicago, Illinois. Exhibits in this museum range from the powder horn carried by a black Revolutionary War soldier, to mementos of a black rodeo rider, to African spirit masks and drums. COURTESY DU SABLE MUSEUM OF AFRICAN-AMERICAN HISTORY

One of the newest of the black American history and culture museums is the Anacostia Neighborhood Museum of The Smithsonian Institution, Washingon D.C. Contantly changing exhibits of interest to black, as well as white, Americans may be seen at the museum. Young visitors to a recent exhibit on African culture study highly stylized Ghanian ancestor figures. COURTESY ANACOSTIA NEIGHBORHOOD MUSEUM

UNDERGROUND RAILROAD TO FREEDOM

On a spring night in 1859, a slave belonging to Jack Tabb of Mason County, Kentucky, went courting on a neighboring plantation. Young and carefree, with a master who was kinder than most, Arnold Gragston had nothing in mind but a pleasant evening with a pretty girl. Instead, an old woman approached him at the house he was visiting. Would he ferry a young slave girl across the river? Arnold knew the request was not as simple as it sounded. Across the river was the free state of Ohio. Anyone caught helping a slave escape across the river was sure to be punished severely, even shot.

Years later, in his own words, Arnold told what happened next. "I was scared and backed out in a hurry. But then I saw the girl, and she was such a pretty little thing, and looking as scared as I was feeling, so it wasn't long before I was listening to the old woman tell me

59

when to take her and where to leave her on the other side. I didn't have nerve enough to do it that night, though, and I told them to wait for me until tomorrow night.

"All the next day I kept seeing Mr. Tabb laying a rawhide across my back, or shooting me, and kept seeing that scared little brown girl back at the house, looking at me with her big eyes and asking me wouldn't I just row her across to Ripley. Me and Mr. Tabb lost, and soon as dusk settled that night, I was at the old lady's house.

"I don't know how I ever rowed the boat across the river. The current was strong and I was trembling. I couldn't see a thing there in the dark, but I felt the girl's eyes. We didn't dare to whisper, so I couldn't tell her how sure I was that Mr. Tabb or some of the others' owners would tear me up when they found out what I had done. I just knew they would find out . . ."

Despite his misgivings, Arnold made it safely across the river, rowing toward a light on the far shore that the old woman had told him he would see. The light was in John Rankin's house, kept burning all night as a beacon for runaway slaves. The trip was the first of many Arnold was to make across the Ohio River on black, moonless nights, carrying as many as a dozen escaped slaves at a time, yet never seeing their faces and never taking anything in payment.

The destination of the fugitive slaves, the John Rankin house in Ripley, Ohio, was one of many homes that served as stations on the Underground Railroad, as the escape route from slavery to freedom was called. For four years Arnold served as a conductor on the railroad, risking his own life so that others could be free. Then one evening in 1863, returning from a trip across the river, he was discovered and had to flee for his life. For weeks he hid out in the fields and woods, sleeping in a cornfield, up in the branches of a tree or buried deep in a haypile. Finally Arnold, now a fugitive slave himself, managed to row across the river to John Rankin's home and freedom.

The Underground Railroad has become a legend in American history. Like most legends, a great deal of myth and folklore has been written about it. Undoubtedly it was never a highly organized, formal arrangement. The main networks of the line all ran north to Canada. From the border states of Missouri, Kentucky and Tennessee, the routes ran through Illinois to Chicago or through Indiana, Ohio, Michigan and western Pennsylvania. The routes ended at Niagara Falls, Detroit and other port cities on Lake Erie, the easiest access ports to Canada.

Another network ran from Virginia and Maryland along the eastern coast through the New England States and upper New York to the Canadian border.

How many slaves escaped north using the Underground Railroad can only be estimated, perhaps from 1,000 to 2,000 a year. Many slaves, fleeing north to Canada or South to Spanish Florida and Mexico, had never even heard of the railroad. They made their own way, relying only on their own courage, ingenuity and fortitude—and the assistance given them by free blacks and slaves along the way.

There were other slaves who tried to escape from the slave ships even before they reached America. One such successful attempt turned into a full-scale mutiny aboard the black-hulled slave ship, the *Amistad*. The escape was managed one dark, starless July night in 1839.

The *Amistad* was off the Cuban coast with a cargo of

61

fifty-three kidnapped slaves chained in the cramped hold. One of the slaves was a powerfully built young man named Cinqué, son of a Mendi chief. Using his strength, along with his powers of persuasion, Cinqué talked the other slaves into breaking their chains, then armed them with deadly sugarcane knives he had found in a nearby cargo hold. Quietly the freed slaves padded above deck. Cinqué killed the sleeping cook with one blow, then killed the captain as he drew his sword. The two remaining seamen jumped overboard.

Two Cuban planters, Montez and Luiz, passengers aboard the ship and owners of the slaves, had their lives spared because the mutineers did not know how to sail the ship. They needed someone to navigate the ship back to Africa. However, Montez would sail the ship east toward Africa by day, but by night he would alter his course and sail northwest.

After seven weeks of this zigzag course, the ship neared the coast of America off Montauk Point, Long Island. The food and water were almost gone, and Cinqué and a party of blacks went ashore to get provisions. While they were ashore, a U.S. Navy Brig discovered the *Amistad*—tales of the strange black-hulled schooner had already spread up and down the coast—and captured the ship as well as Cinqué and the rest of the mutineers.

Cinqué was convinced he would be killed immediately and bid farewell to his men. Instead, he and his men were taken to New Haven, Connecticut, to stand trial. Newspapers picked up the story, and Lewis Tappan of New York, a man who hated slavery, formed a committee to raise money to defend the "Amistad Africans", as they were called.

Spain claimed the slaves were its legitimate property and demanded that the United States return them. The case finally reached the Supreme Court, where Cinqué and his men were defended by John Quincy Adams, who had been the sixth president of the United States. In an eloquent four-hour speech, Adams denounced President Martin Van Buren, who had secretly planned to return the slaves to Cuba, and accused the president of trying to "appease the vengeance of African slave-traders."

John Quincy Adams won his case, and the Amistad Africans were ordered by the Court to be set free. They attended school in Farmington, Connecticut for a year, and then with money raised from the residents of Farmington and elsewhere, they returned to Sierra Leone, along with several missionaries who hoped to spread Christianity among the Mendi people.

The Amistad mutineers were more fortunate than most. There were other slaves who escaped in groups from plantations but never made it back to Africa. In the seventeenth and eighteenth centuries, groups of runaway slaves who hid out in the swamps and mountains of the South formed free or "maroon" communities.

The maroons were greatly feared by the planters because they stirred up other slaves to revolt and run away. The maroons plundered isolated plantations for supplies, and for many years successfully fought off troops of militia sent to destroy them. Although eventually, after better roads and communications were established in the South, the larger bands of maroons were hunted down and destroyed, some smaller groups continued living unmolested, in inaccessible swamp areas.

Whatever the exact count of escaped slaves who fled the plantations, certainly enough ran away for a so-called scientist named Samuel Cartwright to declare solemnly that slaves suffered from a peculiar disease called Drapetomania, or the Disease Causing Negroes to Run Away! And for Southern senators in Congress to push for the passage of the Fugitive Slave Law in 1850 in an attempt to put a halt to the Underground Railroad and runaway slaves. Under the Fugitive Slave Law, anyone who helped escaped slaves, even in free states, could be jailed or heavily fined.

In spite of the colorful and at times exaggerated stories about the railroad, like most legends, it is based on a hard kernel of truth. Hundreds of underground stations did actually exist in homes and barns, churches and schools, stores and caves. And slaves of all description, young and old, women, men and children, in groups and alone, field hands and house slaves, were spirited by conductors from station to station.

Sometimes the fugitives would stay at a station only overnight, sometimes remain for weeks at a time, depending on how safe it was to proceed further. Because homes of slave sympathizers were often visited unexpectedly by proslavery neighbors or by the law, particularly after passage of the Fugitive Slave Act, places of concealment for escaped slaves had to be found. Secret rooms were built into attics and basements and barns, often with connecting passageways. One station used a hollowed-out hayrick in the barn as a hiding place, another had a woodpile with a room in the center. Slaves were hidden in the galleries of churches and the bell towers of schools.

Once they were given directions to the next station, the fugitives often went on foot, following the North Star, hiding by day, traveling by night. The more fortunate might travel hidden in the false bed of a farm wagon or peddler wagon, or beneath a load of produce, hay or grain. One enterprising conductor transported a group of fugitives concealed in a funeral procession!

If the escaped slaves were fair in coloring, they would be passed off as white and dressed accordingly. The Quakers, who were some of the most efficient conductors, were known to dress an escaped slave in the garb of a Quaker woman, the veiled bonnet effectively hiding the face.

As for the conductors themselves, they were a mixed lot. Young and old, women and men, black and white, their only bond was the conviction that slavery was an abomination in the sight of God and man. Most of them were ordinary, law-abiding citizens. However, when it came to helping men, women and children escape the horror of the auction block and the degradation of being treated as less than human, they were willing to put moral law above man-made law.

Among the black conductors, the best known was Harriet Tubman, certainly one of the most unique and valiant heroines in American history. An escaped slave herself, she returned south time and time again and led to safety several hundred passengers. Rewards for her capture began at $1,000 and reached as high as $40,-000, but "General" Tubman could boast that she never lost a passenger or ran her train off the track.

On one of her first trips south, she helped her own parents escape. When her mother was unwilling to leave behind a feather bedtick and her father his tools, Harriet bundled up bedtick, tools, mother, father and all and landed them in Canada.

It is said that Harriet Tubman's motto was "Keep Going." If her passengers grew weary as she led them toward freedom, she would urge, "Children, if you are tired, keep going; if you are scared, keep going; if you want to taste freedom, keep going." Of course, the story is also told of the time one of her passengers grew faint-hearted and wanted to turn back. Whereupon a resolute Harriet drew out a pistol, saying just as firmly, "You go on or die!"

Although Harriet Tubman was perhaps the best known, there were many other black conductors. There was, for example, Josiah Henson. As a child, he had seen his mother beaten for trying to prevent the sale of her children. After escaping to Canada, he returned south to free other slaves and bring them to a safe haven. Most of the ex-slaves fleeing to Canada settled along the western peninsula of Ontario or moved inland, along the valley of the Thames River. Here communities of ex-slaves were formed, land farmed and schools and churches built.

Josiah Henson established such a community at Dresden, Ontario, with the help of money from church people in Great Britain. He set up a vocational school, sawmill and gristmill and a church for the town's black residents.

In the cities of the North, there were many free black men who successfully ran underground stations from their home; they included William Still and Robert Purvis in Philadelphia, William Wells Brown in Buffalo, David Ruggles and Theodore Wright of New York, John Jones of Chicago, and George DeBaptiste and William Webb of Detroit.

In Boston the home of escaped slave Lewis Hayden became a center for the Boston Vigilance Committee, a group of black men and women who aided escaped slaves with food, clothing and jobs. Two famous escaped slaves who took shelter under Hayden's roof were William and Ellen Craft. Ellen, posing as a white man, with her husband pretending to be her loyal slave, had escaped from their plantation owner in Georgia to come to Boston. When deputies came to the Hayden house to reclaim the Crafts, they found the house barricaded with kegs of gunpowder—and beat a hasty retreat.

Among the white conductors, the most widely known are John Rankin of Ripley, Ohio, Thomas Garrett of Delaware and the Quaker Levi Coffin of Fountain City, Indiana. It is estimated that several thousand slaves passed through the Rankin parsonage and the Coffin home while the two operated as underground stations. One young woman who fled across the frozen Ohio River to the Rankin home with her baby in her arms became the character Eliza in *Uncle Tom's Cabin*.

Not only individuals but whole towns were involved in the Underground Railroad. Waukesha, Wisconsin, was called that "Abolition Hole" because of its reputation for helping runaway slaves. In southern Iowa, the towns of Clinton, Tabor and Grinnell were part of the underground route used by John Brown and a group of escaped slaves in 1858.

Colleges, too, were used as underground stations. A guide-board directing fugitive slaves to Oberlin, Ohio, was set up by authorities 6 miles out of town. The fugitive slaves were hidden in the homes of teachers and students at Oberlin College. Knox College and the town of Galesburg became the principal underground station in Illinois. The Mission Institute at Quincy, Illinois, was so noted as a haven for escaped slaves that on a winter's night a group of proslavery Missourians crossed the Mississippi River and burned the institute to the ground.

A great many of the names of the conductors have been lost to history, but each conductor was well aware of the fate awaiting him if he were caught hiding or transporting escaped slaves. Conductors were fined heavily and thrown into jail for five to twenty years. Many were tarred and feathered, beaten half to death, their homes and businesses ruined.

One conductor, Charles Torrey, died in prison; another, ship's captain Jonathan Walker, who helped slaves escape to the Bahamas, was publicly beaten and had his hand branded with SS for slave stealer. A group of residents of Marshall, Michigan, who fought a pitched battle to prevent the seizure of runaway slaves Adam Crosswhite and his family, were arrested, brought to trial and fined several thousand dollars.

The runaway slaves themselves, if recaptured, could expect harsh punishment, even death, at the hands of their owners, to serve as a warning to their fellow slaves not to attempt the same.

Yet, in spite of the relentless opposition, the Underground Railroad continued to flourish, with countless slaves "voting for freedom with their feet." The railroad didn't go out of business till slavery was finally abolished in the United States.

Over the years, almost all physical evidences of the railroad have vanished. Farmhouses and buildings, once active stations on the underground, have been razed, replaced by subdivisions and shopping centers. Tunnels that ran from hayshed to barn to serve as escape routes have fallen into ruin.

Occasionally, though, one can find plaques that mark sites where the railroad once ran, and even homes still standing that were once active stations on the underground.

If you visit these historic landmarks, stand quietly for a moment in the place where the slaves were hidden. If you listen carefully, you can almost hear the hushed breathing of those who once feared recapture there; perhaps you can even imagine a frantic mother trying to keep a crying baby quiet, while their pursuers ransack the area, searching for their escaped property. Then perhaps you will begin to sense a little of the fear and courage, the hope and despair of those long-ago men and women who gambled their lives to make the perilous trip from slavery to freedom.

LEVI COFFIN HOME

The Quakers Levi and Catherine Coffin ran such a successful underground railroad station in their home in Indiana that Mr. Coffin has been called the unofficial "President of the Underground Railroad." Not one of the hundreds of slaves that passed through the Coffin home was ever recaptured.

The attic of the house was often used as a hiding place for the fleeing slaves, even the space between the strawtick and featherbed, if necessary. If there was no immediate danger of recapture, an exhausted refugee might stay for weeks with the Coffin family, building up strength to resume his journey north.

The Coffin house, built in 1839, is now a Registered National Historic Landmark. It has been completely refurnished in furniture of the period when the Coffin family lived there and acted as conductors on the Underground Railroad.

Location: Levi Coffin Home, Fountain City, Indiana, 9 miles north of Richmond, one block north of the traffic light on U.S. 27, east side of the street.

Small admission charge. School group rates.

JOHN RANKIN HOUSE

In 1828 the Presbyterian minister John Rankin built a house on the crest of a hill overlooking the town of Ripley, Ohio, and the Ohio River. A wooden staircase climbed up the hillside from the river to the house. Each night a light beamed from an upstairs window, acting as a beacon to guide slaves across the river from the slave state of Kentucky to a safe haven in Ripley. After the Fugitive Slave Law was passed and escaped

69

slaves were no longer safe even in a free state like Ohio, a cellar was concealed in the barn behind the Rankin house. Here fugitive slaves were hidden when pursuers approached too closely.

From 1824 to 1865 more than two thousand slaves were sheltered in the Rankin house, fed, clothed and sent north to freedom in Canada. John Rankin's whole family assisted him in his work.

Today the Rankin home has been restored by the Ohio Historical Society and looks much as it did when the Rankin family lived there. Visitors may even follow the route of the escaping slaves by climbing the newly rebuilt "staircase to liberty."

Location: Rankin House State Memorial, Ripley, Ohio. Small admission charge.

MILTON HOUSE MUSEUM

In 1844 Joseph Goodrich built a most unusual inn in Wisconsin, constructed with six sides in the shape of a hexagon. A log cabin was connected to the inn by an underground tunnel.

Before the Civil War, the Milton Inn served as a station on the Underground Railroad. Fugitive slaves hid in the basement of the inn. A basement entrance to the tunnel was hidden behind stacks of grain. When pursuers appeared at the inn, the slaves would escape through the tunnel. A small trapdoor in the floor of the log cabin led to the tunnel below. There were no steps. The slaves had to use a rope to climb out of the tunnel.

The Milton Inn, log cabin and underground passageway have been preserved as historic landmarks by the state of Wisconsin.

Location: Milton House Museum, at the intersection of highways 59 and 26, Milton, Wisconsin.

Small admission charge. Group tours by reservation.

THE TALLMAN HOUSE

William Morrison Tallman was a successful land speculator in Wisconsin and an ardent abolitionist. Abraham Lincoln was a guest in his lavish, twenty-six-room house in 1859. Legend has

70

it that the Tallman house also sheltered some not so famous guests—escaped slaves.

If it was safe for the slaves to come into the house, a lantern signal would be given at a window on the second floor. The fugitive would be hidden in the basement or the servants' bedrooms in the back wing. One of the servant's bedrooms had a steep staircase concealed in a closet. If an alarm was raised, the fugitive would climb up the staircase to a small room in the attic, until it was safe to move on. Sometimes the escaped slave's next stop was the Milton Inn.

The Tallman House, completely furnished, is now open to the public.

Location: Tallman House, 440 North Jackson Street, Janesville, Wisconsin.

Small admission charge. Group tours by reservation.

HARRIET TUBMAN HOME

Harriet Tubman's home, in which she lived the last years of her life, was restored in 1953 and is maintained as a museum by the Auburn A.M.E. Zion Church. Many of Mrs. Tubman's possessions are still in the house.

Harriet Tubman, "the Moses of her people," died in 1913 and was given a military funeral at her burial in Fort Hill Cemetery, Auburn, New York. The next year the city of Auburn unveiled a plaque at the Auburn Courthouse in honor of one of the most remarkable women in America's history.

Harriet Tubman's home is open to the public, usually in the afternoon and by appointment on Sunday. However, it is best to write in advance and make sure of the hours. The gentleman in charge of the museum is also the minister of the Auburn A.M.E. Zion Church and has other duties in addition to serving as a museum guide.

Location: Harriet Tubman Home, 180–182 South Street, Auburn, New York.

Free-will donation.

COMMODORE PERRY MEMORIAL HOUSE

The port cities along Lake Erie were used by escaping slaves as exit points into Canada. One of the way stations where fugitives hid until they could secure ship's passage was a tavern in Erie, Pennsylvania, owned by Josiah Kellogg. The walls of the tavern-inn were honeycombed with secret passages. Double fireplaces with secret openings led into stone-walled tunnels, which led to the bay where the fugitives could board ships to take them to Canada.

During the War of 1812, many of Commodore Perry's staff stayed at the inn before the battle of Lake Erie, which was a turning point in the war.

In 1924 the city of Erie acquired the inn and turned it into a museum commemorating Commodore Perry. The building has been restored with furnishings of the many families who have lived in the house. One of the false-walled tunnels used by fugitive slaves may still be seen.

Location: Commodore Perry Memorial House, Second and French streets, Erie, Pennsylvania.

Small admission charge. Group tours by reservation.

CHICAGO HISTORICAL SOCIETY

There were many black conductors in the Underground Railroad. One such man was John Jones, whose portrait hangs in the Chicago Historical Society Museum.

John Jones made a small fortune in the tailoring business in Chicago. He became acquainted with John Brown and Frederick Douglass and worked with them in the abolitionist movement, as well as using his home as a station on the Underground Railroad. Chicago, located on Lake Michigan, was an important in-transit point for slaves escaping into Canada. After the Civil War, Mr. Jones entered politics and worked for the abolishment of segregation in the schools of Chicago.

In addition to the portraits of Mr. Jones and his wife, the Chicago Historical Society Museum houses many interesting exhibits from slave days, items from the lives of John Brown and President Abraham Lincoln, as well as photographs of black soldiers who served in the Civil War.

A plaque commemorating the role Chicago played in the Underground Railroad may be seen at 9955 South Verley Avenue, Chicago.

72

UNDERGROUND RAILROAD TO FREEDOM

Location: Chicago Historical Society Museum, North Avenue and Clark Street, Chicago, Illinois.

Admission charge to museum.

OWEN LOVEJOY HOMESTEAD

After the death of abolitionist publisher Elijah Lovejoy in Alton, Illinois, his brother, Owen, moved to Princeton, Illinois, where his home served as a station on the Underground Railroad. In 1843 Owen Lovejoy was indicted by a grand jury for harboring two slave women in his home, but was acquitted at his trial. In 1863 Mr. Lovejoy, who had been elected to Congress, introduced the bill that led to President Lincoln's signing of the Emancipation Proclamation.

Owen Lovejoy's house, looking much as it did when Mr. Lovejoy sheltered escaped slaves there, was opened to the public in 1972.

Location: Owen Lovejoy Homestead on State Route 6, east edge of Princeton, Illinois.

Small admission charge. Special group rates.

ROKESBY, THE ROBINSON HOMESTEAD

Four generations of a remarkable Vermont family have lived in this house. One of the most interesting members of this family was Rowland T. Robinson, a Quaker and abolitionist, who sponsored an antislavery convention in Vermont and made his home, Rokesby, a major stop on the underground railroad.

The fugitives were housed in an upstairs room. Entrance to the room was gained by a secret stairway and long hall, which only certain members of the household knew about. The Underground Railroad that ran through Vermont had its exit point at the town of St. Albans, across the frontier from Canada.

The Robinson home is now open to the public, and mementos of its days as a station on the underground may be seen, along with many other fascinating historical items from the Robinson family.

Location: Robinson House, Rokesby, U.S. 7, Ferrisburg, Vermont.

Small admission charge. Special group rates.

73

KNOX COLLEGE

The town of Galesburg, in which Knox College is located, was a principal station for the Underground Railroad in Illinois. The majority of the residents of the town were antislavery, and refugees from Missouri knew they could find shelter in the homes of the town as well as at the college itself.

It was at Knox College that Abraham Lincoln and Stephen Douglas held a famous debate while campaigning for the U.S. Senate in 1858. During this debate, Lincoln declared prophetically, "A house divided against itself cannot stand. I believe that this government cannot endure permanently half-slave and half-free." Because this is the only site from those historic debates still standing, the Old Main Building at Knox College has been declared a Registered National Historic Landmark. Documents about the debate are on display in the building.

Location: Old Main Building, Knox College, Galesburg, Illinois.

No admission charge.

WAUKESHA, WISCONSIN

There were many reasons why a slave sought freedom. Sixteen-year-old Caroline Quales made her break for freedom when her mistress, in a fit of temper, cut off Caroline's long, shining black hair. Caroline managed to cross the river from St. Louis to Alton, Illinois, but was pursued by slave catchers when her mistress put up a reward of $300 for Caroline's return.

Underground conductors passed Caroline along from one station to another. At Waukesha, Wisconsin, Lyman Goodnow, traveling at night, escorted Caroline the last 600 miles to safety in Detroit.

Today there is a marker with a bronze plate on Lyman Goodnow's grave, honoring the memory of this first conductor on the Wisconsin Underground Railroad.

Location: Lyman Goodnow's grave, Prairie Home Cemetery, Waukesha, Wisconsin.

74

UNDERGROUND RAILROAD TO FREEDOM

CROSSWHITE BOULDER

Even after a slave escaped into a free state, he was not always safe. He could be recaptured and returned to his former master. In 1847 an attempt was made in Marshall, Michigan, to recapture Adam Crosswhite and his family, escaped slaves from Kentucky who had lived in Marshall for several years. When the slave catchers broke down the door of the Crosswhite home and attempted to physically capture the Crosswhite family, a crowd of angry Marshall citizens gathered and successfully prevented the seizure.

Crosswhite and his family were spirited away to safety, but members of the crowd who prevented their capture were arrested and fined heavily for helping escaped slaves. Public interest in the case spread throughout the South, and the action of the citizens of Marshall is said to have brought about passage of the Fugitive Slave Law of 1850, which made it a federal crime to help runaway slaves.

Today in the town of Marshall there is a boulder with a plaque on it at the approximate site of the battle in defense of the freedom of Adam Crosswhite.

Location: The boulder with plaque is located in a triangular park at the junction of East Michigan and East Mansion streets, Marshall, Michigan.

RALEIGH TOWNSHIP CENTENNIAL MUSEUM

The Reverend William King of Louisiana did more than free his slaves in 1849. He brought them to Canada, purchased land and began the Elgin Settlement, which became a haven for runaway slaves before the Civil War. By 1862 there were 1,000 men, women and children living in the community called Buxton, and together they owned 2,000 acres of land. Each fugitive slave as he arrived at the settlement was encouraged to buy a piece of land and then expected to farm the land and build a house. A school and three churches were built by and for the settlers.

After the Civil War some of the Buxton settlers returned to the United States to help educate their recently freed friends and neighbors. The people of North Buxton today are for the

75

most part descendants of the former slaves who elected to remain in Canada.

In 1967 a museum was officially opened as a memorial to the Elgin Settlement, designed to preserve the history and accomplishments of this small group of fugitive slaves who built a flourishing community from the wilderness.

Location: Raleigh Township Centennial Museum, Village of North Buxton, Ontario, Canada, 401 to Bloomfield Road, south on Bloomfield, west on 8th Concession, south on County Road No. 6.

Admission: Donation box at door.

UNCLE TOM'S CABIN MUSEUM

Many fugitive slaves who escaped to Canada settled there permanently. One such slave was Josiah Henson, more popularly known as Uncle Tom, because it was his life that Harriet Beecher Stowe used as the background for her main character in *Uncle Tom's Cabin.*

Josiah Henson returned south to help other slaves escape and, with financial help from church people in England, set up a vocational school, sawmill and gristmill at Dresden, Ontario, where ex-slaves could be taught to support themselves.

To raise money for the Dresden settlement, Josiah Henson made several trips to England, and was invited by Queen Victoria for a personal visit at Buckingham Palace.

After the war, Mr. Henson visited the plantation where he had lived in slavery. The plantation was in ruins, only the widow of his former master remained to greet him. "Si," she said surprised, "you are dressed like a gentleman." "Ma'am," said Josiah respectfully, "I always was."

The Dresden settlement has been restored to look much as it did when Josiah Henson was alive, with the Henson home, agricultural buildings, the church where Uncle Tom preached and the cemetery where he and his family are buried.

Location: Uncle Tom's Cabin Museum, Highway 21, Dresden, Ontario, Canada, approximately 60 miles east of Detroit, Michigan.

Small admission charge. Group rates.

76

UNDERGROUND RAILROAD TO FREEDOM

CHATHAM-KENT MUSEUM

So many slaves escaping into Canada settled in the town of Chatham on Lake Erie in Ontario that it became known as the capital for fugitive slaves.

In the Chatham-Kent Museum are displays centering around these communities of escaped black men and women. One of the most important of these settlements was the Buxton Settlement begun by the Reverend William King, who not only freed his slaves in Louisiana but brought them north to Canada and set them up on farms. There are also exhibits about Josiah Henson's Dresden Settlement.

Still standing on King Street in Chatham is the First Baptist Church where John Brown and a group of supporters met in May 1858. The outcome of this meeting was John Brown's raid on Harper's Ferry. A plaque in the church commemorates this meeting.

Location: Chatham-Kent Museum, 59 William Street North, Chatham, Ontario, Canada, about 60 miles east of Detroit, Michigan.

Small admission charge.

GRAVE OF AFRICAN NAMED FOONE,
ONE OF CINQUÉ'S SLAVE MUTINEERS

Joseph Cinqué and his rebel slaves from the *Amistad* mutiny lived in Farmington, Connecticut, for two years before and after their trial, which decided that they should be freed.

The appearance of the mutineers from the *Amistad* and their trial caused a sensation in the sleepy New England town. In Farmington Joseph Cinqué and his companions attended the First Church of Christ, Congregational, and were taught English in a small church school. After their acquittal, local citizens supplied them with equipment and money to return to Africa and start a mission school near Sierra Leone.

Unfortunately, during their stay in Farmington, one of the African rebels drowned while swimming. He is buried in the Farmington Cemetery and a marble headstone erected by the townspeople marks his grave.

Location: Farmington Cemetery, Farmington, Connecticut.

THE AMISTAD MURALS

In 1939, the centennial of the *Amistad* incident, Hale Wood-ruff, the distinguished black artist, painted a series of murals depicting the *Amistad* mutiny and the subsequent trial at Farmington, Connecticut. The murals catch the dramatic action of the battle aboard the slave ship and the sharp psychological tension of the courtroom scene in a variety of remarkable black and white faces, postures, gestures and expressions.

Location: The Amistad murals may be seen at the Savery Library, Talladega College, Talladega, Alabama.

NEW HAVEN COLONY HISTORICAL SOCIETY

A portrait of Joseph Cinqué, who led the *Amistad* mutineers, may be seen at the New Haven Colony Historical Society. The portrait was painted in 1839 or 1840 by a man named Jocelyn, who was a local artist. Jocelyn was active in the defense of the *Amistad* mutineers, and the portrait was painted for Robert Purvis, a prominent black abolitionist in nineteenth-century Philadelphia. The painting was given to the society by his son in 1898.

New Haven is approximately 30 miles from Farmington, where Cinqué and the other mutineers lived for two years before, during and after their trial, and where one of the mutineers is buried.

Location: New Haven Colony Historical Society, 114 Whitney Avenue, New Haven, Connecticut.

No admission charge.

A stereotype cut that was used on handbills before the Civil War advertising escaped slaves. The hundreds of handbills and advertisements placed in newspapers over the years by slave owners trying to recapture runaway slaves serve to disprove the myth that black people in slavery were contented with their lot.

Not all captured black people submitted to slavery without a fight. Some fifty-five slave mutinies aboard ships were recorded for the years 1699–1845. One of those mutinies, aboard the ship *Amistad* in 1839, is dramatically shown by black artist Hale Woodruff. The complete set of Amistad murals may be seen at the Savery Library, Talladega College, Talladega, Alabama. COURTESY TALLADEGA COLLEGE

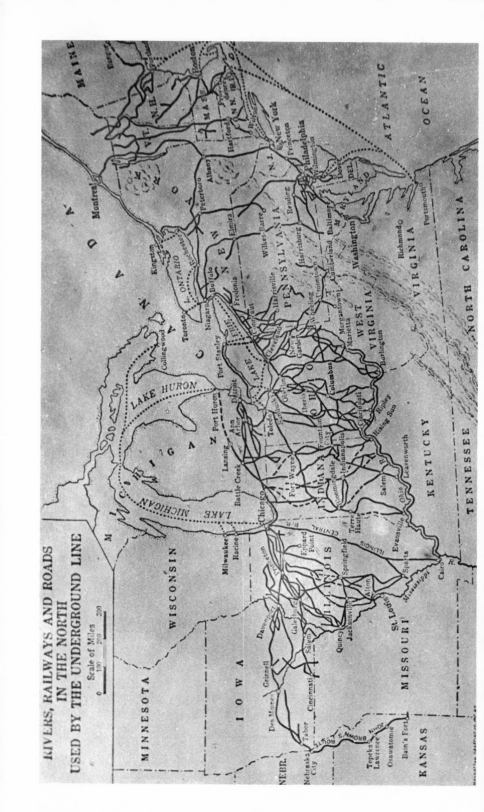

RIVERS, RAILWAYS AND ROADS
IN THE NORTH
USED BY THE UNDERGROUND LINE

Scale of Miles
0   100   200   300

This map shows the many underground routes that black people used in escaping slavery by fleeing to Canada. The map appeared in a history of the Underground Railroad written shortly after the Civil War. COURTESY WILBUR H. SIEBERT: *The Underground Railroad*

— wanted dead or alive.

HARRIET TUBMAN — Reward $40,000.

One of the outstanding heroic people in American history, Harriet Tubman continually and courageously risked her own life and safety to return south time and time again to guide other fugitive slaves to safety. Her home at Auburn, New York, with mementos from her days as a conductor on the Underground Railroad, has been preserved much as she left it when she died in 1913. PHOTO COURTESY TONY BETANCOURT

It was from an upstairs window of the Rankin house that a light always shone at night, a beacon for runaway slaves. So successful was the Reverend John Rankin in running his Underground Railroad station that slaveholders put a price on his head for his capture or death. PHOTO COURTESY TONY BETANCOURT

The Levi Coffin home at Fountain City, Indiana, once a busy station on the Underground Railroad, is today a Registered National Historic Landmark. During the period before the Civil War, when Quaker Levi Coffin and his family lived in this house, several thousand refugee slaves found shelter here before being passed on north.

The log cabin and the Milton Inn (which may be seen in the background) as they look today. Before the Civil War, the inn served as a station on the Underground Railroad, and the nearby log cabin was part of the escape route. When pursuers drew too close, the slaves would escape through an underground tunnel, which led from the inn to the log cabin. COURTESY GAF CORPORATION

A visitor to the Tallman House, Janesville, studying the narrow, hidden staircase from a servant's room to the attic. Fugitive slaves, sheltered at Tallman House, would use this staircase to hide in the attic when there were guests visiting the Tallmans. A wardrobe pushed against the wall hid the door from view.

After the mob murder of abolitionist editor Elijah Lovejoy, his brother, Owen Lovejoy, moved to this house in Princeton, Illinois. The house served as one of the way stations on the Underground Railroad in northern Illinois. COURTESY OWEN LOVEJOY HOMESTEAD, PRINCETON, ILLINOIS

Josiah Henson, the escaped slave who became the "Uncle Tom" in Harriet Beecher Stowe's famous book, made several trips south after his own escape to bring other enslaved black people north to Dresden, Ontario, Canada. COURTESY UNCLE TOM'S CABIN MUSEUM

In Dresden, Ontario, Canada, not far from the American border, Josiah Henson began a settlement where free black people could buy their own land and learn new occupations. Uncle Tom's home, school, church and a small museum may still be seen today, typical of the many small settlements begun by escaped slaves in Canada. COURTESY UNCLE TOM'S CABIN MUSEUM

This portrait of John Jones hangs in the Chicago Historical Society, Illinois. In addition to being a successful businessman and black political leader in Chicago, Mr. Jones was active on the Underground Railroad. He used his palatial home, and sometimes his tailor shop as a hiding place for slaves escaping into Canada. COURTESY CHICAGO HISTORICAL SOCIETY

Not all slaves relied on the Underground Railroad. Henry Brown, a slave in Virginia, had himself "boxed" by friends and shipped via Adams Express Company from Richmond, Virginia, to abolitionists in Philadelphia, Pennsylvania. He arrived safely after an uncomfortable trip that took twenty-four hours. COURTESY LIBRARY OF CONGRESS

Slaves often used daring ruses to make their escape. Ellen Craft, a fair-skinned black woman, dressed herself as a Southern gentleman. Her husband traveled with her, posing as her devoted servant. Because she could not write, Mrs. Craft carried her right arm in a sling so she would not have to sign her name on hotel registers. The Crafts were not safe, even in the North, and were sent to England by the abolitionists. After the Civil War, the Crafts returned and opened a school for black children near the plantation in Georgia where they had been slaves.
COURTESY WILBUR H. SIEBERT: *The Underground Railroad*

THE ABOLITIONISTS, CRUSADERS FOR FREEDOM

On a freezing November night in 1837, an angry mob surrounded a three-story stone warehouse in Alton, Illinois, on the banks of the Mississippi River. When the small group of men trapped within the warehouse refused to surrender themselves, the mob began throwing stones and shooting through the windows of the building. Still the men inside would not be dislodged. Finally one of the mob climbed a ladder and attempted to set fire to the roof of the warehouse. Several of the defenders slipped out into the darkness and pushed over the ladder. A second time a volunteer climbed a ladder to the roof. This time only one man tried to stop the arsonist. But when he stepped outside the door of the warehouse, he was spotted by a sniper. The sniper shot five times, and the man was killed instantly.

Who was this man and what crime had he committed

that a mob should turn upon him so furiously, and finally kill him? The man was Elijah Lovejoy, his crime that he was an abolitionist.

After killing Lovejoy, the mob surged forward into the warehouse. They dumped into the river the printing press on which Lovejoy had planned to continue publishing the *Alton Observer,* an abolitionist newspaper. Three other presses owned by Lovejoy had already been destroyed by proslavery mobs like this one.

But if the mob thought that by killing Lovejoy they had stilled his voice, they were mistaken. There were others to take up the cause. Four years earlier, in December 1833, a group of men who hated slavery as much as Lovejoy did had met in Philadelphia. The organization they formed spoke out in a voice that would not be stilled. Eventually it shook the very foundation of slavery—and finally destroyed the institution completely.

The group of men called themselves simply the American Anti-Slavery Society. There were sixty-three delegates from eleven states, and they met only during the daylight hours and under police protection because, like Lovejoy, they had been threatened with violence if they held their meetings. After three days, the delegates ratified and signed a document whose boldly stated objective was: "the entire abolition of slavery in the United States." This Declaration of Sentiments, as it was named, was signed at Adelphi Hall, not far from Independence Hall, where the Declaration of Independence had been signed fifty-seven years before.

Both black and white delegates attended the historic meetings at Adelphi Hall. Three noted black delegates who signed the Declaration were James G. Barbados, James McCrummell and the youngest delegate of all,

88

twenty-three-year-old Robert Purvis. Other black leaders, John Vashon, Peter Williams and Abraham Shadd, were named to important positions within the Society.

The Declaration of Sentiments, authored chiefly by William Lloyd Garrison, was as revolutionary and shocking a document as the Declaration of Independence had been in its day. For in nineteenth-century America, abolitionists—men and women who sought to abolish slavery—were considered radicals. They were regarded as subversives, part of the lunatic fringe of society, in much the same way that some responsible citizens considered critics of the Vietnam War and student protestors to be rabble-rousers and troublemakers.

It was understandable that plantation owners in the South with a great deal of money invested in slavery would consider abolitionists as dangerous. But many Northerners, too, hated and feared the abolitionists. Northern industrialists found it profitable to preserve friendly economic relations with the South. The workingman in the Northern cities feared the influx of free blacks into the labor market, competing for his job. And then there was always the great silent majority of citizens, apathetic and indifferent, only interested in maintaining the status quo.

Men and women who spoke out against slavery were vilified and abused, their lives threatened, their homes and businesses destroyed. William Lloyd Garrison, the fiery abolitionist who had founded the New England Anti-Slavery Society and published the antislavery newspaper *The Liberator,* was set upon by a mob and dragged through Boston at the end of a rope. Angelina Grimke, speaking at an antislavery meeting, was stoned and the building in which she was speaking was set on fire. A black abolitionist, Lunsford Lane, was almost

89

killed by a mob in North Carolina because he had delivered abolition lectures in Massachusetts.

Despite the threats and harassment, abolitionism spread across the Northern states. More and more anti-slavery societies were formed—in Pennsylvania, New York, New Jersey and as far west as Michigan and Ohio. By 1836 the abolitionists could boast of 300 such societies.

Women—who in some ways were slaves as much as the blacks in nineteenth-century America—were among the first to join the crusade, with antislavery societies of their own. In 1837 the first Anti-Slavery Convention of American Women was held in New York.

Probably the two best-known women abolitionists were Sojourner Truth and Harriet Beecher Stowe. They could not have been less alike. Sojourner was born a slave in 1797 and ran away to freedom when she was grown, taking her youngest child with her. In 1843 she experienced a spiritual awakening that made her declare, "I felt as if the power of the nation was with me." She renamed herself Sojourner Truth and began a pilgrimage across the country, speaking out against slavery whenever and wherever anyone would listen.

A tall, gangling woman in sober Quaker clothes, she could not read or write and hardly seemed the sort of speaker who would impress an audience. Yet audiences listened gladly to her low-pitched, forceful voice, enjoyed her quick wit, her courage in replying to hecklers. When derided for being black, she replied proudly, "I am colored. Thank God for that! I have not the curse of God upon me for having enslaved human beings."

Harriet Beecher Stowe, on the other hand, was the daughter of an illustrious New England family. She described herself as "a little bit of a woman . . . as thin and dry as a pinch of snuff." Her whole family was involved with the abolition movement; her brother, Henry Ward Beecher, a minister, preached abolition from the pulpit of the Park Street Church in Boston.

A modest, quiet woman, Mrs. Stowe was urged by her family to write a book that would show the nation "what an accursed thing slavery is." When she finally finished the book, which she had written in snatched moments between her duties as wife and mother to six children, she was sure she had failed, "that nobody would hear, nobody would read, nobody would pity."

She could not have been more mistaken. The book, *Uncle Tom's Cabin,* published in 1852, became almost immediately a runaway best-seller, not just in America but around the world. The book, which told of slave life in Kentucky from the viewpoint of the slaves, was one of the most important and successful weapons in the arsenal of the abolitionists. People who had never seen a slave, or thought much about slavery, read the book—or saw the play made from the book—and began to hate all slave owners. They began to sympathize with, and even join, the abolitionists.

Sojourner Truth and Harriet Beecher Stowe were only two of many women abolitionists. Sarah Forten, Frances Ellen Watkins Harper, Sarah and Angelina Grimke, Lucretia Mott, as well as others, worked as fervently for the abolitionist cause as any man, and faced even more abuse, because they were women and therefore were expected to sit quietly at home and tend to their knitting.

The fight for abolition of slavery, of course, did not begin with the American Anti-Slavery Society. Many early colonial patriots had spoken out against slavery, and free blacks themselves had for many years bitterly attacked slavery. In 1829 David Walker, a free black, published his famous *Appeal,* calling upon slaves to revolt against their oppressors: "It is no more harm for you to kill a man who is trying to kill you than it is for you to take a drink of water when thirsty," he stated defiantly.

The Southern states refused to allow the *Appeal* to be circulated throughout the South—but David Walker was not alone. Other free blacks held local meetings, wrote petitions, published books and gave money to the cause of abolition. The money given him by black leaders James Forten and John Vashon helped William Lloyd Garrison publish his antislavery newspaper, *The Liberator.* Black subscribers kept the fighting newspaper alive during its first years.

Some of the early black and white abolitionists tried another way to help. They believed that sending free blacks to settlements outside the United States was the only solution. Paul Cuffee, a wealthy black sea captain, used his money and influence to attempt colonization of free blacks in Africa. His attempts failed, but the American Colonization Society for Free People of Color was organized, and in 1821 the country of Liberia on the coast of Africa was founded by free black Americans.

However, in 1817, at a crowded meeting in Bethel A.M.E. Church, Philadelphia, James Forten, as well as other prominent black leaders, had spoken out strongly against such colonization. Such an idea, they pointed out, threatened the free blacks in America with exile and meant turning their backs on the sufferings of their fellow brethren still held in bondage.

Bishop Richard Allen put it even more strongly when he said, "We were stolen from our mother country and brought here. We have tilled the ground and made fortunes for thousands. . . . This land which we have watered with our tears and our blood, is now our mother country."

The colonization movement eventually died away, not to be revived again until after the Civil War.

These first antislavery movements, though, were too scattered to arouse many people in America to action. It took a highly organized national organization with state memberships, such as the American Anti-Slavery Society, to pull the movement together—and awake the conscience of America. Particularly it took the efforts of one man—Frederick Douglass.

Born a slave in Maryland of a slave mother and a white father, young Douglass led a half-starved, brutalized life as a child. As he grew up he was passed from master to master, and each owner attempted but never succeeded in breaking his spirit. The only happy moments in those years was a short time spent working for the Auld family in Baltimore, where he was taught to read and write by Mrs. Auld until her husband forbade her to continue the instruction.

At the age of sixteen, returned by the Aulds to his old master, he tried to escape but his plan failed, and he was sent to work in the shipyards of Baltimore. Here he faced the hostility of white employees, who resented slave laborers. Nevertheless, he continued his education on his own, reading whatever he could lay his hands on. When he was twenty-one, he again attempted to escape and this time succeeded, making his way to New Bedford, Massachusetts.

Douglass was not content, though, with just achieving freedom for himself. He wanted all black men and women in America to be free. To that end, he began speaking at antislavery meetings in Massachusetts, though he knew the danger of recapture when a fugitive slave appeared openly in public. His skill as a lecturer was immediately obvious. A broad-shouldered, distinguished-looking man, he was soon asked to speak all over New England at antislavery meetings. Later he wrote a book about his experiences as a slave and published a newspaper with Martin Delaney called *The North Star*.

His whole life was devoted to abolishing slavery, as well as fighting discrimination against free black Americans. As early as the 1840s, he refused to ride in the Jim Crow car on the Eastern Railroad from Boston to Portland. He had paid for a first-class ticket, and he insisted upon riding in a first-class coach. When the conductor and a half-dozen men attempted to throw him off the train, Douglass, a powerful man, held on so tightly that, as he wrote later, "in removing me I tore away two or three of the surrounding seats." In Indiana, after giving a speech against slavery, he was almost beaten to death by an angry mob, waiting for him outside the hall. Nevertheless, Frederick Douglass continued his crusade.

At first most abolitionists leaned toward a moderate view of working within the system to bring about an end to slavery. They were believers in nonviolence, in passive resistance against slaveholders.

Gradually, though, the abolitionists changed from quiet words to angry protest, particularly after the Fugitive Slave Act of 1850 and the Dred Scott decision of 1857. Dred Scott was a slave from Missouri who had been taken by his master to live in the free state of Illinois. He sued for his freedom because of his residency in a free state. The case was tried first at the Courthouse in St. Louis, Missouri, and the final decision from the

U.S. Supreme Court in 1857 was that since Dred Scott wasn't a citizen, he could not bring a case before the Court.

This decision only seemed to prove that the black American, free or slave, would never be allowed full citizenship through courts of law. Outraged abolitionists put moderation and reason aside and began to take matters into their own hands.

In Boston two runaway slaves were rescued from a courtroom by men with guns and borne safely away to freedom. In 1854 another attempt to rescue an escaped slave, Anthony Burns, failed when the storming of the courthouse by abolitionists was repulsed by armed deputies. The day Burns was taken in chains from the courthouse to be returned to his owner in Virginia, the shops in Boston were hung in black and police lined the street to prevent further violence.

One of the most militant of the black abolitionists, Henry Highland Garnet, added further fuel to the fire with his impassioned speeches, urging, "Brethren, arise, arise! Strike for your lives and liberties. Rather die free men then live to be slaves."

Finally the most devoted abolitionist of them all, John Brown, a white man, conceived a daring plan. He had worked for years in the abolitionist cause in Kansas and Missouri. At last he decided to form a small "Army of Liberation" and invade the South itself. With only twenty-two men, including five black men and his own three sons, he planned to capture the federal arsenal at Harpers Ferry, West Virginia. Once he had the rifles and ammunition stored there, he expected the slaves in Virginia to rise and join him in open rebellion, fighting guerrilla fashion from the mountains against the slave owners.

He and his men reached Harpers Ferry on a cold, drizzly Sunday night in October, taking the town by surprise. Although Brown was able to seize the arsenal, during the exchange of gunfire, a popular local black man was killed. Instead of slaves rising to join him, a contingent of ninety marines, commanded by Lieutenant Colonel Robert E. Lee, arrived the next night and besieged the arsenal engine house where Brown had his headquarters.

After the marines battered down the engine-house door, Brown and five of his men were captured. The rest were already dead or dying. John Brown was tried in nearby Charles Town for murder, treason and conspiring with slaves to commit treason. On December 2, 1859, he was executed by hanging. Of the five black men who fought with John Brown, Dangerfield Newby and Lewis Sheridan Leary were killed in the attack. Shields Green and John Anthony Copeland, Jr., were executed with Brown. The fifth man, Osborn Anderson, escaped and served with distinction as a noncommissioned Union officer in the Civil War.

Later, Frederick Douglass was to say, "John Brown began the war that ended slavery and made this a free Republic."

Alive, John Brown had been called a fanatic. Dead, he was a martyr to the abolitionist cause. There were those who still considered him a madman, but public opinion in the North was shifting slowly but surely against slavery. Abolitionists, once derided as lunatics and traitors, were now being called patriots. Their final victory came when President Abraham Lincoln signed the Emancipation Proclamation on January 1, 1863, freeing three-fourths of the slaves, and with the passage of the Thirteenth Amendment to the Constitution in 1865 which freed all slaves.

Unfortunately, the abolition of slavery, as it turned out, was only the first step in the long, hard road toward freedom for black Americans. And the abolitionists, often split among themselves, were never more than a fighting few. Yet this small, brave band of men and women and the cause for which they fought represented the very highest ideal upon which America was founded —the love of freedom and the hatred of tyranny.

There are historic sites around the United States that bring back memories of the abolitionist movement— Sojourner Truth's grave; Harriet Beecher Stowe's home and museum; Cedar Hill, the Frederick Douglass home; monuments to John Brown; and the National Historic Park at Harpers Ferry, among others.

There is, however, no one monument dedicated to the memory of the abolitionists and the cause for which they fought so valiantly. If there were, no better inscription could be found for it than these words taken from a speech by Frederick Douglass, and inscribed upon his statue at Rochester, New York:

ONE, WITH GOD, IS A MAJORITY.

PAUL CUFFEE MONUMENT

Paul Cuffee (sometimes spelled Cuffe), the son of an ex-slave father and an Indian mother, was sixteen when he shipped out to sea for the first time in 1775. By the time he was thirty-five, he owned his own whaling ships and a farm near Central Village, Massachusetts.

Although he loved the freedom of the sea, Paul Cuffee was well aware of the lack of freedom experienced by his fellow black countrymen on land. He was one of the earliest fighters for the abolition of slavery. He and his brother refused to pay their taxes because they were denied the right to vote; they started their own school for black children when the children were not allowed to attend the village school.

After visiting Africa, Captain Cuffee, using his own money, began transporting black American families to a new colony he started at Sierre Leone, where he felt black people could live in more freedom than in America. However, the War of 1812 cut short his dream of colonizing a new, free land.

Paul Cuffee was a Quaker, and at his death in 1817, he was buried in the cemetery next to the Quaker Meeting House. The Society of Friends have dedicated a monument to his memory, which stands by his grave. There is also a plaque honoring Paul Cuffee in the Town Hall.

Location: Society of Friends Church, Central Village, Westport, Massachusetts.

FREEDOM TRAIL, BOSTON

Boston was the chief port for the importation of slaves, but the city also produced some of the most vigorous leaders in the abolition movement. Today there is a well-marked 1½-mile foot trail, called the Freedom Trail, which runs through old Boston. The trail stops at many historic sites, such as the Boston Massacre Site and the Old Granary Burying Ground, both closely connected with black American history. A black man, Crispus Attucks, was the first man killed at the Boston Massacre, and he and the other men who fell with him that day are buried in a common grave at the Old Granary Burying Ground.

The trail also visits Park Street Church, Faneuil Hall and the Old State House. All three sites have connection with the abolition movement. William Lloyd Garrison (who published his abolitionist newspaper, *The Liberator,* in Boston) gave his first antislavery address at the church in 1829. Frederick Douglass spoke out against slavery at Faneuil Hall. The Boston Vigilance Committee to assist fugitive slaves, composed of black Bostonians, was formed at the Hall on October 21, 1850. Today the Hall is a military museum with historical paintings of famous battles, including a painting of the shooting of Crispus Attucks.

The Old State House today is a museum with many fascinating historical displays from early America. One exhibit concerns the abolitionists, with one slightly morbid artifact from John Brown—the heavy iron hook on which he was hanged!

Location: Park Street Church, Park and Tremont streets.

Location: Faneuil Hall, Faneuil Hall Square at Merchants Row.

Location: Old State House, Washington Street at State Street. There is a circular plaque set onto the cobblestoned street in front of the Old State House at the exact spot of the Boston Massacre.

Location: Old Granary Burying Ground, Tremont at Bromfield Street.

No admission charge to any of the above.

BLACK HERITAGE TRAIL

There is a Black Heritage Trail, sponsored by the Museum of Afro-American History, which intersects with the Freedom Trail and covers points of interest relating to black American history. The trail begins at the Old African Meeting House, Smith Court, Boston. For more information on this Black Heritage Trail, see the description of the Museum of Afro-American History in Chapter One.

FREDERICK DOUGLASS HOME

As George Washington led the fledgling country of America toward freedom and independence for white men, Frederick Douglass, one of the greatest of the abolitionists, led America toward freedom for all men—black and white.

After the Civil War he continued fighting and working not just for the education and welfare of the newly freed black men, but for women's rights and world peace. The last years of his life Frederick Douglass lived in a nine-acre hillside estate near Washington, D.C., called Cedar Hill. For many years after his death in 1895, the home lay neglected, but through the combined efforts of the National Association of Colored Women's Clubs, the Douglass Memorial Association and the federal government, the home is now a National Shrine. It was refurbished and reopened to the public in February 1972.

99

The home is decorated just as it was when Frederick Douglass lived there, including the library where he worked, his original desk and many other personal possessions that were part of his life at Cedar Hill.

Location: Cedar Hill, 1411 W Street, S.E., Washington, D.C. The home can best be reached from D.C. by crossing the 11th Street (Anacostia) Bridge to Good Hope Road, turning left on Good Hope Road to 14th Street, and right on 14th Street to W Street. The home is on top of the hill at 14th and W streets, S.E. Public transportation is available to within a short distance of the site.

No admission charge. Guided tours.

FREDERICK DOUGLASS MONUMENT

There are several plaques, statues and buildings dedicated to the memory of Frederick Douglass around the country. One of the most impressive statues and monuments is located at Rochester, New York, and was dedicated in 1899 by the then New York Governor, Theodore Roosevelt. The youngest Douglass son, Charles, posed for this handsome bronze statue of his father, which has bronze tablets around the base with excerpts from speeches by Douglass.

Location: Frederick Douglass Statue, Highland Park Bowl, Rochester, New York.

FREDERICK DOUGLASS GRAVE

Although Frederick Douglass died of a heart attack at his home, Cedar Hill, he is buried in Rochester, New York. This was the city where he published and edited his newspaper, *The North Star,* in 1847.

Location: Mount Hope Cemetery, 79 Mount Hope Avenue, Rochester, New York.

SOJOURNER TRUTH MONUMENT AND EXHIBIT

No other abolitionist speaker—with the possible exception of Frederick Douglass—could sway audiences against slavery as did Sojourner Truth.

Her faith in ultimate victory never wavered although she

100

admitted, "It takes a little while to turn about a great Ship of State." During the Civil War, she nursed wounded soldiers, and after the war, continued her lectures and travels for the welfare of freed slaves as well as for women's rights. Finally, she retired to her cottage at 10 College Street, Battle Creek, Michigan, where she died in 1883.

In 1929 the Sojourner Truth Memorial Association was formed and placed a handsome granite marker on her grave. An exhibit case with items from her life and work was placed on display on the second floor of the Kimball House Historical Museum, honoring one of the most unusual and outstanding women in American history.

Location: Sojourner Truth's grave, Oakhill Cemetery, Battle Creek, Michigan.

Location: Kimball House Historical Museum, 196 Capital Avenue, N.E., Battle Creek, Michigan.

Free-will donation.

ELIJAH LOVEJOY MONUMENT

Thirty years after Elijah Lovejoy met his death at the hands of a proslavery mob in Alton, Illinois, efforts were begun to have a monument dedicated to the martyred publisher. In 1897 the present Lovejoy Monument was dedicated, with a bronze-winged statue of Victory crowning the 93-foot main granite shaft. In 1969 the monument was refurbished and re-dedicated by the Lovejoy Memorial Association in cooperation with the *Alton Evening Telegraph* newspaper and Pride, Inc. Around the granite columns are bronze panels that tell of the life of Elijah Lovejoy.

The Lovejoy Memorial Association has also set up a college scholarship fund in Lovejoy's name, and the *Alton Evening Telegraph* has established a Lovejoy Press Award. The first of these awards was given to Carl Rowan, a well-known black journalist.

The grave of Elijah Lovejoy is about 75 yards behind the monument, down a graveled lane.

Location: Lovejoy Monument, Alton Cemetery, 5th and Monument streets, Alton, Illinois.

LOVEJOY PLAQUE

The death site of Elijah Lovejoy is marked on the bank of the Mississippi River at Alton. The Sigma Delta Chi, National Journalistic Society, has inscribed on the plaque ". . . without compromise he fought human slavery by the printed and spoken word and with his life defended his press against the mob which shot and killed him . . . 'I can die at my post,' he said, 'but I cannot desert it.' "

OLD COURTHOUSE (DRED SCOTT CASE)

It was at the Old Courthouse, St. Louis, Missouri, that the slave Dred Scott filed suit to gain his freedom in 1847. Although Dred Scott finally lost his case, the decision handed down by Judge Taney turned many Northerners into abolitionists and increased the widening split between the North and South over the issue of slavery. Ironically, Dred Scott himself was set free by his owner a few weeks after the decision was rendered and died a year later.

The Old Courthouse today houses a museum that includes a display about the Dred Scott case. The courtroom in which Scott was tried is no longer open to the public, but on the second floor are two courtrooms furnished in the same manner as the one in which the Scott trial was held. They are open to the public.

The Old Courthouse is part of the Jefferson National Expansion Memorial, which includes the impressive 630-foot stainless-steel Gateway Arch and a museum under the Arch.

Location: Old Courthouse, Broadway and Market streets, St. Louis, Missouri.

No admission charge to Old Courthouse. Small admission charge to ride to the top of the Gateway Arch.

JOHN BROWN MUSEUM, JOHN BROWN MEMORIAL PARK

In the years before the Civil War, the state of Kansas was torn by guerrilla warfare between the antislavery and proslavery groups. Among the more militant leaders in the antislavery group were abolitionist John Brown and his five sons. Brown

102

not only fought in several border skirmishes near the town of Osawatomie, Kansas (in one of which a son was killed), but raided into Missouri, freeing eleven slaves and leading them to safety in Canada.

Today the "John Brown Cabin" in Osawatomie serves as a museum and memorial to Brown's life in Kansas. The cabin originally stood a short distance northwest of the city, but in 1912 it was dismantled and moved to its present location at the John Brown Memorial Park. The interior of the cabin remains much as it was when John Brown was alive. There was once a cellar under the smaller room in the rear where fugitive slaves were hidden.

There is also a life-size statue of the abolitionist in the park.

Location: John Brown Museum, 10th and Main streets, John Brown Memorial Park, Osawatomie, Kansas.

No admission charge. Picnic facilities available at park.

HARPERS FERRY NATIONAL HISTORICAL PARK

In 1796 under the urging of President George Washington, a gun factory was established at the small town of Harpers Ferry, Virginia. By 1810 production had reached 10,000 muskets a year, and by 1819 the Hall Rifle Works was turning out 1,000 breach-loading flintlocks, using interchangeable parts.

It was this important arsenal that John Brown attacked, captured and then lost in 1859. He and his men withdrew to the engine house of the armory complex and used it as their "fort," but were unable to withstand the attack of Colonel Robert E. Lee and a force of ninety marines.

Brown and the survivors of his army of liberation were tried at nearby Charles Town and found guilty. Just before his hanging, John Brown prophesied, "I, John Brown, am now quite certain that the crimes of this guilty land will never be purged away but with blood." His prophecy came true with the Civil War, one of the bloodiest in the history of the world.

Today Harpers Ferry and John Brown's Fort are National Monuments and under development as a National Historical Park.

The Visitor Center has exhibits and a film on the life of

103

John Brown as well as a walking-tour map of nearby points of interest.

Location: Harpers Ferry National Historical Park, Harpers Ferry, West Virginia. The Visitor Center is on Shenandoah Street.

No admission charge. Conducted tours in the summer.

JOHN BROWN WAX MUSEUM

A privately owned wax museum presents the life story of John Brown from youth to gallows in true-to-life wax figures.

Location: John Brown Wax Museum, High Street, Harpers Ferry, West Virginia.

Small admission charge. Special group rates for schools.

JOHN BROWN'S GRAVE

John Brown's final wish was to be buried on his farm in North Elba, New York. The farm was part of thousands of acres set aside by wealthy abolitionist Gerritt Smith to be a free community for ex-slaves. The settlement, called Timbucto, did not succeed because the climate was too harsh and there were no markets for the farm products.

Today the farm is run by the state of New York as a historic site, with the Brown home restored to its appearance when the Brown family lived there. John Brown and several of his sons and companions who died at Harpers Ferry are buried in a grave site near the Brown home.

Location: John Brown's farm and grave, North Elba, New York, 6 miles south of Lake Placid on Route 86A.

No admission charge.

JOHN BROWN MEMORIAL

A single stone column in the center of a walled stone terrace was erected to the memory of John Brown in Akron, Ohio. In 1938 the monument was rededicated by the Negro 25 Year Club and a circular bronze plaque with John Brown's likeness added to the memorial. Cut into the stone tablet are these words: "He died to set his brothers free and His Soul goes marching on."

Location: John Brown Memorial, Perkins Park, Akron, Ohio.

THE ABOLITIONISTS, CRUSADERS FOR FREEDOM

MONUMENT TO THREE OF THE BLACK MEN WHO DIED
AT HARPERS FERRY

Three of the five black men who fought with John Brown are buried in Oberlin, Ohio: Lewis Leary, a native of Oberlin; John Anthony Copeland, Jr., a student at Oberlin College; and Shields Green, a fugitive slave from South Carolina.

The residents of Oberlin, who had long been active in the abolition movement and the underground railroad, were proud of the fact that several of their sons had fought with John Brown. In 1859 a cenotaph to the three black men who fought at Harpers Ferry was erected in Westwood Cemetery by their graves. The monument was restored and moved to the City Park, where it was rededicated in October 1972.

The Oberlin College Library has an outstanding collection of antislavery pamphlets and documents. The college maintains a visitors information center in the Student Union, Wilder Hall, on West Lorain Street. During the summer, guided tours are conducted.

Location: Oberlin College, Oberlin, Ohio. Monument: City Park, Oberlin, Ohio.

ABRAHAM LINCOLN HOME AND GRAVE

Although many black abolitionists, including Harriet Tubman, considered John Brown their true emancipator, there is no doubt that Abraham Lincoln did sign the Emancipation Proclamation of 1863.

Abraham Lincoln had strong personal feelings against slavery, but his political convictions in the beginning were not so much to abolish slavery as to prevent its spread. Once he was elected president, however, he was under constant pressure from the abolitionists to abolish slavery once and for all. Finally, realizing as he himself had said that the Union could not endure "half-slave, half-free," Lincoln issued on January 1, 1863, the long-awaited Emancipation Proclamation.

Lincoln's death by assassination at Ford's Theatre on April 14, 1865, caused grief, horror and anger among the black Americans he had freed. In the funeral procession to the Capitol, pacing at the head of the column was a regiment of black

105

troops with arms reversed. At every stopping place of the funeral train as it moved across the country taking Lincoln to his final resting place at Springfield, Illinois, black Americans waited to pay their respects. In Springfield every black person in town stood in line to see the funeral procession pass by.

Abraham Lincoln lived in Springfield from 1844 to 1861, when he left for the White House. His home in Springfield is furnished as it was when Lincoln and his wife, Mary, lived there.

Location: Lincoln Home, 8th and Jackson streets, Springfield, Illinois.

No admission charge.

ABRAHAM LINCOLN MUSEUM

This museum offers the complete story of Lincoln's life through dioramas and personal effects, as well as a comprehensive view of slavery and the Civil War.

Location: Abraham Lincoln Museum, 8th Street between Capitol and Jackson streets, Springfield, Illinois.

Small admission charge.

LINCOLN TOMB

Abraham Lincoln, his wife and three of his children are buried here. Construction of the tomb was started in 1869 and it was dedicated in 1874. Lincoln's body, however, was moved to various locations within the tomb. Once it was moved to foil a gang of counterfeiters who attempted to steal Lincoln's body with the idea of holding it for ransom! The body was not placed in its present, permanent location until 1901.

Location: Lincoln Tomb, Oak Ridge Cemetery, about 2 miles north of the capitol, Springfield, Illinois.

EMANCIPATION STATUE

The oldest memorial to Abraham Lincoln is a statue in Washington, D.C., financed by voluntary contributions of emancipated slaves. Immediately after Lincoln's assassination, the first five dollars toward the statue was received from a former slave. The bronze statute shows Lincoln holding the Emancipa-

106

tion Proclamation in one hand and placing his other hand on the shoulder of a freed slave. It was executed by Thomas Ball, and dedicated in 1876.

Location: Emancipation Statue, Lincoln Square between 13th and 11th streets, centering on East Capitol Street, Washington, D.C.

LINCOLN MEMORIAL

This magnificent memorial with the colossal seated statue of Abraham Lincoln is a shrine for all Americans, black and white. On the walls of the memorial are carved the Gettysburg Address and Lincoln's Second Inaugural Address, with murals depicting the themes of Emancipation and Reunion.

Thousands of people visit the Lincoln Memorial daily, but perhaps the largest amount of visitors came on August 28, 1963. On that day more than 200,000 Americans of all races, colors and creeds marched on Washington, D.C., to stage a civil rights protest on the steps of the Lincoln Memorial. The chief organizers of the march were Bayard Rustin and A. Philip Randolph, but the most compelling speech of the day was given by Dr. Martin Luther King, Jr., on the steps of the memorial. His famous "I have a dream" speech, included the moving words, "I have a dream that one day this nation will rise up and live out the true meaning of its creed: 'We hold these truths to be self-evident; that all men are created equal.' "

Visitors today to the Lincoln Memorial may hear interpretive talks given hourly beginning at 8 A.M. until midnight.

Location: Lincoln Memorial is directly on a line with the Capitol and the Washington Monument, Washington, D.C.

FORD'S THEATRE

It was while attending a performance at this theater that Lincoln was fatally shot by the actor John Wilkes Booth on April 14, 1865. The theater has recently been restored to the way it was furnished and decorated the night Lincoln was assassinated, including the box in which he and his wife were sitting when the shot was fired.

On the lower level of the theater is a Lincoln Museum, which

107

contains mementos from Lincoln's life, as well as a sound-and-light program depicting events surrounding the assassination.

Plays are once more being presented in the theater, and sometimes it is closed in the afternoons for rehearsals.

Location: Ford's Theater, 511 10th Street, N.W., Washington, D.C.

Admission charge to performances held within the theater. No admission charge to museum.

HOUSE WHERE LINCOLN DIED (PETERSEN HOUSE)

Across the street from Ford's Theater is the small house where Lincoln was carried after he was shot. The home has been restored, including the room in which he died.

Location: Petersen House, 516 10th Street, N.W., Washington, D.C.

THE EMANCIPATION PROCLAMATION

The Emancipation Proclamation only freed slaves in territories not held by federal troops. It was the Thirteenth Amendment to the Constitution, passed December 18, 1865, which placed slavery outside the law. However, there is no doubt that the Emancipation Proclamation spelled the end of slavery in the United States.

Lincoln signed the proclamation in his bedroom in the White House on New Year's Day, 1863. He had been shaking hands at a New Year's Reception since 9 A.M. that morning and his right hand was almost paralyzed. Twice he took up the pen to sign the document and twice put it down. Turning to Secretary of State William H. Seward, he explained, "If my hand trembles when I sign, all who examine the document will say 'he hesitated.' " A third time he grasped the pen and signed his name slowly but firmly.

There were three drafts of the Emancipation Proclamation. The earliest of these is the draft that Lincoln read to his cabinet on July 22, 1862. This draft is on permanent exhibit in the main building of the Library of Congress.

The second, preliminary draft is the only surviving copy in Abraham Lincoln's handwriting. It was purchased by Gerritt

108

Smith, the friend and patron of John Brown, and is now temporarily housed in a vault at the State Library, Albany, New York. When the new Cultural Center building is completed, the document will be on display there.

The original January 1, 1863, version of the proclamation was donated by Lincoln to be sold in Chicago to raise money for soldiers wounded in the Civil War. The document was on display at the Soldiers Home in Chicago when it was destroyed by the great Chicago fire of 1871. Fortunately, the official engrossed copy of this Final Proclamation is in the National Archives in Washington.

Location: The Library of Congress Building faces the Capitol and is across East Capitol Street from the Supreme Court Building.

Free conducted tours available.

HARRIET BEECHER STOWE HOME AND MUSEUM

For information about the Stowe Home and Museum, Cincinnati, Ohio, see Chapter Seven.

There are several statues and monuments in honor of Frederick Douglass around the country. One of the most imposing is this life-size statue on the campus of Morgan State College, Baltimore, Maryland. COURTESY MORGAN STATE COLLEGE

Frederick Douglass spent the last— and some of the happiest—years of his life at his home, Cedar Hill, in Washington, D.C. Today the house has been restored much as it looked when Frederick Douglass lived there and was regarded as the George Washington of black America. COURTESY NATIONAL PARK SERVICE, U. S. DEPARTMENT OF THE INTERIOR

Sojourner Truth and Frederick Douglass were two of the most persuasive abolitionist speakers in the movement. This portrait of Sojourner Truth shows her in the simple Quaker clothes in which she traveled the country, speaking "the truth" about slavery, no matter the hardships. A monument to her memory may be seen at Battle Creek, Michigan, where she spent the last years of her life.
COURTESY BATTLE CREEK CHAMBER OF COMMERCE

Captain Paul Cuffee was a New England sea captain who, instead of bringing black people in chains to America, reversed the process and in 1815 transported a colony of black Americans to settle in Africa. There were many free black men, like Captain Cuffee, who fought for the abolishing of slavery in the United States.
COURTESY LIBRARY OF CONGRESS

Captain Paul Cuffee, was a lifelong Quaker and much respected in his community. The Quakers were one of the first groups in America's history to speak out against slavery. After Captain Cuffee's death, a monument to his memory was erected near the Society of Friends Church in Central Village Westport, Massachusetts. COURTESY GEORGE SALVADOR

In 1837 a proslavery mob in Alton, Illinois, managed to kill abolitionist editor Elijah Lovejoy and destroy his press, but they did not stop the voice of the free press. COURTESY LIBRARY OF CONGRESS

The winged statue of Victory on the monument erected to Elijah Lovejoy at Alton, Illinois, symbolizes the triumph of the cause for which he fought and died—the freedom of black people and the freedom of the press. PHOTO COURTESY TONY BETANCOURT

It was on these steps of the Old Courthouse, St. Louis, Missouri, that slaves were sold to settle estates before the Civil War. And it was in a courtroom of the Old Courthouse that the slave Dred Scott sued for his freedom, in 1847. PHOTO COURTESY TONY BETANCOURT

The famous Dred Scott case did more than decide the fate of one black man. Although Scott lost his case in court, the decision turned many people against slavery and toward abolitionism. The Old Courthouse is now a museum with several courtrooms restored to look much as they did during Dred Scott's trial. PHOTO COURTESY TONY BETANCOURT

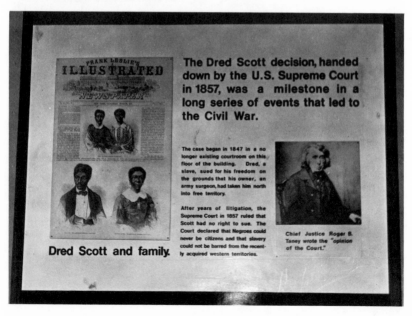

Dred Scott and family.

The Dred Scott decision, handed down by the U.S. Supreme Court in 1857, was a milestone in a long series of events that led to the Civil War.

The case began in 1847 in a no longer existing courtroom on this floor of the building. Dred, a slave, sued for his freedom on the grounds that his owner, an army surgeon, had taken him north into free territory.

After years of litigation, the Supreme Court in 1857 ruled that Scott had no right to sue. The Court declared that Negroes could never be citizens and that slavery could not be barred from the recently acquired western territories.

Chief Justice Roger B. Taney wrote the "opinion of the Court."

It took a company of marines under the command of the then Lieutenant Robert E. Lee to smash their way into "John Brown's Fort" at Harpers Ferry, West Virginia, where John Brown, the militant abolitionist, and his raiders had barricaded themselves. Five of the men who fought with Brown at Harpers Ferry in 1859 were black. COURTESY FRANK LESLIE'S WEEKLY NEWSPAPER, 1859

"John Brown's Fort" was actually the armory fire-engine house. This is how it looks today, a part of the Harpers Ferry National Historical Park, Harpers Ferry, West Virginia. COURTESY HARPERS FERRY NATIONAL HISTORICAL PARK

Thousands of black and white tourists visit Abraham Lincoln's tomb at Springfield, Illinois, yearly, in tribute to the "Great Emancipator." Scores of black people mourned the death of President Lincoln and silently lined the streets of Springfield when he was brought home to be buried in 1865. COURTESY TUESDAY MAGAZINE

MILITARY HEROES—
AND THE FIGHT
FOR THE
RIGHT TO FIGHT!

The Civil War began with the bombardment of Fort Sumter, South Carolina, on April 12, 1861. Two days later the fort surrendered to the Confederacy, and President Lincoln issued a call for volunteers for the Union Army.

Within thirty-six hours, a mass meeting was held by black citizens of Boston at the Twelfth Baptist Church. They pledged themselves "to raise an army in the country of 50,000 colored men ready to go at a moment's warning." In Philadelphia, New York, Cleveland and many other cities, black men rushed to enlist. By the time the war ended, 186,000 black soldiers had served in the Union Army, 29,000 in the navy. Altogether they fought in more than fifty-two military engagements and hundreds of minor skirmishes.

Yet for many years after the war ended, so little was

known about the black man's role in the Civil War that a historian wrote in 1928, "American Negroes are the only people in the history of the world, so far as I know, that ever became free without any effort of their own."

Black men had once again become the invisible soldiers in American history. Although they had fought and died in the early colonial wars—black men had served in the Massachusetts militia of 1652, had helped protect New Amsterdam armed with "half pikes and tomahawks" in 1689, were slaughtered in the Deerfield Massacre of 1704 and fought in the South Carolina militia in the Yamassee Indian Wars—these facts are seldom mentioned in history books. No doubt early white colonists felt uneasy about arming slaves who might be tempted to turn their guns against their masters, but it was a case of whom they feared most—their slaves or the Indians!

When the colonists began to fight England instead of Indians, it was a black man, Crispus Attucks, who was the first to be killed by a British bullet. The shooting of Crispus Attucks and the four white men killed with him at the so-called Boston Massacre on March 5, 1770, was clearly shown in a famous engraving Paul Revere did of the scene. The picture was widely and effectively circulated throughout the North and South to arouse the colonists' anger against the British. However, when the engraving was distributed in the South, there had been a slight change. All the men shown lying dead or dying in the snow were white men. Crispus Attucks had become the first invisible black hero in American military history.

When the Revolutionary War started, black minutemen fought and died at Lexington and Concord. At the battle of Bunker Hill (actually Breed's Hill), two black

118

soldiers, Salem Poor and Peter Salem, were commended for special gallantry. Black soldiers were with Nathan Greene when he captured Fort Ticonderoga, suffered the cruel winter at Valley Forge and crossed the frozen Delaware with George Washington to capture Trenton.

Yet at first blacks were barred from serving in the Continental Army by General Washington because the Southern colonies feared slave uprisings if the blacks were armed. Then in 1775 the English Lord Dunmore offered freedom to any slave who joined the British cause. So many slaves ran away to join "Dunmore's Ethiopians" that Washington was forced to reverse his decision and allow recruitment of free blacks. Slave owners were also allowed to enlist their slaves in the army as substitutes for themselves or to gain bounties of land. In the Northern states, free blacks flocked to the colors. In New Hampshire, almost every black male of military age, free and slave, joined the Continental Army.

In most cases the black soldiers fought in integrated units side by side with white soldiers. They fought in almost every important battle of the war from Fort Mercer—where they courageously withstood an assault of four Hessian regiments—to the siege of Savannah, Brandywine and Monmouth and the final battle of the war, Yorktown.

Black sailors also served with distinction in the young American Navy. One such sailor was James Forten of Philadelphia, who enlisted as a powder boy at age fifteen. He was captured with his ship, but was saved by the admiral's son from being sold into slavery in the West Indies, the fate of the other black sailors captured on his ship.

Because they were not as likely to be suspected, slaves

119

also served as spies, infiltrating British fortifications and bringing back news of enemy troop strength and other information to the American camp. There was even a black Molly Pitcher. A young black woman, Deborah Gannett, enlisted in the Continental Army as a regular soldier under the name of Robert Shurtliff. She served for seventeen months and after the war was cited for "an extraordinary instance of female heroism."

Many black soldiers and sailors were granted their freedom for serving with the American forces. Ironically, after black men had fought and died in battle, later in Philadelphia a constitution was approved that would keep black Americans in slavery for almost a hundred years more. On the other hand, if Great Britain had won the Revolutionary War, the slaves would have received their freedom much sooner, since England abolished slavery in her colonies in 1833.

When the Revolutionary War ended, the black soldier was almost eliminated from the army, although black sailors continued to serve on American merchant ships. These experienced seamen provided an invaluable source of manpower when the War of 1812, fought primarily on the seas, broke out.

The American frontier along Lake Erie was wide open to an invasion by the powerful British Navy. Commandant Oliver Hazard Perry, recognizing the danger, asked his commanding officer for reinforcements and was sent a number of black seamen. When Perry complained about "the motley crew of blacks, soldiers and boys," his commanding officer, Commodore Chauncey, replied tartly, "I have yet to learn that the color of the skin or the cut and trimmings of the coat can affect a man's quality or usefulness." With his "motley crew"

Perry managed to win a decisive victory, turning the tide of war in America's favor.

In New Orleans General Andrew Jackson also found his more than 600 black troops, commanded by black Creole line officers, extremely useful in winning the Battle of Chalmette against the British. Tragically, the battle was fought and won after a treaty of peace had already been signed ending the War of 1812. General Jackson did not hesitate to commend the black soldiers for "manifesting great bravery in the face of the enemy."

Black men did not fight with the American Army again until the Civil War, but they fought *against* American troops much earlier than that—in the Seminole Wars, which lasted from 1816 through 1845.

The Seminole Wars were fought not only against the Seminole Indians in Florida but against a slave insurrection. As early as 1690, escaped slaves from Georgia had joined with the Indians and Spanish in occupying Fort Moosa in St. Augustine, Florida. Many more slaves fled south and settled along the Apalachicola River. Although some were again enslaved by Indian tribes, they were still allowed much more freedom then they had known on the plantations.

Others of these escaped slaves intermarried with the Indians, and some assumed positions of responsibility and leadership in the tribes. An escaped slave named Abraham, renamed Chief Micanopy by the Indians, became a diplomat and emissary between the Seminoles and the United States government.

When the British left Fort Blount in Florida after the War of 1812, some 30 Creek Indians and 300 fugitive slaves from Georgia took over the installation. The fort became such a haven for escaped slaves that it was known as "Fort Negro." Southern slaveholders angrily insisted that the government not only see that their "property" was returned but that the Florida Indians were removed to Indian land in Oklahoma.

In the summer of 1816, Fort Negro was attacked by American soldiers and gunboats. After a four-day battle, a cannonball struck a powder magazine and the fort, with almost all its black and red defenders, was destroyed. The black commandant of the fort was executed, and the survivors were resold into slavery.

On a further slavecatching expedition, Andrew Jackson led an invasion across Florida to Pensacola, burning Indian villages and Spanish forts along the way, determined to end what he called "this perpetual harbor for our slaves." Although there were those who pointed out that Jackson's military expedition into Spanish-held Florida was illegal—Congress had never authorized an American armed invasion of a foreign country—still Jackson was a popular American hero and his march brought about the end of the Seminole War. Or so it was thought.

However, even after Spain ceded Florida to America in 1821, the Seminole War continued. Some of the Indian tribes agreed to the treaty that would move them west, but others refused because they would have had to agree to turn over the ex-slaves—along with any Seminole who had Negro blood—to the Americans to be sold into slavery. One young chief, Osceola, was so contemptuous of such a treaty that he thrust his hunting knife into the document.

The Second Seminole War dragged on for seven years, the most costly Indian war in American history. Black men fought side by side with the Indians, and one American officer commented that "The Negroes, from the commencement of the Florida war, have, for their numbers, been the most formidable foe, more blood thirsty, active, and revengeful than the Indian."

The Indian and black warriors used guerrilla tactics, engaging in small skirmishes, then vanishing into the swamps and everglades. The war turned out to be a political embarrassment to Jackson, now president, who sent general after general down to Florida, all of whom failed to win a decisive victory. One general, Thomas Jessup, announced flatly, "This, you may be assured, is a Negro, not an Indian war."

Finally, in 1842 the war drew to an end, with no clear-cut victory on either side. The Seminoles had been starved into submission. They agreed to move west to the Indian territory in Oklahoma, although some of the tribes never did sign the peace treaty and remained hidden deep in the Florida swampland. The Seminoles who did leave were allowed, however, to take their "Indian slaves" with them. Many black pioneer homesteaders in the Oklahoma territory were the descendants of these determined fighters for freedom in the Seminole Wars.

The Seminole Wars were a shameful episode in American history, and as such are often overlooked in history books. But in another twenty years, a war broke out on American soil that could not be ignored and that completely altered the course of American history. The war was, of course, the Civil War.

President Lincoln was afraid that his use of black soldiers would turn the wavering border states against the Union, so, as in the Revolutionary War, the black man at first was refused the right to fight for his country and his own freedom. Other leaders, ignorant of the courageous role that the black soldiers had played in the Revolutionary War, believed that the black man would not fight.

123

Nevertheless, immediately after the firing on Fort Sumter, free black men rushed to enlist in the Union Army. They were turned away from the recruiting offices. In Cincinnati they were told bluntly that it was "a white man's war."

The first year of the war, however, was disastrous for the North. The South, with fewer men, was outfighting the North at every turn. In addition, Southern slaves had been pressed into building fortifications and roads, working in factories and fields, releasing much-needed manpower for the Confederate Army. Under pressure from the abolitionists and leaders like Frederick Douglass, President Lincoln began to reconsider.

The first black combat troops to be attached to the Union Army were the Corps D'Afrique, formed in New Orleans in May of 1862. Other regiments soon followed: the 1st Kansas Infantry Regiment and the 1st Regiment of South Carolina Volunteers. One of the most famous was the 54th Regiment of Massachusetts, led by Colonel Robert Gould Shaw. Although some of the all-black regiments had black officers, most were commanded by white officers like Colonel Shaw. These hastily formed black regiments, ill-equipped and with little formal training, were soon bloodied in battle.

At Port Hudson, Louisiana, held by Confederate troops, a fort built by slave labor was situated high on a bluff overlooking the Mississippi River. In the spring of 1863, a line of Union troops, including two black regiments from Louisiana, made repeated assaults against the fort under murderous fire. After the battle, reporting on the action of the black troops, Major General Nathanial Banks stated, "No troops could be more determined or daring."

Two weeks later at Miliken's Bend, Louisiana, 1,000

ex-slaves, many of whom had received their muskets only a few days before, fought 2,000 Texans. When their ammunition ran out, the black soldiers used their guns as clubs, and the battle turned into bloody hand-to-hand combat, one of the hardest fought in the war.

At Fort Wagner, South Carolina, Colonel Shaw and his men of the 54th Massachusetts marched for two days through mud and swamp to reach the battle, then led the assault at sunset against the fort. Killed in the first wave of the assault, Colonel Shaw was buried with his fallen comrades in arms.

These and other battles in every theater of the war proved beyond a doubt that the black man would fight and die courageously for the Union cause. Perhaps these men fought even more bravely because they knew that if they were captured, the enemy would show them little mercy. At Fort Pillow, Tennessee, the rebel cry against black soldiers defending the fort was "No prisoners, no quarter." A wholesale slaughter of black prisoners resulted when the fort fell to the Confederate troops. Black supply troops guarding Union Army wagon trains at Poison Spring and New Edinburg, Arkansas, received the same treatment. One Confederate soldier wrote home afterward, "No orders, threats or commands could restrain the men from vengeance on the Negroes."

Black soldiers fought even though they were paid less than white soldiers, and in some cases received no pay at all.

In the navy black sailors made up one-fourth of the seamen. They took part in the hardest-fought naval engagements of the war, aboard the *Kearsarge,* the *Monitor* and with Admiral Farragut at Mobile Bay. The first naval hero of the war was a slave, Robert Small, who worked as a seaman aboard the Confederate transport

Planter. On May 13, 1862, when the Confederate crew was ashore, Small smuggled his family and relatives aboard the *Planter*. Then sailing slowly past the gauntlet of fortifications in the harbor so as not to arouse suspicion, he took the ship to sea, finally surrendering the *Planter* to the Union fleet outside Charleston harbor.

Women like Charlotte Forten and Sojourner Truth nursed the wounded in the hospitals and "contraband" camps where refugee black families were gathered. Harriet Tubman and Elizabeth Bower acted as spies and scouts for the Union Army.

By the end of the war, the United States Colored Troops (USCT), as they were known, could boast of twenty-one Congressional Medals of Honor. In all 29,-000 black soldiers and sailors had lost their lives, either through disease or in battle. As one correspondent from the *New York Tribune* reported at the battle of Port Hudson, after viewing the grim and silent lines of dead black soldiers, "A race ready to die thus was never yet retained in bondage and never can be."

But even as black soldiers were fighting for their freedom from slavery, another race of people on the American continent was fighting a last-ditch battle to preserve their freedom. In the far west, during and after the Civil War, Indian tribes began to join forces against their common enemy—the white man.

The Indian Wars lasted for three decades, from the 1860s through the 1890s. Among the most intrepid fighters in those wars were the all-black troops of the 9th and 10th cavalry regiments and the 24th and 25th infantry regiments. Although these "Buffalo Soldiers," as they were called, were primarily military men, they played such an important part in the winning and settling of the western frontier that their story will be told in the next chapter, which covers the black role in pioneer and frontier American history.

General Pershing served as a lieutenant with the 10th Cavalry in Montana. He was so proud of the reputation of the black soldiers that he became known as "Black Jack" Pershing. In 1898 he risked his career to get reassigned to the 10th Cavalry so he could go to Cuba with them when the Spanish-American War began with the sinking of the U.S. Battleship *Maine.*

Black sailors went down on the *Maine,* and black troopers fought their way up San Juan Hill with Theodore Roosevelt and his Rough Riders. In fact, some members of the 10th Cavalry reached the blockhouse on top of San Juan Hill before the Rough Riders!

Despite their proven fighting ability, during World War I blacks were at first brought into the army only as laborers, and once again had to insist upon their right to bear arms in combat. When black combat units were finally formed and sent overseas to France, they were, as usual, segregated. Although by this time there were black officers in the service, white officers were generally placed over the all-black combat units.

The most famous of these combat units was the "Fighting 369th," which remained in the frontline trenches under constant attack for 191 days, longer than any other regiment, white or black.

The Americans might have had doubts about the black man's fighting ability, but the French and Germans had none. The Germans offered a special award of 400 marks for the capture alive of a black soldier, and the French awarded the Fighting 369th their highest medal of honor, the Croix de Guerre.

Black soldiers, however, returning from World War I, discovered that although they may have helped make

127

the world "safe for democracy," the United States was still not a safe or democratic place for its black citizens. In 1919 seventy blacks were lynched or burned alive, including ten soldiers in uniform. In what became known as the "Red Summer," twenty-six race riots broke out across the country. Twenty-three blacks were killed in a Chicago riot alone.

Within the military, black regiments began to wither away. The proud 9th and 10th cavalry regiments had been broken up much earlier. Although three black men had graduated from West Point during the nineteenth century, there wasn't another one until the graduation of Benjamin Davis in 1936.

Segregation in the Armed Forces continued into World War II. And, as in every war, black soldiers had to prove all over again their courage and fighting ability. For the first time, blacks were accepted as pilots, learning to fly at separate if not equal facilities at Tuskegee Army Air Field. The 99th Squadron, the first of three all-black squadrons, flew over 500 combat missions.

In the Merchant Marine blacks faced less segregation, serving on the small, crowded Liberty ships, eighteen of which were named for black heroes. But in the Navy—the last holdout against integration—blacks still served primarily as mess personnel. It was one such messman, Dorie Miller, who became one of the first naval heroes of the war. When his ship, the *Arizona,* was under fire during the Japanese attack on Pearl Harbor—the attack that brought about America's entry into World War II—Miller manned a machinegun. He brought down four Japanese planes, receiving the Navy Cross for his action.

Black leaders pressed for complete integration of the Armed Services but were told by General George C.

Marshall, Army Chief of Staff, that, "The Army couldn't be expected to solve a social problem which had perplexed the American people throughout the history of the nation."

By the end of 1942, one-half million blacks were in the Army, but only 5 percent had been sent overseas. There were theater commanders who made it clear they didn't welcome black troops. Morale among black units hit a new low, with the white officers distrusting their enlisted men, and the enlisted men distrusting their officers. One black soldier said bitterly, "Just carve on my tombstone, here lies a black man killed fighting a yellow man for the protection of a white man."

There were other commanders, though, like General Douglas MacArthur who welcomed black troops, and General George Patton who bluntly told the black tank battalion sent to him that he didn't care what color they were, as long as they killed Krauts. Black engineer battalions constructed roads and ammunition dumps. Transportation units like the famous "Red Ball Express" trucked supplies to all battlefronts, at times under heavy enemy fire.

Segregation in the armed forces was officially ended by President Truman with Executive Order 9981 in 1948—at least on paper. Segregated units, however, were still to be found during the Korean War. Black and white troops might work together during the day, but in their quarters and recreational facilities they were still separate.

It wasn't until the Vietnam War that the American Armed Forces became completely integrated. And for the first time, the black soldier became "highly visible" as the war was brought home to the American people daily on the television screen. It was impossible to overlook the number of black faces staring grimly out from under helmets as they returned from patrols, or to ignore the fact that blacks, as well as whites, were dying in a war that grew more unpopular with each year.

Although the integration of the armed forces during the Vietnam War could not solve an American "social problem," it could and did banish once and for all the myth of the superiority of the white over the black soldier. And perhaps it also banished another myth—that the black man would ever again fight overseas for the freedom of a foreign people and then come back to his own country and accept second-class citizenship.

Abraham Lincoln said of the Civil War veterans that they "have demonstrated in blood their right to the ballot." A veteran of the Vietnamese War put it even more simply: "I've paid my dues. I'm going to have my freedom."

The monument to Crispus Attucks in Boston is probably the best-known monument to a black man who, although not in uniform, became in his own way a military hero. But there are other monuments around the country, not so familiar. There are also museums with mementos and battle flags from famous black regiments, and old military cemeteries with rows of graves marked simply with a name and USCT.

Perhaps most interesting of all, there are actual battlefields, once resounding to the roar of cannon and the shriek of battle, now silent, historic shrines. The following is not intended to be a complete list of all the skirmishes and battles in which black soldiers have fought. Rather, it is a list of restored battlefields and battlefield museums that may be readily toured by visitors.

Admittedly, in some cases one has to read very carefully among the exhibits in the museums to find any mention of black soldiers having taken part in the battle. Yet black soldiers were there. The ground of these battlefields was stained with the blood of black as well as white soldiers, who fought and died—often side by side.

REVOLUTIONARY WAR

CRISPUS ATTUCKS MONUMENT

Little is known of the life of Crispus Attucks but it is believed he was an escaped slave, a seaman and a stranger in Boston. He was in front of the mob gathered before the Customs House, protesting the presence of British soldiers in Boston. The protestors were armed with cordwood sticks, bottles and icy snowballs. The ten soldiers guarding the Customs House were armed with muskets. When a soldier was struck with a thrown object and fell, the other soldiers, frightened, lowered their muskets into firing position. A British captain, Thomas Preston, appeared on the scene and cried, "Don't fire!"

His cry came too late. A barrage of musket fire rang out in the cold night air. Crispus Attucks was the first man to die. Four white men also died—Samuel Gray and James Caldwell were killed immediately, and Samuel Maverick and Patrick Carr died later from wounds received that March night in 1770.

In 1888 a monument was dedicated, honoring these five men. The names of the men are listed on the monument, with Crispus Attucks' name leading the rest.

The five men are buried together in the Old Granary Burying Ground, where many leading patriots of colonial days rest. The actual site of the Boston Massacre is marked by a plaque in the center of the street in front of the Old State House, Boston.

Location: Crispus Attucks Monument, Boston Common, Boston, Massachusetts.

Location: Old Granary Burying Ground, Tremont Street at the head of Bromfield Street, Boston, Massachusetts.

FORT TICONDEROGA

In 1775 Ethan Allen and his Green Mountain Boys took the British fort of Ticonderoga in a surprise attack. There were several blacks with the Green Mountain Boys, including Lemuel Haynes, Primus Black and Epheram Blackman. Some of the cannons were removed from the fort and in the dead of winter were transported 300 miles, to provide much-needed armament for General Washington and the Continental Army.

The fort has been restored, and the museum contains one of the finest collections of weapons, uniforms and historic battle mementos in America, particularly dealing with the colonial period of American history.

Location: Fort Ticonderoga may be reached via an entrance 1 mile northeast of the city of Ticonderoga, New York, off state routes 73, 22 and 9N.

Admission charge. Guided tours during summer months.

BATTLE OF LEXINGTON AND CONCORD

On April 19, 1775, British troops were sent to Concord, Massachusetts, to destroy patriot munitions stored there. Paul Revere and other riders alerted the countryside. At the town of Lexington and at Concord Bridge a group of patriots called Minutemen assembled to stop the British soldiers. The British finally dispersed the Minutemen, but the Americans continued fighting as the British marched away from Concord. They fought in the way they had learned from the Indians, sniping from behind stone walls, hedges, trees and buildings, the red coats of the British soldiers making easy targets for their musket fire.

Black men fought side by side with the Minutemen at Lexington and Concord—Peter Salem, Samuel Craft, Lemuel Haynes, Caesar Ferrit and his son, John, and Pomp Blackman, among others. They all helped fire the "shot heard round the world."

Location: Battle of Lexington, Lexington Green, Center at Massachusetts Avenue and Bedford Street, Lexington, Massachusetts. A Visitor Center on Merriam Street provides tour information.

132

Location: Battle of Concord. The reconstructed North Bridge spanning the Concord River with the famous statue representing The Minutemen can be found one-half mile northwest on State 2A, Concord, Massachusetts.

MINUTE MAN NATIONAL HISTORICAL PARK

A recently completed national park covers 750 acres of the battle area between Lexington and Concord. A new Visitor Center has an auditorium where a film made in newscast style provides background information about the battles of Concord and Lexington. The museum also has exhibits from the battles, including information about the black soldiers who fought on Lexington Green.

Location: Visitor Center, Minute Man National Historical Park, located in the Battle Road Unit of the park, near the Fiske Hill area of Lexington, Massachusetts.

No admission charge.

BUNKER HILL MONUMENT

On the nights of June 16 and 17, 1775, the Americans had fortified Bunker Hill (actually Breed's Hill) in Boston. The next afternoon under a broiling sun, the lines of British soldiers in full-dress uniform and heavy knapsacks advanced up the hill against withering fire from the Americans aimed at their waistlines.

By the time the British finally swept over the soldiers entrenched on the hill, 1,054 of the attackers had been killed or wounded. The Americans lost 441 men. Among the black soldiers who fought at Bunker Hill were Salem Poor, Grant Cooper, Caesar Brown, Barzillai Lew (a soldier and fifer who remained in the army for six full years), Titus Coburn, Prince Estabrook, Seymour Burr, Prince Hall and Peter Salem.

Caesar Brown and Prince Estabrook died at Bunker Hill, the first full-scale battle of the Revolutionary War. It was a "dear bought victory" for the British and proved to the American soldier that he could stand up against the British regular soldier.

Location: Bunker Hill Monument, commemorating the bat-

133

tle, stands at Monument Square, Charlestown (across the river from Boston), Massachusetts.

Small admission charge to ride to the top of the monument.

PETER SALEM GRAVE SITE

A hero of the battle of Bunker Hill, Peter Salem was a resident of Framingham, Massachusetts, and is buried among other patriots in the Old Burying Ground at Framingham. His grave is maintained by the Daughters of the American Revolution.

Location: Peter Salem grave site, Old Burying Ground near Buckminster Square, Framingham, Massachusetts.

BATTLE OF TRENTON

At the beginning of the Revolutionary War, recruitment of blacks into the Continental Army was discouraged, but so many blacks, slave and free, had gone over to the British Army (in 1776 the British Army on Staten Island had 800 former American slaves enlisted) that General Washington had to reconsider.

In addition, by the end of 1776 the war was going badly for the Americans. General Washington had been retreating for almost six months. New York City had been lost to the British, and the battle of Long Island in August 1776 had almost crushed Washington's forces—140 black soldiers were among those who covered his retreat from that battle. If he was to hold his army together, he desperately needed a victory.

Across the Delaware River from Washington's camp in Pennsylvania, was the town of Trenton, New Jersey, where a Hessian brigade was in winter quarters. Washington decided to gamble. At 7 P.M. on Christmas Day, in a full gale, Washington and his men began to cross the ice-filled river. Despite the order against black soldiers, in Washington's boat were two black men, Prince Whipple and Oliver Cromwell.

The half-frozen army marched 9 miles over icy roads in a freezing rain to take the Hessian troops by surprise. Washington captured over 900 prisoners and lost only two men. They froze to death.

The victory at Trenton raised America's morale, and new recruits flocked to Washington's army. In 1777 Washington asked the Continental Congress to approve enlistment of Negroes in the army, and Congress agreed. In the same year a Hessian officer wrote home that there was no regiment among the Americans "in which there are not Negroes in abundance, and among them are able-bodied, strong and brave fellows."

Location: Trenton Battle Monument is located at the intersection of North Warren and North Broad streets, Trenton, New Jersey.

Small admission charge to top of observatory.

Location: Washington Crossing State Park, 8 miles northwest of the Trenton Battle Monument. Follow Penn Route 32 until left turn at Washington's Crossing. The location of the historic crossing includes a park and a museum.

Small admission charge.

BRANDYWINE BATTLEFIELD

In the fall of 1777 the tides of war turned once again against General Washington. At the battle of Brandywine in September, Washington lost from 1,200 to 1,300 men and was forced to retreat, losing Philadelphia to the British.

Edward Hector, a black soldier attached to the Third Pennsylvania Artillery (with only a few exceptions most black soldiers in the Revolutionary War served in integrated units), took a notable part in the battle of Brandywine.

When Hector's regiment was ordered to pull back, he disobeyed and, making use of weapons discarded by fleeing soldiers, he managed to save his ammunition wagon for the Americans. Many years later the Pennsylvania legislators voted him a forty-dollar reward.

Today the battlefield site may be visited, along with the headquarters of Lafayette, who served at Brandywine under General Washington.

Location: Brandywine Battlefield State Park, U.S. 1, Chadds Ford, Pennsylvania.

No admission charge.

VALLEY FORGE

In December 1777, after a series of defeats in the Philadelphia campaign, Washington and his army went into winter quarters

135

at Valley Forge. Here, exhausted, often starving, ill-clad or with no warm clothes at all, 2,500 out of the 10,000 soldiers died.

Black soldiers suffered and died along with white soldiers at Valley Forge, including Salem Poor, who had fought at Bunker Hill and other engagements. It is a mark of the great respect with which Washington was regarded by his soldiers that he was able to hold his ragged, unpaid army together that terrible winter.

Black soldiers were also winning respect for their courage and fortitude, and it was from Valley Forge in the spring of 1778 that General James Varnum left to raise a black regiment from Rhode Island.

Today the campsite at Valley Forge is a state park where the remains of the lines of entrenchment may be seen, as well as national and state monuments honoring the men who endured that terrible winter of 1777. In the museum, which was once Washington's headquarters, can be seen exhibits and mementos of the native-born and foreign-born, white, black and American Indian soldiers who supported the cause of independence.

A visitor center offers hourly slide shows on the history of Valley Forge and buses take visitors on a narrated ride covering all points of interest in the park.

Location: Valley Forge State Park, Park Reception Center at the junction of state routes 23 and 363, Valley Forge, Pennsylvania.

Admission charge for bus tour.

BATTLE OF MONMOUTH

On a blistering hot day in June 1778, the British, under Lord Clinton, with an armed column that stretched for 12 miles, were withdrawing from Philadelphia to the safety of New York through Monmouth County. General Lafayette and General Charles Lee, under orders from Washington, attacked the British column. The British beat back the Americans, and Lee ordered a retreat that was stopped when Washington appeared on the scene and rallied the American forces to return to battle. The fighting continued until darkness, and in the darkness the British pulled out.

136

The Battle of Monmouth was the last major engagement in the North, and in number of troops engaged was one of the largest battles in the war. There were at least 700 black soldiers among the 13,500 American troops in the Monmouth campaign. By 1778 Washington's Continental Army averaged about 50 black soldiers per battalion.

The Monmouth Battle Monument, dedicated in 1884, is on the site where some of the fiercest fighting of the battle took place. Bronze markers tell of important moments in the battle. Also nearby are historic homes, standing since the time of the battle, and a historic museum that includes exhibits from the battle.

Location: Monmouth Battle Monument, 70 Court Street, Freehold, New Jersey.

Location: Monmouth County Historical Association Museum, across the street from the monument, 70 Court Street, Freehold, New Jersey.

BATTLE OF RHODE ISLAND

In August of 1778 plans were made by General Washington to send a large force of militia and a portion of the French fleet to attack the British forces at Newport, Rhode Island. Although the militia attacked as planned, the French fleet was unable to support the militia because of a severe storm at sea and the sudden appearance of the British fleet. The American land forces were forced to withdraw under cover of night, pursued by a strong British attacking force from Newport, composed of British regular soldiers and Hessian soldiers.

Among the New England militia was a newly raised Rhode Island regiment of more than 200 black soldiers. (This Rhode Island unit and one from Massachusetts were the only two segregated units in the Revolutionary War.) The Hessians attacked the line held by these black soldiers, and the Rhode Island regiment was commended for showing "desperate valor" in repelling three "'furious assaults" for four bitter hours by Hessians.

Location: Battle of Rhode Island Monument, just off the junction of routes 114 and 24, Portsmouth, Rhode Island.

137

STONY POINT BATTLEFIELD

In the dark of a moonless night, June 15, 1779, General "Mad" Anthony Wayne and a light infantry brigade attacked and captured the British fort at Stony Point, New York. The attack was carried on with such secrecy that all neighborhood dogs had been killed to keep them from alerting the British troops at the fort of the Americans' approach. The fortification was taken after a brief but violent hand-to-hand struggle. Among the 600 captured British soldiers were several black soldiers.

Although by 1779 all the colonies had black troops in uniforms (with the exceptions of Georgia and South Carolina), slaves still continued to escape to the British lines. In 1778 Thomas Jefferson estimated that 30,000 slaves escaped from Virginia. Tragically, many of the slaves who joined the British and left America with them, hoping for freedom, were disappointed. After the war some of the British officers made fortunes selling the American slaves as captured booty in the West Indies.

At Stony Point, however, a slave named Pompey Lamb worked for the American cause by serving as a spy before the battle. He sold his vegetables to the British garrison and then returned to the American forces with information about the garrison, which helped the Americans to surprise the enemy.

Location: Stony Point Battlefield Reservation and Museum is 3¼ miles northeast of U.S. 9W, Stony Point, New York. A museum on the reservation contains interesting paintings, murals and relics of the Revolutionary period.

No admission charge.

FORT GRISWOLD MASSACRE

During the last engagements in the war in the North, a British force under the command of General Benedict Arnold (who had defected to the British the year before) attacked Fort Griswold near Groton, Connecticut, to gain possession of its military stores. The British finally overwhelmed the defenders of the fort. When Lt. Colonel Ledyard offered his sword to the victorious Tory officer, Lt. Van Duskirk, the lieutenant accepted the weapon, then plunged it into Ledyard's body. Then the victors massacred the garrison men, leaving eighty-five Americans dead.

One of the defenders of the fort was a black man, Jordan Freeman, who had killed a British officer during the battle. Legend has it that another black soldier, Lambert Latham, avenged Ledyard's death by killing the treacherous Tory officer.

Groton Monument on the hilltop near Fort Griswold is dedicated to the victims of the massacre. It bears a tablet with their names. The tablet also shows black orderly Jordon Freeman spearing the British officer.

The monument house contains relics of the Ft. Griswold massacre.

Location: Fort Griswold State Park, site of the massacre, Groton, Connecticut.

No admission charge.

SIEGE OF YORKTOWN

At Yorktown, Virginia, on October 19, 1781, Lord Cornwallis surrendered to Washington and Lafayette after a ten-day siege. Eight thousand British prisoners were taken, and the Revolutionary War was ended.

Black soldiers were among those present at the surrender of Cornwallis. One of them, a Rhode Islander named Bristol Rhodes, lost an arm and a leg in the siege.

Today the Yorktown battlefield is part of the Colonial National Historic Park. A National Park Service Visitor Center at the Yorktown terminus of the Colonial Parkway supplies information about the battlefield. There are also special exhibits, historic buildings dating from the time of the siege, and a self-guided battlefield tour available to visitors.

Location: Colonial National Historic Park, Colonial Parkway, Yorktown, Virginia.

Small admission charge.

WAR OF 1812

CHALMETTE BATTLEFIELD (BATTLE OF NEW ORLEANS)

This battle fought at Chalmette plantation on January 8, 1815, was the greatest land victory of the War of 1812. It was also

139

the last battle of the war—actually fought after the war had already ended, although the participants did not know this.

English General Sir Edward Pakenham with a force of 7,500 veteran soldiers hoped to attack and capture New Orleans, thus controlling the mouth of the Mississippi River. When the British reached Chalmette plantation, General Andrew Jackson and 4,000 members of the militia formed a defensive line against the British. Pakenham sent 5,400 of his soldiers head-on against the American line. The expert rifle and artillery fire from Jackson's militia, recruited from free blacks, Creoles, Indians, Kentucky backwoodsmen and even pirates, killed or wounded 2,000 of them within thirty minutes. General Pakenham himself was killed. General Jackson's victory at Chalmette assured the safety of Louisiana.

Interestingly enough, black soldiers fought on both sides of this battle. The British had black troops, the 1st and 2nd West Indian Infantry Regiments, and General Jackson had several hundred black soldiers organized as the Louisiana Battalion of Free Men of Color.

Chalmette was designated a national historical park on August 10, 1939. Today the park contains portions of the American defensive line built of fence rails, posts, wooden kegs and mud. The beautiful Beauregard House on the battlefield site has been restored as a visitor center and museum. Within the museum there are exhibits about the battle, including information about the black troops who helped win the day for General Jackson.

Location: Chalmette National Historical Park is 6 miles from New Orleans, Louisiana. From Canal Street follow the main thoroughfare that begins at Rampart Street and merges into St. Claude Avenue, then into St. Bernard Highway, which passes directly in front of the park.

No admission charge.

BATTLE OF LAKE ERIE

In this naval battle fought on September 10, 1813, Oliver Hazard Perry and his fleet of nine vessels won a decisive victory over a British naval squadron. The victory gave America control of Lake Erie, which was vital to winning the War of

1812. Perry's own flagship, the *Lawrence,* bore the brunt of the fight. When his ship became a floating wreck, with four-fifths of its crew out of action, Perry transferred to the *Niagara* and continued the fight. In another fifteen minutes the battle was won. From the deck of the *Niagara,* Perry wrote to General Harrison the now well-known words, "We have met the enemy and they are ours."

One-fourth of the men aboard Perry's small fleet of ships were black sailors. Originally Perry had not been enthusiastic about using black sailors, but after the battle he said of his black crew members, "They seemed absolutely insensible to danger."

The Battle of Lake Erie has been commemorated by a monument of granite, a column 352 feet high. Carved on the walls inside the rotunda of the shaft are the names of the vessels and of the sailors killed or wounded in the Battle of Lake Erie. The column is floodlit at night and is one of the world's greatest battle monuments.

Location: Perry's Victory Memorial is located on Put-In-Bay, South Bass Island, in Lake Erie, Ohio. To reach the island, automobile ferries operate from Catawba Point and Port Clinton, Ohio.

Small admission charge.

THE U.S.S. CONSTITUTION (OLD IRONSIDES)

The U.S.S. *Constitution* was launched in 1797 and fought against the pirates of Tripoli and in the War of 1812, winning forty-four battles in all. One black sailor, buried in Mt. Pisgah A.M.E. Cemetery, Lawnside, New Jersey, was so proud of having served aboard Old Ironsides in the War of 1812 that he had the fact engraved on his tombstone.

Today, restored and still seaworthy, the ship is a historic shrine. Uniforms, cannon and newspaper accounts of the War of 1812 are exhibited aboard her.

Location: U.S. Naval Shipyard, across the Charles River at Wapping and Chelsea streets, Charlestown (Boston), Massachusetts.

No admission charge.

141

FLAGSHIP NIAGARA

Perry's second flagship, the one in which he continued the fight at the Battle of Lake Erie with black and white sailors serving under him, has been restored. Visitors today may see the square-rigged wooden warship with its thirty two-pound guns, quarter deck and crew quarters, dispensary, sail bin and all the other facilities aboard the ship at the time of the battle.

Location: Flagship *Niagara* rests near the foot of State Street and Public Dock, Erie, Pennsylvania.

Small admission charge.

SEMINOLE WARS

FORT GADSDEN

When the British abandoned this fort in Spanish-held Florida in 1814, it was taken over by Indians and runaway slaves from the United States and called Fort Negro. Colonel Duncan Clinch and troops from Fort Scott were sent on gunboats to crush the fort. On July 27, 1816, a shell from a gunboat landed in the magazine of the fort, and as Colonel Clinch wrote later, "The explosion was awful and the scene horrible beyond description." Of the 300 men, women and children in the fort, only 30 survived the explosion.

Later the fort was used as a provision base by Andrew Jackson during the Seminole War, and still later it was occupied by Confederate troops during the Civil War.

Today the site of the fort is part of a state park. The remains of the earthworks and a network of trenches that once were part of the fort may still be seen.

Location: Fort Gadsden State Park, 6 miles southwest of Sumatra, Florida, on State Route 65.

No admission charge.

DADE BATTLEFIELD

One of the bloodiest battles of the Seminole War took place here on December 28, 1835, when Major Francis Dade and a troop of soldiers were ambushed by a group of Indians and escaped slaves who had joined the Seminoles. By the time the attack

142

ended, Dade and his company were all dead, except for three men who managed to escape.

The Dade Massacre touched off the second Seminole War, which lasted until 1841, when the Seminoles and their black "slaves" were removed to Oklahoma. (Descendants of these black Indians were later hired by the U.S. Army in 1870. Known as "Seminole Negro Indian Scouts," they were some of the hardest fighters against the Plains Indian tribes, and the most decorated military unit ever placed in the field.)

Today Dade Battlefield is marked by monuments and interpretive exhibits. A museum contains mementos from the battle.

Location: Dade Battlefield State Historic Site is 1 mile south of Bushnell, Florida, then a quarter mile west of U.S. 301.

Small admission charge to museum.

CIVIL WAR

SHAW MONUMENT (BATTLE OF FORT WAGNER, SOUTH CAROLINA)

In July of 1863 in an attempt to capture the harbor of Charleston, South Carolina, Union troops attacked Confederate-held Fort Wagner on Morris Island.

Spearheading this attack group was Colonel Robert Gould Shaw and the 54th Massachusetts Colored Infantry Regiment. They were new troops and in a forced march to reach the battle had had no rest and little food for two days.

When the regiment came within 200 feet of Fort Wagner, they were caught by a withering blast of musket fire from the ramparts and a crossfire from Confederate guns on nearby Sullivan's Island.

Colonel Shaw and about 90 men, including Lewis Douglass, the son of Frederick Douglass, and Sgt. William Carney, who won the Congressional Medal of Honor for his heroism that night, managed to claw their way to the parapet of the fort. Colonel Shaw was fatally wounded, while the remainder of his men fought in hand-to-hand combat until almost every one of them was killed. In all 1,500 Union soldiers were killed or wounded in the assault; 245 of these were men from the 54th.

Although the battle was a defeat for the Union forces, it was a victory for the black soldiers who fought and died at Fort

143

Wagner. Nationwide attention was focused on the battle, and no longer could it be claimed that black men were not as willing as white men to lay down their lives for freedom.

Almost twenty years after the battle, the city of Boston commissioned a bronze memorial to be raised to Colonel Shaw, born and reared in Boston, and the men of the 54th Massachusetts Volunteers. The artist, Augustus Saint-Gaudens, took fourteen years to complete the bronze bas-relief. When the memorial was unveiled in 1897, the remaining veterans of the 54th, some still bearing their battle scars, came, and as one man stood at attention.

Location: Shaw Monument on Beacon Street facing the State House, Boston, Massachusetts.

FORT SUMTER

The actual battle site of Fort Wagner on Morris Island no longer exists. However, it was under the guns of nearby Fort Sumter (where the first shot of the war had been fired) that black pilot Robert Smalls captured the Confederate steamboat *Planter* and steamed her out of Charleston harbor.

Regular tours are made daily to historic Fort Sumter, which is a National Monument.

Location: Boats leave for Fort Sumter from the Municipal Yacht Basin located on Lockwood Drive just off Highway 17 near the Ashley River Bridge, Charleston, South Carolina.

Admission charge for boat tour.

BATTLE OF BAXTER SPRINGS

In October 1863 the headquarters of Union General Blunt was being moved from Fort Scott to Fort Smith, Kansas, when the train the troops were riding came under attack. Although the attackers wore Federal uniforms, they were actually members of the infamous Quantrill raiders.

At a nearby camp, 100 Union troops, two-thirds of whom were from the 2nd Kansas Colored Infantry Regiment, also were attacked, surprised as they were having dinner. The defenders had to run a gauntlet of enemy fire to get to their weapons before they were able to drive the attackers away.

144

Most of the white and black troops who were killed fighting off Quantrill's raiders are buried in the Baxter Springs National Cemetery. There is a monument at the cemetery in their honor.

Location: Baxter Springs National Cemetery, Baxter Springs, Kansas.

OLUSTEE BATTLEFIELD

On February 20, 1864, on a flat, sandy field, studded with palmetto trees, was fought the largest battle to occur on Florida soil during the Civil War. Three of the nine Union regiments were black: the 1st North Carolina (Colored), the 54th Massachusetts Volunteers and the 8th U.S. Colored.

The 8th U.S. Colored troops, who were among the first in the battle, were mostly raw recruits who had never had an hour's practice in loading or firing their weapons. They lost more than 300 men out of 550, and were retreating in confusion when the 54th Massachusetts arrived on the scene and took over their positions. The 54th managed to hold the area until dark, covering the retreat of the rest of the corps, and were the last to leave the battle scene.

Today the battlefield is well marked and an interpretive museum has artifacts and dioramas of the battle.

Location: Olustee Battlefield State Historic Site, U.S. 90, 2 miles east of Olustee, Florida.

No admission charge.

JENKINS FERRY BATTLE

In April 1864 Union General Steele's forces were attacked along the Sabine River in Arkansas as they withdrew from the Battle of Marks Mill, or Poison Springs as it was called. It was at Poison Springs that Confederate forces overran a Union wagon supply train, manned by the 1st Kansas Colored Regiment, killing captured and wounded black soldiers.

In retaliation, when General Steele's forces were attacked at Jenkins Ferry along the Sabine River, black troops from the 1st Kansas, shouting "Remember Poison Springs," attacked and overran a Confederate battery.

The 1st Kansas Colored Regiment was the first black unit to

145

see action in the Civil War, at Island Mounds, Missouri. By the time the war ended, they ranked twenty-first among Federal regiments in percentage of total enrollment killed in action.

Location: Poison Springs Historic Marker, Poison Springs State Park, Camden, Arkansas.

Location: Jenkins Ferry State Park includes the battleground at Jenkins Ferry and is located 10 miles southwest of Sheridan, Arkansas, on State 46. There is a small museum in Sheridan, Arkansas, which has some items from the Jenkins Ferry Battle on exhibit.

No admission charge.

MANSFIELD BATTLE PARK

In 1864 President Lincoln wanted Federal troops sent into Texas to stop any French threat to the Union from Emperor Maximilian of Mexico. Major General Banks was put in charge of the Red River Campaign, as it was called. His troops included four infantry regiments of black troops.

After a great loss of lives on both sides, General Banks' advance was halted at the battle of Mansfield (or Sabine Cross Roads as the Union Army called it) on April 8, 1864. The next day at Pleasant Hill, Federal troops, including the four black regiments, repulsed a Confederate attack, then withdrew to the south.

At the Mansfield Battle Park Museum exhibits, dioramas, maps and exhibits from the battle may be seen.

Location: Mansfield Battle Park Museum, 4 miles southeast of Mansfield, Louisiana, on State 175, 3 miles southeast of the junction with U.S. 84.

Small admission charge.

PETERSBURG NATIONAL BATTLEFIELD PARK

In June 1864 General Grant encircled Petersburg, Virginia, in an attempt to cut off General Lee's communication and supply lines and force the surrender of the Confederate capitol at Richmond, Virginia. Four days of bitter fighting only forced the Confederate lines back a mile, and the Union forces settled in for a grim ten-month siege. For both the Confederate and

146

Union soldiers, it meant sloshing in steaming mud in trenches in the summer and freezing in ice and snow in the winter, bad food—and sudden death from rifle bullets and mortar fire. Involved in this siege were thirty-two black infantry regiments and two black cavalry units.

In July coal miners from the 48th Pennsylvania Infantry dug a tunnel underneath the Confederate lines and planted four tons of gunpowder there. It was hoped that the Union troops could rush in after the explosion before the Confederates recovered from the shock. The plan was a complete disaster. The mine exploded and formed a huge crater in the ground, but the Confederates quickly rallied.

Federal troops, rushing forward, were trapped in the crater and unable to climb out the steep sides. Confederate artillery soon had the range, and mortar shells exploded among the massed bodies within the crater. Despite the fact that the Union soldiers were now caught in a deadly cross fire and unable to retreat, the worst was yet to come.

General Edward Ferrero's all-Negro 4th Division was ordered forward and the men were soon facing musket fire from their front and a cross fire of shell and grape from their flanks. The soldiers who reached the crater found themselves facing Confederate infantry. In an orgy of shooting, clubbing and bayoneting, the crater became choked with the dead and dying.

Those who were able to fight their way out of the crater retreated in confusion to the Union lines. The losses among the black troops were staggering: 209 killed, 697 wounded and 421 missing.

Today the Petersburg Battlefield is a 1,500-acre park, established to preserve and interpret the battlefields involved in the ten months of siege warfare. Many original earthworks remain, as well as many battle points, including a reconstructed tunnel to the crater where so many black and white soldiers lost their lives. Exhibits along the way explain one of the most incredible episodes in the Civil War.

During the summer, there is a Living History Program conducted at the battlefield by the National Park Service. The life of Civil War soldiers is relived in surroundings like those during the siege. Included in this Living History Program are several blacks who vividly retell to visitors the story of the black soldier at Petersburg.

Location: Petersburg National Battlefield Park, entrance off State 36, Petersburg, Virginia. The Visitor Center at Battery Five (near entrance) has a park museum with exhibits from the campaign, electronic map presentation and battlefield relics. No admission charge.

RICHMOND NATIONAL BATTLEFIELD

Many small and large battles were fought around Richmond, Virginia, during 1864–65 as the Union forces fought to gain possession of Richmond, and the Confederate forces fought just as desperately to hold on. Many of these battles included black troops.

In July 1864 at Deep Bottom, Virginia, four black regiments withstood an enemy assault, which took three hundred lives. Six weeks later at New Market Heights, a brigade of black troops helped take Confederate Fort Harrison. Later, Secretary of War Stanton said of the day's action: "The hardest fighting was done by the black troops. The parts they stormed were the worst of all." Thirteen Congressional Medals of Honor were awarded to the black soldiers after the battle of New Market Heights.

Several other battles near Richmond in which black troops engaged were the battle of Chafin's Farm with the 8th U.S.C.I. (which had suffered such disasterous losses at Olustee), and in October, the battle at Darbytown Road with the 29th Connecticut C.I.

Richmond surrendered on April 3, 1865, and the 5th Massachusetts Cavalry, a black regiment, was among the first to enter the city. Today the historic sites, forts, breastworks and other landmarks of the many battles around Richmond have been incorporated into the Richmond National Battlefield Park.

There is a small visitor center at Fort Harrison to help tourists visiting the battlefield. There is also a headquarters visitor center at 3215 East Broad Street, Chimborazo Park, Richmond, containing an audiovisual program and exhibits about the fighting around Richmond.

Location: Richmond National Battlefield is 5 miles north of

148

the headquarters visitor center on U.S. 360, Richmond, Virginia.

No admission charge.

BATTLE OF NASHVILLE

On the fifteenth and sixteenth of December 1864, Union and Confederate forces fought outside of Nashville, Tennessee. Eight black regiments, recruited mainly from Tennessee and Missouri, were a part of the Union army.

The 13th U.S. Colored Infantry led the line of Union troops that attacked Overton Hill, which was strongly fortified by the Confederates. The troops had to fight their way up the hill against musket fire while threading their way through the abatis—tangled fences of knife-sharp branches placed along the hillside. Within thirty minutes, 25 percent of the black brigade had been lost, but the remaining men succeeded in reaching the parapet of the hill.

Some of the old forts and breastworks, trenches, monuments and historic markers may be seen on a portion of the Nashville, Tennessee, battlefield. A map of the battlefield showing the location of battle sites and markers may be secured from the Metropolitan Historical Commission, Stahlman Building, Nashville, Tennessee, for twenty-five cents.

APPOMATTOX COURTHOUSE

The Civil War ended on Palm Sunday, April 9, 1865, at the small village of Appomattox, Virginia. General Robert E. Lee's formal surrender to General Ulysses S. Grant brought to a close a war that had caused the deaths of 94,000 Confederate soldiers and 360,222 Union soldiers, including 29,000 black soldiers.

Today Appomattox village is a National Historic Park and has been restored to look as it did on that fateful Palm Sunday in 1865. Appomattox Courthouse serves as the Visitor Center with a museum and theater where a program about Appomattox is shown regularly.

During the summer months, local villagers turn the village into a "living history" area, including the role that free blacks played in village life during the Civil War.

149

Location: Appomattox Courthouse National Historic Park, on State 24, 3 miles northeast of Appomattox, Virginia.

Small admission charge to certain areas.

MOBILE BAY NAVAL BATTLE (FORT MORGAN AND FORT GAINES)

At the start of the Civil War, when blacks were refused enlistment in the army, many turned to the navy. By the end of the war, one-fourth of the sailors in the Union Navy were blacks, serving as firemen, landsmen, seamen and all ranks short of petty officers.

By the end of the war five black sailors had been awarded the Congressional Medal of Honor. One of these was John Lawson, who served on board Admiral Farragut's flagship, the *Hartford,* on August 5, 1864. On that day the Federal fleet of fourteen vessels attempted to pass Fort Morgan and Fort Gaines, defending the Confederate seaport of Mobile, Alabama.

When an enemy shell from a Confederate ironclad exploded in the midst of a six-man crew, Lawson, though wounded, refused to go below. He remained at his station until the battle was won and the forts were surrendered.

Today both Fort Morgan and Fort Gaines have been restored much as they were during the Civil War with gun emplacements and other fort relics, as well as a museum at each fort containing old photographs, uniforms and naval battle displays.

Location: Fort Morgan State Park, on Route 180, 20 miles west of Gulf Shores, Alabama.

Location: Fort Gaines, Dauphin Island, Alabama. Dauphin Island is reached by Dauphin Island Bridge.

Small admission charge to both forts.

ANDERSONVILLE PRISON PARK AND CEMETERY

Black soldiers fighting in the Union Army often faced more than prison if captured. Some were resold into slavery or shot. Those Union soldiers, black or white, who ended up in Southern prison camps found life there barely endurable. (Northern prisoner-of-war camps were not much better.)

One of the most notorious of the Southern prisoner-of-war camps was Andersonville. The prison consisted of an uncovered enclosure surrounded by pine log walls fifteen feet high. Twenty-six percent of the men imprisoned at Andersonville died from starvation, disease or exposure.

Corporal James Henry Gooding of the 54th Massachusetts Volunteers, wounded and taken prisoner at the Battle of Olustee, Florida, was one of these prisoners.

In September 1863 Corporal Gooding had written a letter to President Lincoln protesting the fact that black soldiers received lower pay than white soldiers. In protest the black soldiers of the 54th had elected to take no pay at all. Therefore, when Corporal Gooding died at Andersonville on July 19, 1864, he had never drawn a day's pay for his military service.

A month after Gooding died, the United States Congress finally passed a bill authorizing equal pay for black soldiers.

Today the site of Andersonville Prison is called Prison Park. Monuments erected by several states beautify the grounds of the park and the National Cemetery nearby where many prisoners are buried.

Location: Andersonville National Cemetery and Prison Park are about a mile north of the town of Andersonville, Georgia.

JEFFERSON BARRACKS MUSEUM AND CEMETERY

In the National Cemetery at Jefferson Barracks is a memorial to 175 soldiers of the 56th Colored Infantry Regiment who died of cholera while stationed at Jefferson Barracks shortly after the close of the Civil War. More white and black soldiers died of disease during the war than of battle wounds.

The Jefferson Barracks Museum houses many historic military artifacts and relics left by soldiers stationed at this post since it was built in 1826. One of the exhibits is about "The Immunes" recruited during the Spanish-American War.

The 7th Regiment of Immunes was a black regiment stationed at Jefferson Barracks in 1898. In those days it was believed that blacks were immune to malaria and yellow fever, which was killing many American soldiers in Cuba.

Although the Immunes never reached Cuba, the all-black 9th and 10th Cavalry and 25th Infantry Regiment did and played a major role in the Spanish-American War.

151

Location: Jefferson Barracks Museum, 533 Grant Road, St. Louis, Missouri.

Small admission charge. Guided tours.

WAR MEMORIAL MUSEUM OF VIRGINIA

The War Memorial Museum of Virginia has 18,000 exhibits and displays, covering every conflict America has seen from pre-Revolutionary times to Vietnam. The museum has one of the most valuable collections of military memorabilia in America today.

Included in the museum is an impressive display on the black role in America's military history, with special emphasis on the 10th United States Cavalry, which served on the western frontier as well as in the Spanish-American War.

Location: War Memorial Museum of Virginia, located on Warwick Boulevard at Huntington Park, Newport News, Virginia.

No admission charge.

CHICAGO HISTORICAL SOCIETY

In the Civil War Gallery of the Chicago Historical Society, there is available to visitors a slide-show presentation called "Years of Anguish and Glory," which includes actual photographs of black sailors, infantry- and artillerymen who served in the Civil War.

Location: Chicago Historical Society, in Lincoln Park at Clark Street and North Avenue, Chicago, Illinois.

Admission charge.

STATE CAPITOL, DES MOINES, IOWA

In the State Capitol at Des Moines are displayed the battle flags of Iowa soldiers who served in the Civil War. Included among these flags is that of the 1st Regiment Iowa Colored Infantry. Iowa lost almost one-third of its black adult male population in the Civil War.

Location: State Capitol, Grand Avenue between East 9th and East 12th streets, Des Moines, Iowa.

No admission charge. Guided tours available.

152

WORLD WAR I

VICTORY MONUMENT

This monument, created by Leonard Crunelle, was erected as a memorial to the black soldiers and sailors from Illinois who died in the line of duty during World War I. At the outbreak of hostilities, the old 8th Illinois National Guard was reorganized into the 370th all-black U.S. Infantry, 93rd Division. They fought in the terrible battle of the Argonne Forest and then pursued the Germans into Belgium. By the end of the war, General Pershing had awarded the Distinguished Service Cross for acts of extraordinary heroism to twelve members of the 370th and sixty-eight of them received the Croix de Guerre from a grateful French government.

Location: Victory Monument, 35th Street and South Park Way, Chicago, Illinois.

NEGRO SOLDIERS MONUMENT

In 1934 a monument was erected by the state of Pennsylvania to honor the black soldiers from Pennsylvania who had fought in America's wars.

One of the bloodiest and most decisive battles of the Civil War took place at Gettysburg, Pennsylvania, in 1863. Although black soldiers had not yet been recruited into the Union Army at the time of the battle, they acted as supportive troops, building barricades, roads, and serving as teamsters, wagoners, carpenters, hospital attendants and blacksmiths. By the summer of 1863, however, after the Gettysburg campaign, black troops were enlisted in the Union Army. Some 8,600 black Pennsylvanians served in the Union armies before the end of the war. Most of them were trained at Camp William Penn on the outskirts of Philadelphia.

Location: Negro Soldiers Monument, Lansdowne Drive, West Fairmount Park, Philadelphia, Pennsylvania.

WORLD WAR II

ARIZONA MEMORIAL

The battleship *Arizona* was one of the ships sunk by the Japanese attack on Pearl Harbor, Hawaii, December 7, 1941. The

153

Arizona sank with 1,102 men entombed aboard. Dorie Miller was a black Messman First Class aboard the *Arizona* when the ship came under attack. After carrying a wounded officer to safety, Miller took over an unmanned machinegun. Although, as a messman, he had not been trained in its use, he managed to shoot down four enemy planes and was awarded the Navy Cross.

By the end of World War II there were 165,000 black enlisted men in the Navy and 53 black officers. However, 95 percent of the black enlisted men in the navy were still serving as messmen. They fared much better in the merchant marine, where in many cases they secured equal ratings with white sailors.

A memorial has been built on the superstructure of the battleship *Arizona,* dedicated to the sailors who gave their lives at Pearl Harbor. Many black sailors were among those killed at Pearl Harbor.

Location: Cruise ships that tour Pearl Harbor and visit the *Arizona* leave Kewalo Basin, Pearl Harbor, Oahu, Hawaiian Islands, daily. The navy also operates a shuttle boat to the memorial several times a day from the memorial landing near Halawa Gate, Pearl Harbor Naval Base, Hawaii.

Admission charge for privately owned cruise ships.

VIETNAM WAR

MILTON L. OLIVE PARK

This park was named in honor of Private First Class Milton L. Olive, a black soldier in the Vietnam War. In October 1965, while Private Olive was part of a platoon moving against the Vietcong, a grenade landed in the midst of the platoon. Private Olive saved the lives of his fellow soldiers by grabbing the grenade in his hand and falling on it, absorbing the blast with his body.

For his heroism, Private Olive was awarded the Congressional Medal of Honor posthumously.

Location: Milton L. Olive Park, Ontario Street on the lakefront. Chicago, Illinois.

The monument to the five men killed in the Boston Massacre of March 5, 1770, may be seen in the Boston Common, Boston, Massachusetts. The name of Crispus Attucks, who was the first man killed that day, leads the rest.

An engraving of the Boston Massacre by Paul Revere hangs in the National Gallery of Art, Washington, D.C. Although the first man killed that day was Crispus Attucks, a black man, all the victims in this engraving are shown as white men. Attucks had become one of the invisible black military heroes in America's history.
COURTESY NATIONAL GALLERY OF ART, WASHINGTON, D.C.

On warships like the U.S.S. *Constitution,* black sailors fought alongside white sailors during the Revolutionary War, the War of 1812; and—in later wars—on steam-propelled ships. Today the U.S.S. *Constitution* is still a commissioned Navy ship as well as an historic shrine, berthed on the Charles River, Charleston, Massachusetts. Black sailors still serve on the U.S.S. *Constitution* today.
OFFICIAL U.S. NAVY PHOTOGRAPH

Peter Salem is credited by some historians with having shot the British commander, Major John Pitcairn, at the Battle of Bunker Hill. Freed by his owners so that he could join the Continental Army, Peter Salem also fought at Lexington and Concord. The Bunker Hill Monument in Boston, Massachusetts, commemorates the white and black soldiers who fought in this famous Revolutionary War Battle.
COURTESY INTERNATIONAL LIBRARY OF NEGRO LIFE AND HISTORY, CHARLES WESLEY

Chalmette Battlefield near New Orleans, Louisiana, was the scene of the greatest American land victory of the War of 1812. Black soldiers fought on both sides of this battle—black West Indians with the British and Louisiana Free Men of Color with General Andrew Jackson.
COURTESY NEW ORLEANS TOURIST AND CONVENTION COMMISSION, PHOTO BY GORDON PURSLEY

Where Fort Negro once stood is today a peaceful, historic park near Sumatra, Florida. Fort Negro in then Spanish Florida was a haven for runaway slaves from Georgia. The fort was defended by free blacks and Indians until the defenders and the fort were destroyed under attack by an American gunboat in 1816.
COURTESY DEPARTMENT OF NATURAL RESOURCES, TALLAHASSEE, FLORIDA

A recruiting poster for black soldiers used during the Civil War. By the end of the war, 186,000 black men had served in the Union Army. COURTESY CHICAGO HISTORICAL SOCIETY

COME AND JOIN US BROTHERS.
PUBLISHED BY THE SUPERVISORY COMMITTEE FOR RECRUITING COLORED REGIMENTS
1210 CHESTNUT ST. PHILADELPHIA.

The Shaw Monument in Boston, Massachusetts, honors Colonel Robert Gould Shaw and the all-black 54th Massachusetts Colored Infantry Regiment. The 54th fought valiantly at the Battle of Fort Wagner, South Carolina, in July 1863. Although the battle was not a military victory for the Union, it was a victory for the black soldier, who proved that he was as willing to fight and die as any white soldier in the Civil War. PHOTO COURTESY FAY FOTO COMPANY

The battlefield at Olustee, Florida, is quiet now but the flat, sandy field is still covered with pines and palmetto trees, as it was in February 1864 when black and white soldiers died here. Visitors can walk along the well-marked battle lines and visit the small battlefield museum. COURTESY DEPARTMENT OF NATURAL RESOURCES, TALLAHASSEE, FLORIDA

One-third of the Union troops at the Battle of Olustee, Florida, in February 1864 were black and mostly raw recruits. The untrained 8th U.S. Colored Troops, who were hastily thrown into the battle, lost more than half their men in a few hours' time. A black soldier later described the battle as "a fight, a licking, and a foot race." COURTESY CHICAGO HISTORICAL SOCIETY

During the summer, the Petersburg National Battlefield, Virginia, has a Living History Program re-creating the life of the soldiers who served here during the Civil War. The young men shown below are playing the role of black Civil War soldiers. Thirty-two black infantry regiments and two black calvary units fought at Petersburg. COURTESY NATIONAL PARK SERVICE, U.S. DEPARTMENT OF THE INTERIOR

A gun emplacement at Ft. Gaines on Dauphin Island, Alabama, with the flags that have flown over the fort since the early nineteenth century. Admiral Farragut and his flagship, *Hartford*, with a crew of white and black sailors, ran the gauntlet of the guns of Ft. Gaines and Ft. Morgan during the battle of Mobile Bay in the Civil War. Black sailor John Lawson won the Congressional Medal of Honor for his part in this famous naval battle. COURTESY CHAMBER OF COMMERCE, MOBILE, ALABAMA

Appomattox, where the Civil War ended on April 9, 1865, is now part of a National Historical Park. During the summer months local residents take the roles of villagers who lived in the hamlet at the time of the surrender. A local schoolteacher re-creates the role of one of the free black residents of the village in 1865. COURTESY NATIONAL PARK SERVICE, U.S. DEPART- MENT OF THE INTERIOR

Charleston, South Carolina, did not fall to Union troops until February 1865. Black soldiers of the 21st U.S. Colored Troops and 55th Massachusetts led the march into the captured city, as shown in a drawing by Thomas Nast displayed in the Museum of Fine Arts, Boston, Massachusetts. COURTESY MUSEUM OF FINE ARTS, BOSTON, M. AND M. KAROLIK COLLECTION

Frederic Remington, the noted Western artist, painted this scene of Captain Dodge's buffalo soldiers of the 9th Calvary charging the Ute Indians at Milk River. The all-black 9th and 10th Calvary and 24th and 25th Infantry regiments spent more than a quarter of a century patrolling and guarding the Western frontier. COURTESY DENVER PUBLIC LIBRARY WESTERN HISTORY DIVISION

An exhibit from the Spanish-American War which may be seen at Jefferson Barracks Museum, St. Louis, Missouri. The black soldier in the exhibit is a member of the 7th Regiment of Immunes who trained at Jefferson Barracks in 1898. (Although the Immunes did not reach Cuba, the all-black 9th and 10th Calvary and 25th Infantry regiments did fight in Cuba.) Five black soldiers won the Congressional Medal of Honor and two sailors the Navy Medal of Honor during the Spanish-American War. PHOTO BY RICHARD J. LYNCH

A monument in Chicago, Illinois, honors the black "Doughboy" of World War I. Black servicemen numbered 370,000 in that war and were the first to receive the French medal for bravery in combat, the Croix de Guerre. COURTESY CHICAGO PARK DISTRICT

Dorie Miller, the first black naval military hero of World War II, was serving aboard the U.S.S. *Arizona* when Pearl Harbor was attacked on December 7, 1941. Later this memorial in honor of the men who lost their lives that day was erected on the sunken superstructure of the *Arizona*. COURTESY HAWAII VISITORS BUREAU

The Korean War was the first since the Revolutionary War in which black and white soldiers once more served together in integrated units. The above photo shows men of the 2nd Infantry who fought near the Chongchon River in Korea.
U.S. ARMY PHOTO

Congressional Medal of Honor winner in the Vietnam War, Private First Class Milton L. Olive, III, has a park named in his honor in Chicago, Illinois.
U.S. ARMY PHOTO

PIONEERS
AND
COWBOYS

When the Civil War ended, the Union and Confederate soldiers returned home to find a changed world. The Southerner found his land in ruins, his towns destroyed, the economy at a standstill. In the North the Industrial Revolution was in full swing, but cheap immigrant and child labor made jobs hard to find for the returning veteran. Many men from both the North and South took their families, pulled up stakes and headed west.

The story of the westward migration in America is well known: the lonely wagon trains crossing arid plains, deserts and mountains; the hardships and perils faced by the pioneers on the long trail from Independence, Missouri. What isn't as well known is that black men, women and children were also involved in this great migration west.

In fact, long before the Civil War, the black man

played an important part in the Western scene. As early as 1536, four men, looking like savages in loincloths and beards, more dead than alive, reached the headquarters of the Spanish government in Mexico. Three of the men were white; the fourth was a black man named Estevan, sometimes called Estevanico.

The four were the sole survivors of the ill-fated 500-man Narvaéz expedition sent by the king of Spain to explore the northern coast of the Gulf of Mexico. Half the expedition had drowned in a shipwreck; the rest, captured by Indians, had died of starvation and disease. The four survivors managed at last to escape and make their way to Mexico.

Three of the four men returned to Spain. Estevan, sold into the service of the Viceroy of New Spain, remained behind in the New World. Estevan's stories of his adventures, particularly tales he had heard from the Indians about the Indian city of Cíbola or "The Seven Cities of Gold" so intrigued the Spanish Governor Mendoze that he decided to send an expedition to search for Cíbola. Father Marcos de Niza was selected to lead the exploring party, and Estevan was chosen to be the guide.

Posing as a medicine man with bells on his arms and legs, Estevan went ahead of the expedition and sent back wooden crosses to Father Marcos. The crosses grew larger in size as he neared his goal. At last a cross arrived at the camp as large as a man, but no further word came from Estevan. Two wounded Indians finally brought back the news. Estevan was never to reach The Seven Cities of Gold. He had been captured and killed as he entered an Indian village.

What Estevan discovered was not Cíbola but the Pueblo city of the Zuñi Indians. Although his discovery

166

brought no gold to the Spaniards, his early, careful mapping and exploration of Arizona and New Mexico led to later explorations of the Southwest by Francisco Coronado and Hernando de Soto.

Estevan was not the first black man to help in the exploration of the New World. Africans had sailed with Ponce de Leon when he discovered Florida. Blacks were part of Cortez' army when he conquered Mexico and they were with Pizarro in Peru. Wherever Spanish settlements put down roots in what is now the Southwestern United States, the African was there, too. A Spanish census of 1792 shows that there were 500 blacks living in Texas and that 18 percent of the people in what is now California were of African descent.

The Spanish village of Los Angeles was founded by forty-four persons, twenty-six of whom were of African ancestry. A black man was mayor of Los Angeles in the 1770s, more than 200 years before another black man, Thomas Bradley, took that office in 1973.

Another black resident, Pio Pica, was Governor of California in the 1840s. In that same period, one of the first millionaires and large landowners in California history was William Leidesdorff; his father was Danish, his mother African. Leidesdorff helped establish the first public school, the first wharf (at Leidesdorff and California streets) and the first hotel in San Francisco. He also assisted in setting up the new government when California became a state.

While the Spanish were seeking gold and spreading the Catholic faith in the Southwest and Florida, the French were establishing themselves as fur trappers in the largely untouched wilderness along the Mississippi River Valley. Jean Baptiste Point Du Sable, of French and African parentage, was one of the earliest of these

167

fur trappers. In 1779, after marrying a Potawatomi Indian, he set up a prosperous trading post at the mouth of the Chicago River. This trading post was the first permanent settlement in what was to become the city of Chicago.

In 1800 Du Sable sold out his fur-trading business and retired to St. Charles, Missouri, but by 1803 the Mississippi Valley was no longer in French hands. By the terms of the Louisiana Purchase of 1803, the American government had gained possession of 909,130 square miles of land, about which they knew very little. Meriwether Lewis and William Clark were sent by President Thomas Jefferson to explore the new American territory. York, a slave of William Clark's, went along on the expedition.

An impressive-looking man, over six feet tall, York was the center of attention when Indian tribes visited the camp of the exploring party. Many of the Indians had never seen a black man before. The Mandan Indians thought he had painted his body with charcoal and were amazed when they were unable to rub the color off. At the end of the two-and-one-half-year expedition, as a reward for the valuable assistance he had given the expedition as hunter and fisherman, as well as by his ability to make friends with the Indian tribes, Clark gave York his freedom. It is said that York promptly returned to the West he had helped explore and took up life with the Indians.

Black men also traveled with John C. Fremont on his three pathfinding expeditions to the West. One man, Saunders Jackson, joined Fremont to make enough money to buy his family from a Missouri plantation owner. Happily, when gold was discovered in California,

Jackson dug enough gold in just a few days to return to Missouri and buy his family's freedom.

Even more than explorers like Lewis and Clark and Fremont, the men who unlocked the secrets of the West were the fur trappers, or mountain men as they were called. An unusual breed of men, they roamed the valleys and mountains with only a big-bored rifle and a shaggy horse for company, setting their traps in icy waters in search of the valuable beaver. Coming and going as they pleased, when they did occasionally meet with other mountain men, they loved to swap tall tales of their adventures.

Two such mountain men, who lived at the same time as Daniel Boone and Jim Bridger, were black men— Ed Rose and James Beckwourth. Rose, reported to be an ex-river pirate, hired out to fur companies as a trapper, scout and interpreter. As a trapper, he was the first black man to explore the Yellowstone region, but he much preferred living with the Indians to living with white men.

Beckwourth was a more restless man, seldom staying in one place very long. He started his fur trapping in the Green River region of Wyoming, married a daughter of a Crow chief, and became a Crow chief himself. He managed a trading post in Montana as well as fighting in both the Seminole Wars and the California Revolution as an Army Scout. He is best known, perhaps, for his discovery in April of 1850 of a pass through the Sierra Nevada Mountains. He led the first wagon train of settlers through the pass. The pass, mountain peak, valley and town nearby are named for him.

In Minnesota the Bonga family, who came to the territory as slaves, gained their freedom, took Chippewa brides and made a fortune in the fur trade, leaving their name on a township in the state.

The relationship between the American Indian and the black man in frontier America has only begun to be explored by historians. Yet there is no doubt that there was a unique and, at times, close relationship between the two groups. Records show that slaves captured by Indians on their raids against Eastern colonial settlements were seldom tortured or killed; instead they were often adopted into the tribe.

Intermarriage between blacks and Indians was not uncommon in colonial days. Paul Cuffee, the prominent New England shipbuilder, took an Indian wife, and was himself the son of a slave and his Indian wife. Edmonia Lewis, the noted sculptress, was of mixed Indian-black parentage, and was reared partly by her mother's tribe. Certainly the freedom enjoyed by the American Indians (until they were finally placed upon reservations) must have held a tantalizing attraction for the enslaved black man.

Mountain men and fur traders were not the only blacks to come west in the 1800s. Black servants were with the Mormons on their long, arduous trek to Utah and their promised land. And when Southern plantation land became exhausted from overplanting, many wealthy planters headed west to Texas to find new land. Coffles of their slaves trudged along behind their wagon trains.

One such slave, Biddy Mason, following her master's wagon train to the California gold fields, had the difficult job of herding the cattle on the long, exhausting trip. When her master decided to give up the gold fields and return home, Biddy convinced the local sheriff that she and her family were entitled to their freedom and remained behind. Through hard work and shrewd land investments, she made enough money to donate schools, churches and nursing homes to the community where she lived.

Other adventurers, black and white, who headed for the gold fields in 1849 were not so fortunate. Many black miners, caught up in the gold fever that swept the country, barely made enough to scrape by. If they were lucky enough to make a strike, they often lost their claims in the gambling halls or to claim jumpers. One black miner, Alvin Coffey, however, held on to his gold. A slave from Missouri who came west with his owner, he earned enough money to finally buy his freedom and that of his wife and children.

Other black miners were fortunate enough to own and operate their own mines or, like Moses Rodgers, became mining experts. Robert Anthony, an ex-slave, built and operated the first quartz mill in California.

The best known of the black miners was ex-hotel-keeper Barney Ford. With a friend, Henry O. Wagoner, Ford filed a gold claim on a hill outside of Breckenridge, Colorado. The claim was supposedly so rich that jealous white miners in the area jumped the claim and forced Ford and Wagoner to leave. Ironically, despite years of searching, no gold was ever found in Barney Ford's Hill, as it is known today. Barney Ford and his friend, however, fared much better than the claim jumpers. They started several successful businesses in Denver, including hotels, barbershops and restaurants. They also lobbied in Washington, D.C., to make sure that when Colorado entered the Union, her black citizens had the right to vote.

The gold fields were a great attraction in the 1840s but so was the promise of free Western land. Black

171

farmers, like an ex-slave named George Washington, followed the Oregon Trail west. Washington established a homestead on 640 acres of land. Later he established the town of Centralia, Washington.

Another farmer and veteran of the War of 1812, George W. Bush, joined a wagon train in 1844 and settled in Puget Sound, Oregon. So respected was Bush for his farming skills and generosity to his neighbors that when the Puget Sound area finally came under control of American law, rather than British, Bush and his family were specially exempted from the Oregon black laws then in effect, which would have taken away his land and citizenship.

Black men entered all occupations in the West. They were editors, like Mifflin W. Gibbs, who published California's first black newspaper, *Mirror of the Times;* they were pony-express riders and stagecoach drivers, schoolteachers and shopkeepers.

And they were not all men. Clara Brown, who as a slave had seen her husband and children sold away from her, finally managed to purchase her own freedom and make her way west. She operated a laundry in Central City, Colorado, and made enough money to bring many of her relatives west on several wagon trains she helped sponsor.

Mary Ellen Pleasant, another ex-slave, raised money for the abolition movement in California, helped finance John Brown's raid on Harpers Ferry and spearheaded a successful drive to repeal California's black laws.

Although the blacks settling in the West before the Civil War were few, compared to their numbers in the South, they joined successfully with white abolitionists in agitating against the spread of slavery from the South into the Western territories.

After the Civil War, the stream of pioneers and settlers moving west became a flood, so much so that by 1890 the primitive Western frontier was no more. In those few short years a hard-fought struggle had taken place between the settlers putting down their roots into a new free land and the Indian tribes fighting desperately to hold on to the last remnants of their freedom and a way of life completely alien to the white man.

The settlers turned to the government, asking for protection against the Indians, and the U.S. Army set up a line of forts along the Western frontier. The troops were to seek out and punish the marauding Indian tribes and to protect the various shaky Indian treaties that were in effect.

Duty at these Western forts was harsh, dangerous and lonely and 20 percent of the soldiers who patrolled this Western frontier were black men. In 1866 Congress had authorized the formation of four all-black regiments, the 24th and 25th infantry regiments and the 9th and 10th cavalry regiments. Almost immediately after their formation, all four regiments were posted to Western garrisons for duty.

Called "brunettes" by the white soldiers, the black troopers were named "buffalo soldiers" by the Indians as a mark of respect, for the buffalo was sacred to the Indian. The Indians had good reason to respect the buffalo soldier. The 9th and 10th Cavalry, although their equipment and horses were often rejects from the more favored 7th Cavalry, developed into one of the hardest-fighting, best-disciplined and most efficient mounted forces on the Western frontier.

The buffalo soldiers developed a legendary ability to arrive in the nick of time to save besieged fellow troopers under Indian attack. At Sandy Creek, Major General George Forsyth and his men were pinned down by an Indian attack for almost a week. Their food and medical supplies gone, half-mad from the heat, the men were forced to eat their dead horses. A messenger finally made it through the Indian lines and reached Fort Wallace. Captain Louis Carpenter and his 10th Cavalry troopers covered 100 miles in two days to rescue General Forsyth and his men.

A company of the 9th Cavalry rode an equal distance, and on the way took part in two Indian fights, to relieve a unit of the besieged 7th Cavalry when it was under Indian attack. By the end of the Indian wars, fourteen buffalo soldiers had won the Congressional Medal of Honor.

But the buffalo soldiers did not only do battle with Comanche, Apache and Sioux. They built forts and roads, and they explored and mapped the Staked Plains of Texas. They escorted settlers and railroad crews and guarded Indian territories against settlers homesteading illegally. In many cases they helped support what little law and order was available in the pioneer West.

Although they served on the most isolated and desolate of posts, the buffalo soldiers had the lowest desertion rate among the military on the frontier. In addition to bad food and harsh punishment, they often faced open hostility from the very white settlers they were there to protect.

In Brownsville, Texas, in a revolt against the harassment of the townspeople, twenty men from the 25th Infantry rode through the town, shooting out windows and killing one man. Military investigation failed to uncover the identification of the men involved and because the three companies of black troopers refused to volunteer any information, 167 black soldiers were dishonorably discharged.

In 1972, sixty-six years later, determining that this mass punishment was not justified, the army changed the discharges to honorable. Only one man, Dorsie Willis, was still alive. He received his honorable discharge and $25,000 in back pay.

Perhaps of all the men on the Western frontier to come down to us in legend and history, none has been more written about than the American cowboy. The cowboy, like the buffalo soldiers, came into prominence after the Civil War. Ranchers returning from the army found their herds of cattle scattered and running wild at a time when Western beef was bringing high prices in Eastern markets. The ranchers began gathering their longhorned steers wherever and however they could. In many cases they branded any cattle they found as a maverick and therefore anyone's property. Then the ranchers herded their cattle north in a desperate gamble to recoup their losses.

The three cattle trails they used moving their cattle north—the Western, Goodnight and Chisholm—have become famous. The cowboys who worked for the ranchers, men who broke the horses, gathered and branded the steers and spent weeks fighting the weather, hostile Indians and rustlers to bring the herds to rail centers at Dodge, Wichita and Omaha have become equally famous.

There is hardly an American alive who has not seen in the movies or on television the highly glorified exploits of the Western cowboy. The cowboy he sees on his movie or television screen, though, is almost inevitably a white man. And the truth is that one out of every four cowboys in the West was a black man.

175

Even before the Civil War, slaves were used on ranches in the West to wrangle horses and tend the cattle. Southerners moving to Texas with their slaves soon discovered that the black man could be as easily trained as a white man to tend cattle without the bother of paying him a wage.

After the war, many of these ex-slave cowboys remained on as cowhands. Since segregation in a small, closely knit group like a cattle drive was difficult, at least along the trail, black and white cowboys received equal treatment and equal pay.

It is estimated that there were 8,000 black men engaged in the cattle industry during the days of the great cattle drives, although few of their names and stories have come down to us. Only one black cowboy wrote an autobiography about his days in the West.

That cowboy was Nat Love, who worked the Texas Panhandle region and claimed to be the original "Deadwood Dick." Born in a Tennessee slave cabin in 1854, at age fifteen Nat Love ran away from home and headed west. At Dodge City he talked his way into a thirty-dollar-a-month job as a cowpuncher and became part of the long cattle drives north from Texas. His autobiography—telling of his adventurous life, fighting off Indians, wild animals and desperate men—is, like other Western sagas written in that period, filled with exaggeration and braggadocio. Still it catches the freewheeling, hard-driven life of the cowboy in the West, whether he was black or white.

Not as well known as Nat Love was James Kelly, top troubleshooter on the Olive Ranch in Texas. Other black cowhands respected for their abilities were "80" John Wallace, who had his own ranch, and Bill Pickett, who developed a unique form of steer wrestling that involved biting the ear of the steer before wrestling it to the ground. He became an international rodeo rider and in his day was called "the greatest sweat and dirt cowhand that ever lived, bar none."

Just as there were numerous black cowhands, there were also black rustlers, gunslingers and cardsharps. Ben Hodges, a confidence man and part-time cattle thief, lived in Dodge City. He was reported to be as sharp at cards as Wyatt Earp. A black rustler, Isom Dart, although supposedly reformed, died in the traditional Western manner, shot down by a hired gun.

The great cattle drives lasted from 1866 until 1895. They ended because of overgrazing, severe winters and, perhaps most important, a new breed of man coming west—the homesteader. He wasn't looking for adventure or gold or a quick fortune in the cattle business. He wanted to sink roots on his own farmland and put up fences across public grazing lands. He wanted churches and schools in his town, not gambling halls and shoot-outs on the public streets.

Many of these homesteaders were emigrants, part of the great immigration from Europe that swept like a tidal wave over the East Coast of the United States between 1870 and 1910. Some, like the Irish, fleeing the famines and lack of freedom in their own country, had come crammed in "coffin" ships, not much better than the "blackbirders" that had brought the African slave to America.

When they reached America, they found no streets of gold, but signs for employment that read, NO NEGROES OR IRISH NEED APPLY. Because their religion and culture were different from the native white Anglo-Saxon Protestant, they were both hated and feared. In some areas they faced much the same sort of hostility that blacks

177

had lived with for years. Many of these emigrants, hoping for a better life, headed west.

There was another group of emigrants who headed west at much the same time. They endured the same, if not worse, hardships as the European immigrants. Unlike the other emigrants, though, they weren't just looking to put down roots in a new land but to find a freedom that was being denied them by their own country. This was the great mass of black migrants who left the South when the Reconstruction period ended in the late 1870s.

Slowly but surely most of the freedoms so dearly won for the black Americans by the Civil War had been withdrawn: the right to vote, to hold public office, to serve on a jury, to secure a decent education for their children. In some cases their very right to survival was threatened by the Ku Klux Klan and lynch mobs. Instead of owning their own small pieces of land, the freed slaves had been forced into sharecropping, kept constantly in debt to their new masters.

This mass movement west came in two waves. The first from 1873–78 was organized by men like Benjamin "Pap" Singleton who, after the war, looked into buying land in Kansas. In 1871 he formed a Real Estate and Homestead Association. Then he gave lectures throughout the South, urging dispossessed blacks to move west to Kansas and Oklahoma. Five black settlements in the West came out of this first wave of black settlers, including the town of Nicodemus, Kansas, in 1877.

The second wave of black migration came a few years later. Unorganized, with little or no money or knowledge of the land to which they were heading, thousands of black families fled west in 1879. This migration was

178

known as the "Great Exodust" and the migrants were
known as "Exodusters."

They flooded into Kansas and were dropped on
wharves along the Missouri River by steamboats. Some
townspeople along the way provided them with food to
keep them from starving; other towns drove them away.
Those that survived hired out as laborers, or, if they
could, purchased land, digging holes in the ground in
which to live until they could build sod huts.

At Wyandotte, Kansas, where 2,000 were stranded,
the wealthy Chicago meatpacker Philip D. Armour reported, "The churches, private houses and halls were
full, and many of them had to lie out on the docks. . . .
I talked with a great many of them and was surprised at
their intelligence. I asked them where they thought they
were going. They said only West to escape persecution."
Armour collected funds in Chicago to help tide the
emigrants over.

Fearful of the loss of their cheap labor, some Southerners tried to stop the exodust by threats and intimida-
tion. In 1879, in Mississippi, a group of mounted and
armed white men blocked river landings and threatened
to sink all boats carrying blacks, effectively closing the
Mississippi River. It took a threat of federal interven-
tion before frightened shipowners continued accepting
blacks as passengers.

Despite the threats and harassment, still they came—
43,000 people in three years' time. Some found their
"promised land" in Kansas and Nebraska; others finally
gave up and returned to the South. Still others pushed
farther west. By 1910 the black population of the Western states had risen to a million.

All-black communities were started in DeWitty, Nebraska; Dearfield, Colorado; and Langston City and

179

Boley, Oklahoma, as a result of the western migration of black families. These were primitive frontier towns like many white settlements in the West, the only difference being that they were run by a black mayor, had a black sheriff and black teachers and pupils.

Booker T. Washington, visiting Boley in 1905, commented that on summer nights from the hills beyond the town there could still be heard the shrill cries of Indian dancers. He also reported that the first town marshal of Boley had been killed in a gun duel with a horse thief.

In the years to come, many of these towns disappeared, as did many rural white communities, as residents moved from the small town and farm to the big city. The towns of Langston City and Boley survived. However, they both felt the effects of white suppression when in 1910 Oklahoma added the Grandfather Clause to her state constitution. The Grandfather Clause prohibited anyone from voting whose grandfather had not been allowed to vote on January 1, 1867. Since in 1867 no blacks had been allowed the ballot, the clause effectively deprived black citizens of their right to vote.

Oklahoma was by no means the only Western state that passed Jim Crow or black laws against its nonwhite citizens. The exodusters who went west expecting to escape racial prejudice and bigotry were soon disillusioned. Prejudice and bigotry often rode west in the covered wagons of the white settlers, prejudice not just against blacks, but also against Chinese immigrants and Spanish-Americans, as well as the Indians. Some of the frontiersmen and homesteaders who thought the only good Indian was a dead Indian, also agreed with Horace Greeley, the famous New York publisher, when he stated that the West "shall be reserved for the benefit of the white Caucasian race."

Black laws were found in the constitutions of almost every Western state until the last year of the Civil War. And after the war, new laws, even more discriminatory and more severe, deprived many blacks of their right to land, education and the vote.

Yet in spite of the obstacles, black men and women stubbornly put down their roots in the hard-bought, alien land. They prospered, raised families, and by their courage, fortitude and determination helped blaze the trail for the settlers who followed after them.

One has to search hard to find any monuments to these early black pioneers—the explorers, mountain men, buffalo soldiers, cowboys and homesteaders. The vital role they played in the winning of the West is seldom mentioned in history books. Yet there are a few monuments, paintings, museums that touch upon the contributions they made, the part they played in American frontier life.

Among the most fascinating of these historic sites are the Western forts still standing today, their buildings, walls and furnishings so carefully restored that if you visit one of them and listen carefully, you might just hear the jingle of the spurs of the legendary buffalo soldier . . .

SAN MARCOS DE APALACHE STATE MUSEUM

Pánfilo de Narváez and the few hundred men remaining in his ill-fated Spanish expedition after a shipwreck, landed not far from this site in Florida in 1528. By 1536 only four men in the expedition were still alive. One of the men who survived was Estevan, a black servant of Andres Dorantes.

Before disease, starvation and hostile Indians killed off Pánfilo de Narváez and his men, they managed to make their way to the junction of the St. Marks and Wakulla rivers and started the first shipbuilding yard in the New World.

181

In 1679 later Spanish explorers built a fort here, the ruins of which may be seen today. The San Marcos Museum contains many unusual Indian and Spanish artifacts from the time of these early Spanish explorers.

Location: San Marcos de Apalache State Museum, off State Route 363, 1 mile southwest on Canal Street, St. Marks, Florida.

ZUÑI PUEBLO

Estevan and the three other survivors of the Narváez expedition finally reached the safety of the Spanish government in Mexico. Three of the men, including Estevan's former master, returned to Spain. Estevan remained in Mexico and acted as guide for an expedition led by Father Marcos de Niza in search of the fabled Seven Cities of Cíbola, whose streets were supposedly paved with gold.

What Estevan actually found was the Zuñi village of Hawikuh. Like other Zuñi Indian settlements, the homes consisted of great terraced communal dwellings several stories high. Although the Zuñi Indians had a highly organized, sophisticated culture long before the Spanish arrived, they had no gold.

Other Spanish explorers, like Francisco Coronado, later came trying to convert the Indians to Christianity as well as to find gold. Like Estevan, most of them found only death.

Today there is only one surviving settlement of the fabled Seven Cities of Cíbola. The Zuñi Indians who still live here manufacture fine-quality silver and turquoise jewelry. Visitors are allowed to visit the pueblo during daylight hours and view some of the ancient masked ceremonial dances—dances that might have been performed at the time the black explorer Estevan visited the Pueblo settlement centuries ago.

Location: Zuñi Pueblo, Zuñi, New Mexico, is intersected by State Highway 53 and is near Gallup, New Mexico.

No admission charge.

STATE CAPITOL, PHOENIX, ARIZONA

The State Capitol Building contains eight colorful murals, showing scenes from the history of Arizona. One of these murals, painted by Jay Datus, depicts the black guide Estevan, who was the first man, other than Indians, to explore the territory that is now New Mexico and Arizona.

Location: State Capitol Building, West Washington and 17th Avenue, Phoenix, Arizona.

No admission charge.

CHICAGO HISTORICAL SOCIETY MUSEUM

Although Jean Baptiste Point Du Sable was the first settler in what is now the great city of Chicago, there are few mementos of this early black fur trader. The most interesting is a small replica of the Du Sable trading post, which is contained in the Chicago Historical Society Museum. In addition to his house, the trading post also included a dairy, smokehouse, stable, barn and mill, making Du Sable and his family almost self-sufficient.

When Du Sable sold the trading post for $1,200 and moved to St. Charles, Missouri, the purchaser was John Kinzie, and today the replica of the fur trading post (and a diorama of the post, which may also be seen at the museum) is sometimes called the Kinzie Fur Trading Post.

Location: Chicago Historical Society Museum, in Lincoln Park at Clark Street and North Avenue, Chicago, Illinois.

Admission charge.

The actual site where the Du Sable Post stood in Chicago is marked by a plaque in the Pioneer Court on the northeast approach to the Michigan Avenue Bridge, Chicago, Illinois.

DU SABLE BURIAL SITE

As the old fur trapper Jean Baptiste Du Sable grew older, he feared only two things: that he would not have enough money to support himself, and that he would not be buried in a Catholic cemetery. Although his first fear came true and he died a pauper, he was buried in the Catholic St. Charles Borromeo Cemetery at St. Charles, Missouri.

EL PUEBLO MUSEUM

The early history of the West is the history of the fur trade. In Colorado in 1842 a fortification called El Pueblo was built by

183

fur traders close to the eastern wall of the Rocky Mountains, near an important fording point over the Arkansas River. The fort was built of adobe with a heavy wooden gate and two towers for riflemen as protection against Indians.

Jim Beckwourth, the black fur trader who was active in beaver trapping along the Arkansas River, is one of the traders credited with building Fort Pueblo.

After the decline of the beaver trade, Fort Pueblo fell into decay, with vagrant Mexican families occupying it. Then on Christmas Day, 1854, a raiding band of Ute Indians slipped inside the fort and slaughtered or kidnapped everyone there.

A full-sized reproduction of Fort Pueblo, complete with adobe walls, sentry posts, living quarters, kitchen, blacksmith shop and stable, has been built within the El Pueblo Museum. The museum is maintained by the State Historical Society of Colorado.

Location: El Pueblo Museum, 905 South Prairie Avenue, Pueblo, Colorado.

No admission charge.

BECKWOURTH PASS

Today the trip over U.S. 395 west of Reno to the California line can be covered in a few hours. When Jim Beckwourth first discovered the pass over the Sierra Nevada Mountains and laid out this trail, it was used by thousands of pioneers, trudging along beside their ox-drawn wagons, and took weeks. Today the pass, mountain peak, valley and nearby town bear the name of Jim Beckwourth. The pass is still used by modern-day motorists and may be found on State Highway 70, the spectacular Feather River Highway, just east of the junction with U.S. 395, several miles north of Lake Tahoe, California. A monument was erected to Jim Beckwourth's memory at the summit of the pass.

MUSEUM OF THE FUR TRADE

This is a one of its kind museum—a museum dedicated to the history of the American fur trade. Exhibits in the museum contain guns, bowie knives, frontier weapons, trade goods used in the fur trade and the furs themselves—buffalo robes, beaver, mink and badger. The grounds include a typical fur trader's house.

The programs of the museum stress the cosmopolitan nature of the Western trapper brigades. These fur traders included French Creoles, "civilized" Indians, Spaniards from the Southwest and such black mountain men as Ed Rose and Jim Beckwourth.

Location: Museum of the Fur Trade, Route 2, Chadron, Nebraska.

Small admission charge.

FORT CLATSOP

The Lewis and Clark Expedition, which included a black man, York, left on the famous Western exploration trip on May 14, 1804, wintered at the Mandan Indian villages, in what is now North Dakota, and finally sighted the Pacific Ocean on November 15, 1805.

The winter of 1805 was spent at Fort Clatsop in the present state of Oregon.

An exact full-scale replica of Fort Clatsop has been built near the site of its original location, following the plans drawn by Captain Clark in 1805. At the Visitor Center a narrated slide program takes the viewer along the expedition's route from St. Louis to Fort Clatsop. An exhibit room contains artifacts from the expedition. The role that York played can be seen in both the exhibits and the slide program.

Location: Fort Clatsop is 4½ miles southwest of Astoria, Oregon. U.S. 101 passes just north of the area.

No admission charge. Special "living history" tours for groups may be arranged with the staff at Fort Clatsop National Memorial by advance notice.

MONTANA HISTORICAL SOCIETY MUSEUM

Part of the Lewis and Clark trail runs across northern Montana. Montana has honored the Lewis and Clark Expedition in a painting by a noted Western artist, Charles Russell. The painting appears on the front wall of the House of Representatives in the State Capitol Building.

The Montana Historical Society has several other paintings by Charles Russell, including one showing the Mandan Indians examining York. There are also dioramas in the museum of the expedition, in which York may be seen.

On the ground floor of the museum are many exhibits from the early days of Montana, including a completely reproduced frontier street of the 1880s.

Location: Lewis and Clark mural, State Capitol Building, Helena, Montana.

Location: Montana Historical Society Museum, 225 North Roberts Street, Helena, Montana.

No admission charge.

TOMBSTONE, ARIZONA

Although Tombstone first gained fame as a silver-mining town, it is best known today as the town where the battle of the O.K. Corral took place between the Earps and the Clantons. Black as well as white prospectors came west to try their luck at gold and silver mining, and Tombstone, in its heyday, was a lusty, brawling town.

One of its sheriffs was John Slaughter, and one of his cowhands was John Swain, who had been born a slave and came west after the Civil War. Despite several near brushes with death in defending his mining claim, John Swain lived to a ripe old age and was buried with honor in Boot Hill by the City of Tombstone.

Today, Tombstone, "The Town Too Tough to Die," has been named a National Historic Landmark. Many of its buildings have been restored, including the Bird Cage Theater, O.K. Corral and the Boot Hill Graveyard. The Schieffelin Hall Museum contains many fascinating exhibits from the history of Tombstone.

Location: Tombstone, Arizona, is located on U.S. Highway 80, a 70-minute drive from Tucson, Arizona.

Admission charge to some of the attractions in the town.

DEADWOOD, SOUTH DAKOTA

Not only black men came west in the gold- and silver-mining days, but black women, too. Sally Campbell, a cook for a con-

186

tractor in the 7th Cavalry, was the first woman in the Black Hills, arriving in 1874. She staked out a gold claim and lived in Galena, South Dakota, till her death in 1888. Her grave marker occupies a place of honor in the Deadwood Museum.

Another black woman whose picture can be seen in the museum is Lucretia Marchbank, better known as Aunt Lou. Although she was a housekeeper for the Father De Smet miners, it was said she could run the mine as well as any man.

Several cowboys claimed the title "Deadwood Dick," including the flamboyant Nat Love, a black cowboy who won prizes for his riding and marksmanship at a Fourth of July celebration at Deadwood in 1876.

Deadwood today has been registered as a National Historic Landmark. Visitors to the town may view an early gold mine, as well as the Adams Memorial Museum, containing displays from the early days of Deadwood. Mount Moriah Cemetery (Boot Hill), where wild Bill Hickok and Calamity Jane are buried, is about 1 mile from town. During the first weekend in August, a special celebration is held called "The Days of '76." Rodeos and parades are included.

Location: Deadwood, South Dakota, is on U.S. 85, near the Wyoming border.

Admission charge to some of the attractions.

CENTRAL CITY OPERA HOUSE

Another well-known black woman who went west to the gold fields was Clara Brown. She found her fortune, not in gold but in running a laundry. Believed to be the first black resident of the territory of Colorado, she used her wealth to bring many of her relatives west and performed many acts of charity.

She was a member of the Colorado Pioneers Association. At her death, the "Aunt Clara" Brown Chair was dedicated and placed in the Central City Opera House, where it may still be seen today, along with other hickory chairs carved with pioneer names.

The Opera House, with its crystal chandeliers and murals, still holds performances.

Other reminders of Central City's lively past can be seen at the Central City Historical Museum.

187

Location: The Central City Opera House, Eureka Street, Central City, Colorado.

There is an admission charge to some of the attractions in Central City and to the performances held at the Opera House.

DODGE CITY, KANSAS

One of the most famous of the wide-open frontier towns of the Old West was Dodge City. Black cowboys, as well as white, raring to let off steam after long, hard months on the trail, brought prosperity—and lawlessness—to this prairie "boom town." Buffalo soldiers from nearby Fort Dodge helped preserve law in the town.

Ben Hodges, a black cowboy, came to Dodge City in the spring of 1872. He lived by his wits, which involved horse stealing, card playing and bilking the gullible. In his old age, Ben Hodges became a respected old-timer, who loved to tell tales of the old, wild days. He died the same year as Wyatt Earp, and the people of Dodge City donated money for a tombstone for Ben Hodges. His grave can be seen in the old Maple Grove Cemetery.

Today Dodge City is a modern cattle town, but its notorious Front Street, one block square, can still be visited, looking much as it did in the 1870s, including the Long Branch Saloon, and the Boot Hill Cemetery, where the "hanging tree" still stands. Beeson Museum contains many relics from the days when Wyatt Earp and Bat Masterson tried to bring law to Dodge City.

Location: Dodge City, Kansas, on U.S. 50.

Some of the historic buildings ask donations. Admission charge to see the variety show at the Long Branch Saloon.

SIMMONS PARTY MEMORIAL

When Missouri passed a law against free blacks settling in the state, George Washington Bush, a wealthy black cattleman, took his family and joined the Simmons wagon train heading west to Oregon in the spring of 1844.

Because of their great respect for Bush, Simmons and the rest of his party decided they would not settle where Bush

188

might be persecuted because of his color. They pushed north-
ward to Puget Sound, which was under British rule and therefore had no restrictive black laws.

George Bush prospered, and during a time of famine in 1852,
had put aside enough wheat so that he could help his less fortunate neighbors. When Puget Sound came under American control and Oregon's black laws were put into effect, Simmons
sponsored a bill in the Oregon Legislature in 1854 that specially exempted Bush and his family from those laws.

A monument was erected in honor of the courage and stam-
ina of the Simmons party and their long trek west.

Location: Simmons party Memorial Monument, Tumwater
Falls Park, Tumwater, Washington.

HARRY S. TRUMAN LIBRARY

It was from Independence, Missouri, that many of the wagon
trains started their long, dangerous trips west. Artist Thomas
Hart Benton painted a mural called *Independence and the
Opening of the West* that may be seen at the Harry S. Truman
Library in Independence, Missouri.

In the center of the mural is shown a blacksmith working
on the wagons. The blacksmith represents a free black man
named Hiram Young who lived in Independence and made a
small fortune building many of the wagons for the pioneers. He
employed as many as fifty men at twenty-five forges.

Not shown in the mural is another black man, scout and
Indian fighter, who lived in Independence. He was Major
"Black" Harris, who led many wagon trains west.

In the museum of the library may also be found materials
relating to the civil rights movement, including the 1946 Executive Order forming the Commission on Civil Rights and the
Executive Order of 1948 directing "equality of treatment and
opportunity" for both black and white soldiers in the Armed
Forces.

Location: Harry S. Truman Library and Museum, northwest
edge of Independence, Missouri, on U.S. 24 and Delaware
Street.

Small admission charge.

189

CENTRALIA, WASHINGTON

In 1850 George Washington, born in slavery but adopted by a white family, headed west to the Oregon territory with his foster parents. There he prospered and eventually founded a town called Centerville. He built streets, churches and a public park, and sold lots at low prices to encourage new citizens. During the Panic of 1873, Washington, although he was then seventy-six years old, helped save his town by buying and shipping food in from other cities and providing jobs for the unemployed.

Although there are other towns in the West that were built by black men—towns like Boley, Oklahoma; Nicodemus, Kansas; and Langston, Colorado—perhaps no other town owes so much to the strength and good will of one man alone.

The park in Centralia, Washington (as the town is now called), bears his name—George Washington Park.

BRIGHAM YOUNG PIONEER MONUMENT

On July 21, 1847, Green Flake, a black man, drove the lead wagon of Mormon pioneers into the Salt Lake Valley, Utah. The Mormons had been driven out of other settlements in the East and Midwest because of their religious beliefs. Three black men went west with this first group of Mormons—two were slaves, Hark Lay and Oscar Crosby, and the third, Green Flake, was a freeman baptized into the Mormon Church.

Green Flake also helped bring a second company of Mormon settlers to Utah. The second company had with it thirty-four black men and women. Green Flake stayed in Utah, owned his own farm and helped to build the magnificent Salt Lake Temple. The land for the farm was given to Green Flake by Brigham Young as a reward for his services to the church.

A monument to the early Mormon settlers who helped found the state of Utah was erected in downtown Salt Lake City. The name of Green Flake, as well as those of other early white and black pioneers, is engraved on the base of the monument.

Location: Brigham Young Pioneer Monument, intersection of Main and South Temple streets, Salt Lake City, Utah.

PIONEERS AND COWBOYS

LOS ANGELES COUNTY MUSEUM OF NATURAL HISTORY

In the eighteenth century, Spain colonized California in order to prevent its seizure by other European powers. Some of the families recruited in Mexico to move north to California were of African descent, people whose ancestors had been brought to Mexico centuries before to work in the mines. The family of Antonio Mesa was among the first to reach the small village in California now known as Los Angeles.

Forty-four persons in all—twenty-six of whom were Afro-Americans—settled at a site that is now the Plaza on North Main Street. Other early black residents like Marie Rita Valdez and Francisco Reynes owned land in California that included sections of what is now Beverly Hills and the San Fernando Valley.

A diorama of the first black and white settlers arriving at Los Angeles may be seen at the Los Angeles County Museum of Natural History, along with other exhibits on the early history of California.

Location: Los Angeles County Museum of Natural History, 900 Exposition Boulevard, Los Angeles, California.

No admission charge.

EL PUEBLO DE LOS ANGELES STATE HISTORIC PARK

The founding site of Los Angeles is today a State Historic Park, which contains historic buildings, plazas, cultural exhibits and shops. Black Governor Pio Pico's home, which later became Los Angeles' first major hotel, may be visited, as well as the original plaza where black and white families first settled in Los Angeles in 1781.

Guided walking tours through Pueblo Park are available. Many special events and fiestas take place in the park during the year that are free to the public.

Location: El Pueblo de Los Angeles State Historic Park is located around N. Main Street and Los Angeles Street at Sunset Boulevard, Los Angeles, California.

191

GOLDEN STATE MUTUAL LIFE INSURANCE AFRO-AMERICAN
ART COLLECTION

The Art Gallery at Golden State is a showplace for the works
of black American artists, historic and contemporary. In addition, the gallery has two priceless murals that dramatically illustrate the black contribution to the growth and development
of California.

The murals by black artists Charles Alston and Hale Woodruff show many prominent historic black figures: Estevan,
James Beckwourth, William Leidesdorff, black gold miners and
pony-express riders, among many, many more.

Visitors are welcome to tour the collection. Group tours may
be arranged by calling the Golden State Mutual Personnel
Office.

Location: Golden State Mutual Life Insurance Company,
199 West Adams Boulevard, Los Angeles, California.

THE OAKLAND MUSEUM

The many black Americans who have contributed to the settlement and growth of California are well represented by exhibits in this museum.

The displays tell the story of Alvin Coffey, a successful black
gold miner who became the only black member of the Society
of California Pioneers; Colonel Allensworth, who founded a
town in California; Grafton T. Brown, black artist and lithog-
rapher; Captain William T. Shorey, the only black whaling
captain on the Pacific Coast; and many others.

Guided tours are available through the museum.

Location: The Oakland Museum, 1000 Oak Street, Oakland,
California.

No admission charge.

ALLEN ALLENSWORTH TOWNSITE AND PROPOSED
HISTORICAL STATE PARK

Allen Allensworth was born a slave in Kentucky in 1842 and
was sold "down river" for attempting to learn to read and write.
During the Civil War, he served in the Union Navy and later,

after becoming a minister, enlisted as a chaplain the army, retiring in 1906 with the rank of Lt. Colonel.

After his retirement, he and his friends established the town of Allensworth in the San Joaquin Valley of California, hoping that black residents who settled there would be free of the discrimination and racial prejudice they faced elsewhere.

The town prospered and was typical of the small farming communities of the time, growing sugarbeets and alfalfa. After World War II, however, the community experienced a critical water shortage. The town might have vanished completely, but in 1970 a bill was passed in the state senate proposing that the town and surrounding land be preserved as a Historical State Park.

Buildings will be restored to reflect the 1908 to 1918 scene, with a museum to illustrate the history of the town and black Americans in California. When the park is completed, it will be the first historical park area dedicated to the black pioneers of the Old West.

Location: The town of Allensworth and the future Historical State Park are located in the southwest corner of Tulare County, California, on State Highway 43, between Fresno and Bakersfield.

WESTERN FORTS WHERE BUFFALO SOLDIERS WERE STATIONED

FORT RILEY, KANSAS

Established in 1853, this fort protected traffic on the Santa Fe Trail from the Indians. For many years it was headquarters of the famed 7th Cavalry and Lt. Colonel George Custer. Both the 9th and 10th Cavalry were also stationed here at various times, the 9th much longer than the 10th.

Fort Riley is still an active army post today and may be toured by the public. A U.S. Cavalry Museum is in Building Number 30 at Fort Riley, with exhibits showing the history of the fort and photographs of the cavalry and other units stationed here. Included are photographs of the 9th Cavalry.

Location: U.S. Cavalry Museum, Building No. 30, Fort Riley, Kansas.

No admission charge.

FORT LARNED, KANSAS

Fort Larned was established in 1859 and was one of the most active posts on the frontier in the 1860s. It was charged with protecting the Santa Fe Trail and served as a base for military operations against the Indians of the Central Plains.

Company A, 10th Cavalry, was stationed at Fort Larned from April 1867 to January 1869. It was during this period that the Indian War of 1868–69 took place, with the Cheyennes, Kiowas, Comanches and Arapahos raiding from Kansas to Texas. The defeat of the Cheyennes at the Battle of the Washita on November 27, 1868, ended organized Indian resistance in the area around Fort Larned.

Today Fort Larned is a National Historic Site, and the Park Service is restoring the fort to its 1868 appearance. Some of the buildings have already been restored, and a museum displays cavalry and infantry equipment and mementos of fort life. One display, "This Month in History," tells what happened at historic Fort Larned during one month in 1868. The actions and movements of the 10th Cavalry are mentioned frequently.

Location: Fort Larned is located 6 miles west of the city of Larned, Kansas, on U.S. 156. Group tours may be arranged in advance.

No admission charge.

FORT ROBINSON, NEBRASKA

Fort Robinson was the home of both the 9th and 10th cavalry regiments at various times. The 9th was stationed here in 1885, and some of their more famous skirmishes were against the Sioux during the Ghost Dance uprising in 1890. It was from Fort Robinson that the 9th Cavalry under Captain Dodge rode 100 miles in thirty hours to rescue a troop of the 7th Cavalry under Indian attack. In 1898 the 9th left Fort Robinson to fight with great gallantry and courage in Cuba during the Spanish-American War.

The 10th Cavalry came to Fort Robinson in the early 1900s and saw service against the Ute Indians.

Charles Young, who later became the first black colonel in

194

the U.S. Army, spent part of his army career at Fort Robinson after graduating from West Point in 1889.

Fort Robinson saw seventy-two years of military history, from the taming of the West to the phasing out of the horse in the U.S. Army. Today the fort and its buildings have been restored and stand in the midst of a state park. The museum offers Indian, pioneer and military displays.

Inside the museum, located in the former post headquarters, there are several exhibits relating to the 9th and 10th cavalry regiments.

Location: Fort Robinson Museum, 4 miles west of Crawford, Nebraska, on U.S. 20.

No admission charge. Free guided group tours may be arranged.

FORT SILL, OKLAHOMA

Work on Fort Sill was begun in 1869 by the buffalo soldiers of the 10th Cavalry; its construction is one of the epic accomplishments in the wilderness service of the Frontier Army. The building of the fort was constantly interrupted because the black soldiers had to take off on Indian expeditions, escort duty, surveys and the pursuit of lawless bands of renegades that infested the border area.

When the fort was finished, the buffalo soldiers at Fort Sill were involved in the Red River Campaign against the Comanches, Kiowas and Southern Cheyenne Indians, a war that finally ended in 1875. After that campaign, the 10th Cavalry Regiment departed for duty stations in Texas.

Today Fort Sill is a modern army post, the U.S. Army Field Artillery Center; but the historic Old Post area has been preserved—the Geronimo Guardhouse, the Cannon Walk, the Old Post stone stockade and corral, among other buildings.

The U.S. Army Field Artillery Museum, one of the outstanding military museums in the world, occupies several of the original buildings of the Old Post. The museum displays many cavalry and Indian exhibits reflecting Fort Sill's history as a frontier cavalry post. Some of the more prominent displays concern the buffalo soldiers, who played an important part in early garrison life at Fort Sill.

195

Not far from the Old Post area are the grave sites of Geronimo and Sitting Bear, along with other valiant Indian chiefs buried with military honors at Fort Sill. The "Chiefs' Knoll," as the burial site is known, has been called the "Indian Arlington."

Location: The historic Old Post area at Fort Sill is located just east of the Main Post of Fort Sill, Oklahoma. The Chiefs' Knoll is located in the Post Cemetery, a few blocks from the museum grounds. Geronimo's grave is on the East Range.

No admission charge. Group tours may be arranged.

FORT CONCHO, TEXAS

One of the most fascinating of old Western forts is Fort Concho, established in 1868 at the junction of the two forks of the Concho River. The city of San Angelo grew up around Fort Concho.

The 24th and 25th infantry regiments, as well as the 9th and 10th Cavalry, all served at Fort Concho at one time or another during their tours of duty in Texas. Colonel Benjamin Grierson and the 10th Cavalry had their headquarters at Fort Concho from 1875 to 1882.

During their tours of duty here, the buffalo soldiers helped make the first thorough exploration of Texas' Staked Plains. They also battled Sioux, Apaches and Comanches and helped capture Geronimo and Billy the Kid.

Today Fort Concho is a National Historic Landmark. Many of the original buildings are still standing or have been restored, including officers' and enlisted men's quarters, schoolhouse-chapel and post headquarters. An excellent museum covering the history of the fort has several exhibits on the buffalo soldiers. The museum is located in the Headquarters Building and the four reconstructed barracks.

Location: Fort Concho, 714 Burges Street, San Angelo, Texas.

Small admission charge. Guided tours available.

OLD FORT RICHARDSON, TEXAS

Fort Richardson was built in 1868, one of a line of forts built in Texas to keep the frontier safe from the increasingly ferocious raids by Comanches, Kiowas and Kiowa-Apaches. Troops from Fort Richardson, including buffalo soldiers, not only fought off Indians but provided escorts for mail and supply trains and protected the military road connecting Richardson with forts Griffin and Concho to the southwest.

The fort was abandoned in 1878 when the frontier became more settled. Eleven of the original forty buildings are still standing; others are being restored. The fort is a state historic site, open to the public, and includes a small museum of military history.

Location: Fort Richardson is 1 mile southwest of Jacksboro, Texas, off U.S. 281.

Free admission to the grounds of the fort; small admission charge to the museum.

FORT DAVIS, TEXAS

Fort Davis was built in 1854 to protect pioneers heading west on the Overland Trail and was a key post in the defense system of western Texas during the Indian Wars against the Mescalero and Warm Springs Apache. The Apaches were cunning and courageous warriors with complete mastery of guerrilla tactics, fighting only when the odds were overwhelmingly in their favor. The Apache Wars began in the early 1850s and ended only with the surrender of Geronimo in 1886.

It was during the period of these wars, from 1867 to 1881, that Fort Davis was garrisoned by black troops of the 24th and 25th Infantry and the 9th and 10th Cavalry. In the one year of 1878 they covered a record 6,724 miles on scouting expeditions against the Apaches. One of the largest military campaigns of black troops from Fort Davis was against the Apache Chief Victorio in 1880. Although Victorio was never captured, he was finally forced to withdraw to Mexico, where he was killed in 1880.

Fort Davis became a National Historic Site in 1963, and today the fort has been restored to look much as it did during the days of the Indian Wars. In addition to the museum and visitor center, which are located in one of the enlisted men's barracks, there are approximately fifty restored and partially

197

restored buildings on the grounds. There is an entire exhibit area devoted to the buffalo soldiers.

Location: Fort Davis lies on the northern edge of the town of Fort Davis and can be reached by Texas 17 or 118, which links U.S. 90 and 290.

Admission charge by the car.

THORNBURGH BATTLEFIELD SITE

Major T. T. Thornburgh and 160 troopers were pinned down here by a war party of Ute in 1879, with 56 men, including the major, dead or wounded. At last, two messengers managed to secure help, and a troop of the 9th Cavalry Regiment, under Captain Francis Dodge, arrived and slipped in among Major Thornburgh's men during the night. With the help of the 9th Cavalry, the Indians were held off for three more days until a company of infantry arrived to drive off the Indians.

One of the 9th Cavalrymen, Sergeant Henry Johnson, won the Medal of Honor for risking his life during this engagement to care for the wounded. In the thirty years that the buffalo soldiers served on the frontier, fourteen noncommissioned officers won the Congressional Medal of Honor for their courage under fire.

Today a granite shaft has been erected on the battlefield site.

Location: Thornburgh Battlefield Site is 17 miles south of Craig, Colorado, on State 13, then left 11 miles to a side road and right .6 mile to the site.

BEECHER ISLAND BATTLE MARKER

It was here that Colonel Forsyth and fifty soldiers were trapped and held under siege by several hundred Indians for eight days. Without medical supplies and food, and with very little water, the command was rescued by the 10th Cavalry arriving from Fort Wallace. The site is marked by a cement monument and five gravestones.

Location: Beecher Island Battle Marker, on Route 53, near Wray, Colorado.

198

CUSTER BATTLEFIELD

Several monuments commemorate the Battle of Little Big Horn, in which General Custer's three battalions were ambushed and massacred by Sitting Bull and his Sioux warriors on June 25, 1876. One of the men killed at Little Big Horn was Isaiah Dorman, a black scout who had joined Custer only a few days before. Dorman had lived among the Sioux. A Cheyenne brave, describing the scene after the battle, tells of seeing Dorman's body: "I saw by the river, on the west side, a dead black man. He was a big man. All of his clothing was gone when I saw him, but he had not been scalped nor cut up like the white men had been. Some Sioux told me he belonged to their people but was with the soldiers."

Nearby Custer Battlefield is the Custer Battlefield National Cemetery, in which many buffalo soldiers who served at forts across the West are buried.

There is a museum at the battlefield, in which may be seen guns, maps and dioramas of the battle. On the field itself are many white headstones, as the soldiers were buried where they fell.

Location: Custer Battlefield National Monument is 13 miles southeast of Hardin, Montana, on State 47.

No admission charge.

A scene from the early history of Arizona showing the black guide and explorer Estevan (*extreme right*) with other missionaries and conquistadors. This mural, painted by Jay Datus, may be seen in the State Capitol Building of Phoenix, Arizona. COURTESY JAY DATUS, ARTIST, AND ARIZONA DEPARTMENT OF LIBRARY AND ARCHIVES.

The Western artist Charles Russell painted the scene *below* of York, the black man who traveled with the Lewis and Clark Expedition. York is being examined with amazement by the Mandan Indians, who had never seen a black-skinned man before. The painting hangs in the Montana Historical Society Museum, Helena, Montana. COURTESY MONTANA HISTORICAL SOCIETY, HELENA

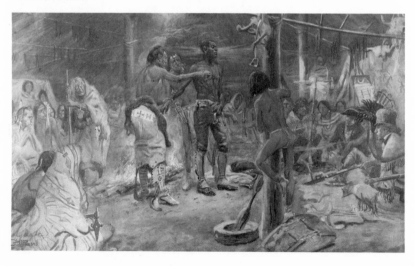

This replica of the John Kinzie home (formerly the Du Sable Fur trading Post) may be seen at the Chicago Historical Society Museum. Jean Baptiste Point Du Sable, a black fur trader, built his post in 1797 and became the first settler of what is now the city of Chicago. COURTESY CHICAGO HISTORI-CAL SOCIETY

One of the early mountain men in the Old West, black James Beckwourth lived with the Indians, trapped furs in Wyoming and Montana, and discovered a pass through the Sierra Nevada Mountains in 1850. A full-scale reproduction of Fort Pueblo, which Jim Beckwourth helped found, may be seen at the El Pueblo Museum, Pueblo, Colorado. COURTESY STATE HISTORICAL SOCIETY OF COLORADO

A diorama in the Los Angeles County Museum of Natural History shows the first settlers coming to Los Angeles in September 1781. Of the forty-four people in this first group of settlers sent out by the Spanish government, twenty-six were of African descent. COURTESY HISTORY DIVISION, NATURAL HISTORY MUSEUM OF LOS ANGELES COUNTY

The Afro-American Art Collection of the Golden State Mutual Life Insurance Company, Los Angeles, California, has several murals on "The Negro in California History." One of these murals, shown above, painted by black artist Charles Alston, shows black pioneers in the early days of California's history. Some of the black pathfinders who can be seen in the painting are Estevanico, James Beckwourth and William Leidesdorff, among many others. COURTESY GOLDEN STATE MUTUAL LIFE INSURANCE COMPANY, AFRO-AMERICAN ART COLLECTION. PHOTO BY HOWARD MOREHEAD

The flamboyant black cowboy Nat Love won the title "Deadwood Dick" for his roping and shooting in the days of the cattle drives north from Texas. He was one of the few early cowboys to write his autobiography. COURTESY NEBRASKA STATE HISTORICAL SOCIETY

A group of genuine old-time cowboys and broncobusters posing for their photograph at Denver, Colorado, in 1901. One out of every four cowboys in the Old West was a black man. COURTESY SOLOMON BUTCHER COLLECTION, NEBRASKA STATE HISTORICAL SOCIETY

COME!

To the Colored People of the United States of America:

This is to lay before your minds a few sketches of what great advantages there are for the great mass of people of small means that are emigrating West to come and settle in the county of Hodgeman, in the State of Kansas—and more especially the Colored people, for they are the ones that want to find the best place for climate and for soil for the smallest capital. Hodgeman county is in Southwestern Kansas, on the line of the Atchison, Topeka & Santa Fe Railroad.

We, the undersigned, having examined the above county and found it best adapted to our people, have applied to the proper authority and have obtained a Charter, in the name and style of "THE DAVID CITY TOWN COMPANY," in the County of Hodgeman, State of Kansas.

One of the posters used to urge blacks to move west to Kansas after the Civil War. Although the black pioneers, in some cases, found only drought and poor soil instead of the rich lands promised them, they did leave behind the restrictive "Jim Crow" laws that were passed after the end of the Reconstruction period. COURTESY KANSAS STATE HISTORICAL SOCIETY, TOPEKA

Black, as well as white, pioneer families headed west after the Civil War.
This is a photograph of black homesteaders, the Shores family, taken in front
of their sod shanty near Westerville, Custer County, Nebraska, in 1887.

The Thomas Hart Benton mural *Independence and the Opening of the West,*
painted for the Harry S. Truman Library in Independence, Missouri, shows
in the right corner a blacksmith hard at work. The man in the painting is
modeled after an actual black man, Hiram Young, who owned one of the
largest blacksmith shops in Independence and made a small fortune building
many of the wagons that took the trail west from Independence.

Green Flake, a free black man, was one of the first settlers to move west to Utah with the first wagon train of Mormons in 1847. His name is inscribed on the Pioneer Monument that may be seen in Salt Lake City, Utah. COURTESY CHURCH OF JESUS CHRIST OF LATTER-DAY SAINTS

A monument to the first Mormon settlers who came west to Utah with Brigham Young in July 1847 may be seen in Salt Lake City. The names of these early settlers are inscribed on a tablet at the base of the monument and include those of black settlers, slaves and free blacks, as well as white settlers. COURTESY CHURCH OF JESUS CHRIST OF LATTER-DAY SAINTS

A guide in the dress uniform of an 1880 cavalry man showing two visitors the Court Martial Room at old Fort Concho, San Angelo, Texas. The all-black 9th and 10th Cavalry, as well as the 24th and 25th Infantry regiments, saw duty at Fort Concho, one of a series of forts built to protect the Western frontier. COURTESY TEXAS TOURIST DEVELOPMENT AGENCY

The restored administration building (now the Fort Concho Museum, San Angelo, Texas), which served as Headquarters for the 10th Cavalry Regiment, 1875–82, under the command of Colonel Benjamin Grierson. While stationed at Fort Concho, the buffalo soldiers fought Sioux, Apaches and Comanches. COURTESY FORT CONCHO MUSEUM

Black soldiers of the 9th Cavalry going on guard duty at Fort Robinson, Nebraska, in the 1890s. Guard duty was only part of the life of the buffalo soldier, which included fighting off Indians, protecting railroad workers, escorting settlers, building forts and roads, and the just plain monotony of everyday garrison life. COURTESY NEBRASKA STATE HISTORICAL SOCIETY

An interior of an enlisted men's barracks at Fort Robinson, Nebraska, home of the 9th and 10th Cavalry, as it appeared in the 1890s. Today many of the buildings at Fort Robinson have been restored, with an extensive cavalry museum in the former post headquarters. COURTESY NEBRASKA STATE HISTORICAL SOCIETY

A mock battle formation of the 10th Cavalry Regiment at Fort Robinson in the early 1900s. In earlier years it was from Fort Robinson that Captain Dodge and men of the 9th Cavalry rode one hundred miles in thirty hours to rescue a regiment of the 7th Cavalry under Indian attack. COURTESY NEBRASKA STATE HISTORICAL SOCIETY

ARTISTS
AND
CRAFTSMEN

While black pioneers were following "Pap" Singleton west to stake their claims along the Kansas frontier, another sort of black pioneer was staking his claim in Philadelphia at the Centennial Exhibition of 1876.

At the Centennial, Edward Bannister was awarded the Gold Medal in art for his landscape painting entitled *Under the Oaks*. When the judges learned that the artist was a black man, they decided to "reconsider" their decision. After all, it was a commonly held belief of the day that the black race had absolutely no talent for producing great works of art. The white competing artists, however, protested this injustice and the award stood. The painting later was sold in Boston for $1,500, an unusually high price for that time.

Edward Bannister, although a black pioneer in the American art world, was not the first accomplished black artist to appear in America. Black art has its roots in the beginnings of our country's history, and beyond that, stretches back to Africa itself. Most of the slaves brought to America came from the coastal area of West Africa, where a high level of art had been reached centuries before the coming of the white man.

The art of Africa was not at all the same as the art of Europe and Western civilization. The tribal artist did not paint in oil on canvas or create great marble statues. He worked with wood, stone and ivory, or cast bronze, brass and other metals. The articles he created were not only for decoration or self-expression. The elaborate masks, altarpieces and figure sculptures of gods, humans and animals expressed religious and social ideas. Art work played a vital role in the daily life of the African. The artist, himself, often spent a lifetime learning his craft and held an esteemed position within the tribe.

The captured slaves sent to America were taken from all walks of life. Warriors, priests, chiefs of royal blood, women, children, artists—almost overnight they were all cut off from the tribal life they had known and forced to accept a new, strange culture. Whatever artistic talents the slaves brought with them, whatever memory of their village life and their own arts and crafts, lay hidden and in time were almost forgotten, erased by years of brutal labor that left little time or energy for artistic creation.

Even among the white colonists, there was little attention given to art and art appreciation. In the early years of America, survival came first—planting crops, building stockades, fighting off Indians, disease and starvation. It was only after the colonies became securely settled by the middle of the eighteenth century that the wealthy Northern merchants and Southern plantation owners turned their thoughts to building mansions for themselves and their families.

It was the hands of skilled black craftsmen that helped create and build these lavish homes, not surpassed in architectural beauty even today. Every plantation of size had its own slave blacksmith, tanner, carpenter, pewterer and silversmith, and brickmaker. Black carpenters created pieces of furniture for the house: cabinets, mantelpieces, tables and chairs rivaling in many cases those being produced at that time in Europe. The unbelievably delicate wrought-iron balconies still to be seen on the Ursuline Convent in New Orleans were produced by skilled slave ironworkers.

In Milton, North Carolina, a master cabinetmaker, Thomas Day, free and black, had his own factory that turned out mahogany furniture sought after by the wealthiest families of the Carolinas and Virginia. In his own way, Thomas Day was also something of a civil rights activist. Blacks, slave or free, were not allowed to sit on the main floor of the white churches in Milton. Yet, when the church body of the local Presbyterian church wanted to replace their old wooden pews, they asked Thomas Day to build them. He agreed to build the church mahogany pews on the condition that he could sit in the front pew. The church fathers reluctantly agreed. It wasn't until much later that they realized Thomas Day had outsmarted them. The church pews, though beautifully carved, were not expensive mahogany at all, but of pinewood.

In addition to extravagant homes and furnishings, the wealthy American of the eighteenth century wanted another important status symbol, paintings of himself and his family. Portrait painters, or limners as they were called, were in great demand. Artists traveled from town

213

to town, painting portraits of the leading citizens. That some of these early limners were black artists has now been proved beyond doubt. Joshua Johnston, a "Free Householder of Colour" of Baltimore, painted at least twenty-one such portraits from 1790 to 1825. Patrick Reason of New York City did engravings of famous abolitionists, which were circulated throughout the world. The pastel of the noted Bishop Richard Allen by G. W. Hobbs was done in 1785 and is the first known American portrait of a black man by a black artist.

By the nineteenth century, black artists, like their white counterparts, were beginning to paint landscapes as well as portraits, and some were also turning to sculpture. When they could possibly afford it, these early American artists preferred to study and live abroad.

Robert Duncanson was one such painter. Educated by his father in Canada, in 1841, at the age of nineteen, Robert returned to his mother's home in Cincinnati, Ohio. At that time Cincinnati, although a thriving art center, was a border city, torn with strife between pro-slavery men and abolitionists. Duncanson was accepted by the white artists in Cincinnati, but found it difficult for a black artist to receive commissions, much less exhibit his work. He finally received support from Nicholas Longworth, a wealthy citizen of Cincinnati, and was sent to study in England and Scotland with funds partly provided by an Anti-Slavery League award. His romantic landscapes were highly praised in England and soon were being bought in America, too.

Another black artist given support by the abolitionists was the sculptress Edmonia Lewis, of half-Chippewa half-African descent. An intense, tomboyish young woman, almost entirely self-taught, her medallion of John Brown and bust of the Civil War hero Colonel

Robert Gould Shaw brought her sufficient recognition to enable her to move to Rome to study. At twenty-four, she completed one of her best-known statues, called *Forever Free,* celebrating the passage of the Thirteenth Amendment, forever freeing slaves.

Of all the expatriate black artists—men and women who left America to study and live in the more sympathetic surroundings of Europe—Henry Ossawa Tanner is undoubtedly the best known. Certainly Mr. Tanner was the first internationally known black American artist. The son of a minister, young Henry became interested in painting when, as a small boy in Pittsburgh in 1872, he watched an artist paint a tree. Henry immediately got some house painter's brushes and tried to paint the same scene, using the back of his geography book as a palette.

His father, knowing the difficulties his son would face in an art career, tried to persuade him instead to become a minister. When he discovered, though, that his son was determined to become an artist, he allowed him to study under the famous Thomas Eakins at the Pennsylvania Academy of Fine Arts. Eakins urged his student to "peer deeper into the heart of American life" for the subjects of his paintings. As soon as it was financially possible, however, Henry Tanner moved abroad. He spent most of the rest of his life in Paris and the Holy Land. His religious paintings, taken from Bible stories, made him one of the best-known artists of his day.

Throughout the 1800s, most black artists, with a few exceptions, looked to Europe and traditional subjects for their inspiration. They avoided black subject matter and racial problems in their work. Duncanson said, "I am not interested in colour [problems] only paint." Black artists who sought Tanner's help in Paris were reminded that, "They could have it as artists, not Negroes."

It wasn't until the early 1900s that the black artist began to look into himself and at the experiences of the black person in America to find subject matter for his sculpture and paintings. When he did, the black art world changed forever.

This renaissance or "golden age" for the black artist began in Harlem, New York. For just as New York City was the center of art, music and literature in white America, so Harlem was the center of culture of black America. After World War I, thousands of black families left the South and headed north. Although they were crowded into tenements in the ghettos of Harlem, they found a freedom to express themselves that they had never known before.

Included in this renaissance were not only black artists but black philosopher-historians like Alain Locke and W. E. B. Du Bois and black poets like Langston Hughes and Countee Cullen. All turned aside from the "mainstream" of American philosophy, literature and art to find the "New Negro," a new way of looking at American life, history and culture. Gradually the renaissance spread to other cities: Chicago, Cleveland, Washington, Atlanta.

Among the best-known artists of the renaissance were painters like Aaron Douglas, Archibald Motley, James Porter and Lois Mailou Jones; black sculptors like May Howard Jackson and Richmond Barthé, to name just a few. Painters and sculptors all broke new ground in the art world. They no longer painted black men and women as stereotypes, that is, the way the white men often saw the black person, as patient "Uncle Toms" or fat "Aunt Jemimas."

They painted the black man and his daily life as it

216

actually was: the joys and the sorrows; the feverish activities of the city streets; the sordid reality of the ghetto;
the exhausted sharecropper; the terror of lynchings; as
well as the proud dignity in the face of the black man,
the beauty in the face of the black woman.

For all its burst of creative talent, the new black art
movement could not have succeeded had it not been for
the support it received from two separate sources. One
was the Amy Spingarn prizes, sponsored by *The Crisis*
magazine, "for persons of Negro descent in order to encourage their aptitude for art expression." The other
was the Harmon Foundation, begun in 1926 by William Harmon, businessman and philanthropist. The
foundation began the first all-black art exhibitions in
America. In addition, the foundation helped support
struggling young artists and promoted art education for
black students in schools and colleges.

The black artist in the 1920s and '30s did not only
look to his own past and present. He began to rediscover
his African heritage. It was during this period that the
term "Afro-American" first came into use. White artists
were also beginning to discover African culture. In Ber-
lin and Vienna great museums started building collections of African art. Art critics were realizing that the
tribal carvings in wood and ivory were not savage or
uncivilized, but a unique stylized art form with a powerful, original beauty.

In the United States Alain Locke urged young black
artists to look to "the art of the ancestors." Traces of this
African influence can be found in the early paintings of
Aaron Douglas and Archibald Motley and the sculpture
of Richmond Barthé and Sargent Johnson.

There were still other artists who found their own
way, not looking to their African heritage or the racial

217

injustice around them as subjects for their work. Such an artist was self-taught Horace Pippin. As a boy he had always wanted to draw, but he was too poor to take any formal art training and a World War I wound left his right arm and hand virtually useless. Laboriously, after many years' work, he taught himself to use his left hand to lift his right hand. Then with a red-hot poker he burned an outline of figures on a piece of wood, finally teaching himself to paint brilliant colors flatly on boards.

His paintings were called "primitives" because he was self-taught, but in his early work he caught the horror of war as few artists have. He also recalled with great skill scenes from his childhood and stories he had been told by his grandmother. One particular story Pippin remembered was of the day his grandmother had watched the abolitionist John Brown going to his hanging. In his paintings of the scene, his grandmother is in the foreground turning sadly away from the sight of John Brown, seated on a wagon, tied up securely, with guards surrounding him.

Horace Pippin painted his first picture when he was forty-three. Critics saw his work, and after that fame came quickly. Even after museums eagerly sought his work, Pippin went his own way. He painted what he felt in his heart, paying no attention to those who wanted to change his style. His style might have seemed simple and childlike, but his pictures were filled with a sensitivity and a powerful use of color that no child could copy.

In the 1930s disaster struck the United States. A great depression swept across the country, bringing massive unemployment in its wake. The people of Harlem suffered even more than the rest of the country, and the black art movement might have foundered completely but for the Federal Works Project. The government provided financial aid to both black and white artists. Commissions to paint murals—pictures which are painted directly on a wall or ceiling—were given to black artists. Colorful murals began appearing on the walls of government buildings, schools, hospitals and libraries all over America.

It was during this period that Aaron Douglas painted his exciting murals at the Countee Cullen Library in New York City. The murals are a pictorial history of the black man in America. In Atlanta, Georgia, Hale Woodruff's murals titled *Shantytown* and *Mudhill* showed the bleak, ugly poverty of the black slums in Atlanta, shocking the conscience of the white community with their message of social protest.

Hughie Lee Smith, Jacob Lawrence, Romare Bearden and Charles White were among other black artists of the 1930s who used their talents to protest the injustices the black man had suffered. But they didn't only paint of oppression. They also brought to black Americans a new sense of pride in their accomplishments. Charles White's outstanding portraits of such black leaders as Frederick Douglass and Sojourner Truth were reminders that there were black heroes, as well as white, in America's history.

In the 1940s and 1950s, black artists continued to grow in stature but were always fighting an uphill battle to be accepted by a white art world. They tried new techniques in their work. And both painters and sculptors constantly explored new ideas and subject matter for their art.

With the growing militancy of the black population in the 1960s, young black artists turned more and more to protest subjects in their work, making bitter social statements in paint and sculpture. There are some critics who object to this, who say that black artists must not be restricted to "African" art or "racial" art. They insist that the creative artist crosses all boundaries, touches all subjects, all mankind.

Other critics say that the black artist cannot be separated from his "blackness," that he must use his talent in the social struggle to free his race. They are equally insistent that "black art must stem from black culture."

Whoever is right, one thing is true. Art is in its own way a short cut to the history of a people. When we look at the sculptured head of a young black woman by Elizabeth Catlett, it is impossible not to see that black is truly beautiful. In viewing the murals by Hale Woodruff showing the mutiny of slave leader Cinqué aboard the *Amistad,* his trial and final freedom, we learn more vividly than from a book that not all slaves submitted meekly to a life of slavery. We can glimpse the proud African past in Sargent Johnson's lacquered statue *Forever Free,* and the sometimes tortured, bitter present in the painting *D-Yard Attica* by Roger Brown.

Today there is hardly a major art museum in the United States that does not have in its collection at least one or several examples of art by black painters or sculptors. A great many museums have representative African art collections. The following, therefore, can be considered only as a select list of museums with outstanding African collections or good to excellent black American art collections.

Also included are those few museums that specialize exclusively in collecting and exhibiting paintings, statues and graphics by black artists. Such museums are something new on the American scene. Some of them are not museums in the traditional sense of the word. They are community or urban centers that combine art exhibits with other cultural activities—such as handicraft workshops and musical and theatrical events, or just neighborhood meeting areas, bringing the museum directly to the people of the community.

All of the following museums are open to the public, some with a small admission charge, some without any charge at all.

ALABAMA

Art Gallery, Carver Museum, Tuskegee Institute, Tuskegee. An excellent collection of African art items, such as jewelry, swords, musical instruments, clothing and ornaments, as well as paintings and sculpture by black American artists of the nineteenth and twentieth century.

Talladega College, Talladega. The Amistad Murals of the Cinqué mutiny, painted by Hale Woodruff, are located in the Savery Library of the college.

CALIFORNIA

Los Angeles County Museum of Art, 5905 Wilshire Boulevard, Los Angeles. The famous Paul Tishman collection of African sculpture and several paintings by black American artists Henry Ossawa Tanner and Charles White.

Oakland Museum, 1000 Oak Street, Oakland. The Oakland Museum has almost 155 works in its collection by black American artists and sculptors, including lithographs by Grafton T. Brown, one of the earliest black artists in California.

San Jose Public Library, 180 West San Carlos Street, San Jose. Three rare statues by Edmonia Lewis, the half-Indian half-black artist, may be seen at this library. The statues were purchased by the library in 1873 when the artist held an exhibit of her work in San Francisco. In 1968 the statues were discovered, coated with grime, in the basement of the library.

Golden State Mutual Life Insurance Company, Afro-American Art Collection, 1999 West Adams Boulevard, Los Angeles. On the walls of the Home Office lobby of this company are two famous murals by Hale Woodruff and Charles Alston, covering the role black Americans played in the exploration and settlement of California. Within the lobby also can be seen the Golden State Mutual's Afro-American Art Collection, which was conceived as a showplace for the works of black artists.

COLORADO

Denver Art Museum, 100 West 14th Avenue, Parkway, Denver. Outstanding collection of African art.

DISTRICT OF COLUMBIA

Anacostia Neighborhood Museum, 2405 Martin Luther King, Jr. Avenue, S.E. The Anacostia Museum is a combined cultural arts center and workshop for neighborhood groups. It offers exhibits by and about Afro-American art and artists in addition to constantly changing exhibits on black American history and urban problems. Also films and other special programs. For more information about the Anacostia Museum, see Chapter One.

Barnett Aden Art Gallery, 127 Randolph Place N.W. One of the difficulties black artists have always faced is finding art galleries that will display their work for exhibit and sale. In 1943 Alonzo Aden opened an art gallery in his mother's old-fashioned Washington home with the purpose of "discovering and presenting new talent, white and colored, to the community." Many of the black artists Mr. Aden presented for the first time have reached international acclaim.

Gallery of Art, Howard University, 2455 6th Street, N.W. One of the finest collections of contemporary black art and African art. The African collection was begun by Alain Locke, the black author, historian and philosopher, who gave his own personal collection to the gallery.

The art of mural painting is being continued by the art department of the university with a series of monumental wall paintings on the black experience in America. The huge murals will average two stories high by 60 feet long and will be affixed to the exterior and interior walls of several buildings on campus.

Museum of African Art, 316–318 A Street, N.E., Capitol Hill. In 1964 the former Washington townhouse of Frederick Douglass was turned into the first public museum in this country to exhibit only African and Afro-American art.

What were once living rooms in the Douglass home have been changed into elegant black and gold galleries, decorated with priceless African spirit masks, magnificent pieces of sculpture, colorful African textiles and jewelry. One room is a special gallery showing the influence of African sculpture on the modern art of the Western world, particularly its influence on such famous artists as Picasso, Modigliani and Klee.

The museum also has a permanent collection of nineteenth- and twentieth-century black American art, including works by Tanner, Bannister, Duncanson and others.

Lectures on African art and demonstrations of African musical instruments are offered in the auditorium of the museum.

Group tours of the museum by appointment.

National Collection of Fine Arts, 8th and G streets, N.W. This museum features a survey of two centuries of American art, and has an extensive collection of paintings and sculptures by black American artists. The National Portrait Gallery is in the south wing of this museum. When the Harmon Foundation was discontinued in 1967, a great many of its paintings, including forty portraits of famous black Americans, were given to the National Portrait Gallery.

Naitonal Gallery of Art, Constitution Avenue at 6th Street. This gallery owns several rare portraits by early black American portrait painters, such as Joshua Johnston, and equally rare watercolor paintings of slave handicrafts from Southern plantations.

National Museum of Natural History, 10th Street and Constitution Avenue. The African galleries in this museum have displays of nineteenth-century African art and figure sculpture exhibited in faithfully reconstructed tribal surroundings.

Phillips Collection, 1612 21st Street, N.W. The Phillips Collection owns thirty of Jacob Lawrence's sixty panels on the "Migration of the Negro," a remarkable collection of paintings on the great migration of blacks from the South to Northern cities. Jacob Lawrence's family moved north with the first migration.

GEORGIA

Art Gallery, Atlanta University, Atlanta. In 1942 when the noted black artist Hale Woodruff was on the faculty of Atlanta University, the university began an annual exhibition of the works of black American artists. Through these exhibitions and through purchases of the prize winning selections, the Atlanta University gallery now represents probably the largest and most important collection of works of contemporary black artists to be found anywhere in America. The gallery has works of Elizabeth Catlett, Charles White, Ernest Crichlow, Henry Ossawa Tanner and John Biggers, among many others. The Art Gallery is located in the lower level of Trevor Arnett Library.

ILLINOIS

Art Institute of Chicago, Michigan Avenue at Adams Street. The museum owns paintings and sculpture by contemporary black artists, as well as earlier artists such as Henry Ossawa Tanner, Richard Hunt, Marion Perkins and Archibald Motley. The museum also owns a large collection of African art.

Du Sable Museum of African-American History, 3806 South Michigan Avenue, Chicago. Although primarily a history museum, the Du Sable Museum also has black contemporary art in its collection, along with examples of African arts and crafts.

Field Museum of Natural History, Roosevelt Road at Lake Shore Drive, Chicago. This museum has an excellent collection of nineteenth-century African sculpture, particularly art of the Cameroons and the Benene bronzes.

Wall of Respect, 43rd and Langley Avenue, Chicago. An outdoor mural of paintings and photographs, created in the summer of 1967 by the Organization of Black American Culture.

The mural painted on a building wall depicts the struggle and the heroes of the black revolution.

The Southside Art Center, 3831 South Michigan Avenue, Chicago

Art and Soul Art Center, 1866 South Komensky Avenue, Chicago

Both are small, neighborhood art centers that encourage young and old black artists by conducting art classes and exhibiting work of local artists.

LOUISIANA

Louisiana State Museum, 751 Chartres Street, New Orleans. Portraits, including a self-portrait, of early nineteenth-century black artist Julian Hudson may be seen in this museum.

MARYLAND

Baltimore Museum of Art, Art Museum Drive, Baltimore. Excellent African art collection.

Gallery of Art, Morgan State College, Baltimore. The gallery includes black American artists in its collection. On campus is a statue of Frederick Douglass by black sculptor James Lewis.

MASSACHUSETTS

Boston Museum of Fine Arts, Huntington Avenue, Boston. This world-famous museum owns a fine collection of African sculpture as well as paintings by Afro-American artists.

Museum of Afro-American History, Smith Court, Boston. In addition to exhibits emphasizing aspects of black American history, this museum also houses a collection of Afro-American paintings and posters, as well as African and Haitian sculpture.

National Center of Afro-American Artists, 122 Elm Hill Avenue, Dorchester. In connection with the NCAAA, an art gallery is being developed that will act as a forum for black artists, exhibit their works and preserve black historical art material for the future. The NCAAA, which was founded with the support of the Museum of Fine Arts, Boston, also

225

houses the Elma Lewis School of Fine Arts, Inc., for training young black students in the dance, music and drama.

Peabody Museum, Harvard University, Cambridge. Includes an excellent African art collection.

MICHIGAN

Detroit Institute of Arts, 5200 Woodward Avenue, Detroit. One of the best African art collections in the country, as well as a collection of paintings by outstanding black artists such as: Jacob Lawrence and his series of paintings on John Brown; Hughie Lee-Smith, *Boy With a Tire;* Romare Bearden, *Black Mother and Child;* Henry Ossawa Tanner, *Flight from Egypt,* among many others.

International Afro-American Museum, Inc., 1549 West Grand Boulevard, Detroit. This new museum maintains a mobile museum as well as an African Art and History exhibit. One of the fascinating resources is a collection of taped interviews with local black artists, whose life stories and experiences illuminate some facets of black history.

MINNESOTA

Minneapolis Institute of Arts, 201 East 24th Street, Minneapolis

Walker Art Center, Vineland Place, Minneapolis
Both have good collections of African art.

MISSOURI

City Art Museum of St. Louis, Forest Park, St. Louis. A good collection of African art and a small collection of works by black American artists.

William Rockhill Nelson Gallery and Atkins Museum of Fine Arts, 4525 Oak Street, Kansas City. A good collection of African art and sculpture by Richard Hunt and the painting *Home Chores,* by the noted black artist Jacob Lawrence.

NEW JERSEY

Newark Museum, 43–49 Washington Street, Newark. An excellent collection of paintings and sculpture by black American artists, including a rare Joshua Johnston portrait and a recent acquisition by Barbara Chase-Riboud, *Monument to Malcolm X, II*. One of the more popular exhibitions held recently at the museum was "Black Artists: Two Generations," which included paintings by Henry Ossawa Tanner, Hale Woodruff, Charles W. White and others.

NEW YORK

Albright-Knox Art Gallery, 1285 Elmwood Avenue, Buffalo. Includes paintings by black artists Horace Pippin and Jacob Lawrence and sculpture by Richard Hunt.

American Museum of Natural History, Central Park West at 79th Street, New York. African art and sculpture from the nineteenth and twentieth century may be seen well displayed in the Hall of Man in Africa section of this museum.

Community Art Gallery, Brooklyn Museum, Eastern Parkway, Brooklyn. Located on the ground floor, east wing of the Brooklyn Museum, the Community Art Gallery is dedicated to exhibits of the work of black artists of quality. These unique exhibits of art and handicrafts have brought thousands of visitors to the gallery who have never been to a museum before.

The Brooklyn Museum, in addition, has a large collection of African art, as well as works by black American artists: *Funeral Sermon* by Jacob Lawrence; *Before the Storm* by Richard Mayhew and *Shoe Shine* by Ernest Crichlow, among many others.

The Cinqué Gallery, 245 Lafayette Street, New York. A small art gallery, located in Manhattan's East Village, that is a "showcase for the works of young minority artists."

Countee Cullen Branch, New York Public Library, 104 West 136th Street, New York. The four famous Aaron Douglas murals can be seen here. They depict black America's history from its African background through slavery, emancipation and the great migration of Afro-Americans from the South to the North that began during World War I.

Metropolitan Museum of Art, Fifth Avenue and 82nd Street, New York. Paintings by contemporary as well as nineteenth-century black artists are included in this enormous collection

227

of world art. A few of the better-known works by black artists in this collection are *Victorian Interior* by Horace Pippin, *Blind Beggar* by Jacob Lawrence, *The Woodshed* by Romare Bearden; sculpture by Richmond Barthé, and photographs by Gordon Parks.

Museum of Modern Art, 11 West 53rd Street, New York. Perhaps the best-known works by black artists contained in this collection are the thirty panels entitled "The Migration of the Negro" by the great social-protest artist Jacob Lawrence. The remaining thirty of these panels are at the Phillips Collection, Washington, D.C. The Museum of Modern Art also includes in its extensive collection other drawings, prints, paintings, sculpture and photographs by a great many Afro-American artists.

Museum of Primitive Art, 15 West 54th Street, New York. Includes art from Africa, Oceania and the pre-Columbian Americas.

The Schomburg Collection, 103 West 135th Street, New York. Includes African art objects of ivory, metal and wood as well as more than one hundred paintings, etchings, lithographs, engravings and watercolors, either by noted black American artists or of black subjects.

The Studio Museum, 2033 Fifth Avenue, New York. This museum was created in 1968 to encourage and support black artists in America and to establish a meeting ground between black art and the community. Constantly changing exhibits of paintings and sculpture are displayed on two upper floors of a loft building in central Harlem. The exhibits include the work of well-known black American artists of today and yesterday—as well as the works of gifted unknown artists.

Whitney Museum of American Art, 945 Madison Avenue, New York. Black artists Jacob Lawrence and Charles White are included in this museum's collection of great American art.

NORTH CAROLINA

The Yellow Tavern, Milton. The Yellow Tavern in its early days was an overnight stop on a stagecoach line. In 1823 Thomas Day, a black carpenter, bought the tavern and turned it into a factory. There, he and his specially trained white and black

228

apprentices made the fine mahogany furniture for which he was famous. So highly respected was Mr. Day that when he threatened to leave Milton because black laws wouldn't allow him to bring his wife (a free black woman) into the state of North Carolina, the citizens of Milton requested and received from the state legislature a special exemption for Mrs. Day.

The Yellow Tavern is now a private home not open to the public. The Presbyterian church, however, where Thomas Day built the pews may be opened by request. There are also other churches in the area that have Thomas Day pews. Mr. Day is buried on a farm he owned near Milton.

OHIO

Allen Memorial Art Museum, Oberlin College, Oberlin. Includes an African art collection as well as works by contemporary black sculptors like Richmond Barthé.

Carnegie Library, Wilberforce University, Wilberforce. The library at Wilberforce has an art gallery of works by black American artists.

Cincinnati Art Museum, Eden Park, Cincinnati. This was the first major art museum in America to display African art. The museum also has paintings by early black artists, such as Robert Duncanson's *Blue Hole, Flood Waters, Little Miami.*

Cleveland Museum of Art, 11150 East Boulevard, Cleveland. Includes a good African art collection.

Karamu House, 2355 East 89th Street, Cleveland. Begun in 1915, the studio at Karamu House has from the beginning successfully completed its purpose: that of discovering and training the creative abilities of the American Negro in art, theater, dance and music. Many talented young artists, sculptors, printmakers and etchers have gotten their start here and held exhibitions sponsored by the Karamu House.

Taft Museum, 316 Pike Street, Cincinnati. Formerly the Belmont mansion owned by Nicholas Longworth. The landscape murals by Robert Duncanson may be found here. Nicholas Longworth was a generous friend to Robert Duncanson and commissioned him to paint the murals in his home when Robert Duncanson was still a relatively unknown artist.

229

OREGON

Portland Art Museum, 1219 S. W. Park Avenue, Portland. Has a very good African art collection.

PENNSYLVANIA

Carnegie Institute, Carnegie Museum, 4400 Forbes Avenue, Pittsburgh. Contains works by contemporary black artists like Norman Lewis and John Wilson, as well as nineteenth-century artists Horace Pippin and Henry Ossawa Tanner. The institute also has an excellent collection of African art.

Museum of the Philadelphia Civic Center, Philadelphia. One of the most significant collections of African musical instruments, as well as over 3,000 examples of African sculpture, craftwork, masks, figurines, textiles, leatherwork, metalwork, pottery, wood carvings and basketry. The museum recently sponsored an Afro-American Art Exhibit and has on display a case containing fifty commemorative medals of noted black people in history.

Pennsylvania Academy of Fine Arts, Broad and Cherry streets, Philadelphia. This museum has religious paintings by Henry Ossawa Tanner, as well as paintings by Horace Pippin, among other noted black artists.

Philadelphia Museum of Art, Parkway at 26th, Philadelphia. Includes African art as well as such works by nineteenth- and twentieth-century black American artists as *The Lynching* by Samuel Brown, *The End of the War* by Horace Pippin and *The Annunciation* by Henry Ossawa Tanner.

RHODE ISLAND

Museum of Art, Rhode Island School of Design, 224 Benefit Street, Providence. Contemporary and historic black American art works, sculpture and paintings, including seven landscape paintings by the nineteenth-century black artist Edward Bannister, who lived in Providence, Rhode Island, and was one of the seven founders of the famed Providence Art Club.

SOUTH CAROLINA

Art Gallery of the The Old Slave Mart Museum, 6 Chalmers Street, Charleston. One of the few museums in this country to exhibit the handicraft of slaves, items actually made and used on plantations. The art gallery also contains works of art by African, West Indian and contemporary black American artists.

TENNESSEE

Carl Van Vechten Gallery of Fine Arts, Fisk University, Nashville. The MacDonald Collection of African sculpture is available for public viewing on the third floor of the Fisk University Library. Contemporary black American art from the Alfred Stieglitz collection may be seen at the Carl Van Vechten Gallery of Fine Arts on the campus. Murals by Aaron Douglas are in the old library, now the administration building.

TEXAS

Houston Museum of Fine Arts, 1001 Bissonnet Street, Houston. Includes African art and a small collection of works by black American artists.

VIRGINIA

College Museum, Hampton Institute, Hampton. This museum houses one of the oldest collections of African art in this country, begun in 1868. Also at the museum are works of art by historic and contemporary black artists: one of Henry Ossawa Tanner's early paintings, *The Banjo Lesson;* and an impressive set of murals by Charles White titled "The Contribution of the Negro to American Democracy"; and others.

WASHINGTON

Seattle Art Museum, Volunteer Park, Seattle. Includes a good African art collection.

WISCONSIN

Milwaukee Art Center, 750 North Lincoln Memorial Drive, Milwaukee. A small collection of paintings by black American artists, including works by Henry Ossawa Tanner and contemporary sculpture by Richard Hunt.

Milwaukee Public Museum, 800 West Wells Street, Milwaukee. An important African sculpture collection.

A young visitor to the Museum of African Art in Washington, D.C., studies a wood carving of a kneeling figure holding an offering bowl in which kola nuts were kept. The act of offering kola nuts to visitors to one's house is a traditional sign of hospitality among many African cultures. COURTESY MUSEUM OF AFRICAN ART, WASHINGTON, D.C.

A modern-day African wood carving and some ancient spirit masks on the wall are part of the African art collection at the Du Sable Museum of African-American History in Chicago, Illinois. Much like contemporary Western art, African art is often symbolic and highly stylized rather than realistic. COURTESY *TUESDAY* MAGAZINE

This bronze Memorial Benin head at the Smithsonian National Museum of Natural History, Washington, D.C., is from seventeenth-century Africa and was made by a sophisticated "lost wax" method. No two heads made by this method are ever exactly the same. A head such as this was used to ornament the ancestral shrines of the royal rulers of the kingdom of Benin, Africa. COURTESY NATIONAL MUSEUM OF NATURAL HISTORY, THE SMITHSONIAN INSTITUTION

Pottery making was developed into a fine art by Africans and was actually an art practiced by the women in a tribe. The influence of the African Effigy pot may be seen in the Afro-American face jug, which was made by an unidentified South Carolina black potter. This face jug, and others, may be seen at the National Museum of History and Technology, Smithsonian Institution, Washington, D.C. COURTESY THE SMITHSONIAN INSTITUTION

The painting of portraits was a thriving business for artists in nineteenth-century America. Black portrait artists Patrick Reason and Joshua Johnston worked in New England, while in New Orleans Julien Hudson, of French-African parentage, not only painted portraits of famous people but did his own self-portrait, which may be seen at the Louisiana State Museum, New Orleans. COURTESY LOUISIANA STATE MUSEUM

Like Robert Bannister, Robert Duncanson's best works are his romantic landscapes, which were so popular in nineteenth-century America. He studied and traveled abroad but his early years as an artist were spent in Cincinnati, where many of his paintings may now be seen. One of his finest paintings, *Blue Hole, Flood Waters, Little Miami*, shown *above*, hangs in the Cincinnati Art Museum. COURTESY CINCINNATI ART MUSEUM

Although both Robert Bannister and Robert Duncanson achieved success as artists, Henry Ossawa Tanner in 1900 was the first black artist to achieve world-wide recognition. Most of his best paintings were on religious subjects. However, an early painting, *The Banjo Lesson,* touches on black family life with warmth and sensitivity. The painting is in the collection of Hampton Institute, Hampton. Virginia. COURTESY HAMPTON INSTITUTE, HAMPTON, VIRGINIA

Sculptors during the Harlem Renaissance turned to more realistic portrayals of black people. Richmond Barthé, one of the leading black sculptors, displays the graceful carriage of a young black woman in his statue *The Blackberry Woman.* The statue is in the collection of the Whitney Museum of American Art, New York City. COURTESY HARMON FOUNDATION COLLECTION, NATIONAL ARCHIVES

One of the black artists who came to the fore during the Harlem Renaissance of the 1920s was Archibald Motley. Unlike previous black artists, artists of the renaissance stressed the black experience in their work: life for the black American as it really was in the ghetto and on a sharecropper's farm. Motley's painting *Chicken Shack* catches the feeling of street life in Harlem in the 1900s. COURTESY HARMON FOUNDATION COLLECTION, NATIONAL ARCHIVES

Some of the Harlem Renaissance artists turned to their African heritage for their inspiration. The African-Egyptian influence can be seen clearly in Sargent Johnson's sculpture *Copper Mask,* and in one of his most famous works, *at left, Forever Free.* A lacquered redwood version of this work may be seen at the Oakland Museum, California. COURTESY HARMON FOUNDATION COLLECTION, NATIONAL ARCHIVES

One of the best-known, self-trained black artists who worked during the Harlem Renaissance and the depression years was Jacob Lawrence. He painted in a two-dimensional style and used episodes of black life and history as themes for his works. His series of paintings "The Migration" covers the migration of the black people from the rural South to the big Northern cities. Thirty of the paintings are in the Museum Modern of Art, New York, and thirty are in the Phillips Collection, Washington, D.C. COURTESY HARMON FOUNDATION COLLECTION, NATIONAL ARCHIVES

Black artists of the Harlem Renaissance and later, in painting of black experi-
ence and history, often turned to portraits of black heroes and heroines in
American history. One such artist, Charles White, in the above drawing caught
the rocklike physical and moral strengths of Harriet Tubman. The ink and
wash drawing may be seen in the Afro-American Art Collection of the Golden
State Mutual Life Insurance Company, Los Angeles, California. COURTESY GOL-
DEN STATE STATE MUTUAL LIFE INSURANCE COMPANY, AFRO-AMERICAN ART COL-
LECTION

The Barnett-Aden Gallery in Washington, D.C., was one of the first private art galleries to display work by black artists. Recently they lent a portion of their collection by black artists to the Anacostia Museum, Washington, D.C., for a special art exhibit.
COURTESY ANACOSTIA NEIGH-BORHOOD MUSEUM, WASHING-TON, D.C.

Horace Pippin's paintings came into prominence in the 1930s and followed no artistic style except his own. One of his most important works, *John Brown Going to His Hanging,* is in the collection of the Museum of the Pennsylvania Academy of the Fine Arts, Philadelphia. Pippin has painted into the foreground of the picture the figure of his grandmother, who is turning sadly away from the scene of abolitionist John Brown riding a wagon to his execution.
COURTESY PENNSYLVANIA ACADEMY OF THE FINE ARTS

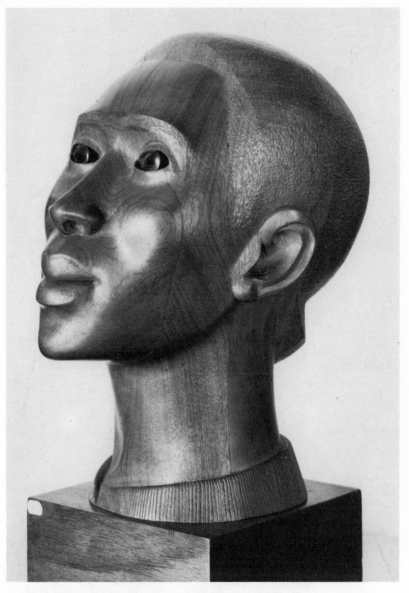

Perhaps no piece of sculpture illustrates more clearly the "black is
beautiful" theme first emphasized in the Harlem Renaissance than this
carving by Elizabeth Catlett. It is called *Negro Woman* and is in
the collection of Atlanta University. In addition to her sculpture,
Mrs. Catlett is also noted for her prints and paintings.
COURTESY ATLANTA UNIVERSITY AFRO-AMERICAN COLLECTION

With the Depression, many black and white artists turned to painting murals in public buildings, sponsored by the government. The murals of Aaron Douglas at the Countee Cullen Library, New York City, tell the story of the black people from Africa, through slavery, Reconstruction days and migration north. The *above* panel shows life for the black American after Reconstruction—the constant labor in the fields, the horror of lynchings and, despite their troubles, the ability of the black man and woman to enjoy laughter and music. COURTESY COUNTEE CULLEN BRANCH OF THE NEW YORK PUBLIC LIBRARY

Another black artist who painted outstanding murals was Hale Woodruff. His *Amistad* mutiny murals at Talladega College, Talladega, Mississippi, were completed in 1943. The *above* scene shows the mutiny leader, Cinqué, facing his accusers in a court of law. The faces in the mural are actual liknesses of the people involved in the Amistad case. COURTESY SAVERY LIBRARY, TALLADEGA, COLLEGE, TALLADEGA, MISSISSIPPI

UP,
-YOU MIGHTY
RACE

During the 1960s, mural painting moved from the interior of buildings to the outside walls of buildings in black neighborhoods. The above is a typical "wall of respect," as it was called, painted by black artists on the wall of a house in St. Louis in 1968. The portraits are of various historic and contemporary black persons, ranging from Phillis Wheatley to Malcolm X.
COURTESY ART DEPARTMENT, ST. LOUIS PUBLIC LIBRARY

Some black artists in the 1950s and 1960s, although they still used black experience as themes for their works, became more militant and bitter in their outlook. Roger Brown, in his painting *D-Yard Attica* in the collection of the Art Institute of Chicago, has chosen the prison riot at Attica, New York, in September 1971 as the subject of his work. COURTESY OF THE ART INSTITUTE OF CHICAGO

Although the small boy in the painting *above,* "Boy with a Tire," is black, he could just as easily be white. Hughie Lee-Smith paints not just on black themes but on universal themes—such as the loneliness and isolation of the human spirit—that touch all people. The Detroit Institute of Arts owns this painting, as well as many other works by black American artists. BOY WITH A TIRE, ARTIST HUGHIE LEE-SMITH (American, b. 1915) COURTESY DETROIT INSTITUTE OF ARTS, GIFT OF DRS. S. B. MILTON, JAMES A. OWEN, B. F. SEABROOKS AND A. E. THOMAS, JR.

THE
STORYTELLERS

In 1761 John Wheatley of Boston brought home a present for his wife. The gift was a young, pretty slave girl, only eight years old but with a frail dignity beyond her years. Mrs. Wheatley became very fond of Phillis, as she named the young girl, treating her more like a daughter than a servant, teaching her to read and write. Phillis learned quickly. By the age of thirteen, she was not only writing English but translating Latin, and she had written her first poem. In 1773 a collection of her poems was published in London. The book was greeted on both sides of the Atlantic with enthusiasm—and amazement.

For just as Americans and Europeans, of the eighteenth and nineteenth centuries, considered the black race to have no artistic ability, they were also convinced that a black man or woman could not possibly compose poetry or write stories. Everyone knew that the continent of Africa, with the possible exception of Egypt, was a vast, uncivilized wasteland with no history of its own. And since Africans had no written language, they could not possibly have any knowledge of literature or literary talent.

This belief that most of Africa was a dark, savage continent was based partly on ignorance—very few Americans or Europeans had ever seen Africa—and partly on stories spread by the slave traders of the time. It was much easier to justify the cruel business of buying and selling human beings if the slave dealers convinced everyone that the people being kidnapped and sold into slavery were from an inferior race. Some Americans who bought slaves were even persuaded that they were doing the slaves a favor by introducing them to the advantages of "civilization."

It wasn't until early in the twentieth century that scholars began studying black Africa at firsthand. They discovered that instead of being without a history, these people had had a flourishing civilization while Europe was still in the dark ages. And that even without a written language, the African tribes for centuries had encouraged a strong oral or spoken tradition of literature among their people.

Poets, storytellers and musicians had been attached to the royal court of Dahomey; in the Ruanda Kingdom the post of court poet was a valued hereditary position, to be passed down from father to son. The Ashantis trained their musicians from childhood in guilds, where they were taught to play a dozen complicated musical instruments. These storytellers and musicians were not only court entertainers. They preserved the history, religious traditions and beliefs of each tribe and handed them down in story, poetry and song from one generation to the next.

Not all the storytellers and poets were professionals. The villagers themselves delighted in telling stories around the campfire at night. Each took his turn, spinning tales of brave and cowardly men and women, of kings and warriors, and of the frightening supernatural. Especially enjoyed were humorous stories about animals.

Often story and song were combined, with the audience joining in the singing when they happened to feel like it. Since the words and music were never written down, each storyteller was free to improvise, to change the story or song to suit the occasion, depending on his or her own dramatic and musical ability.

When black people were brought to America, very few were given the opportunity to learn to read and write. They therefore continued their oral tradition, telling stories aloud rather than writing them down. In time the African themes, settings and even the characters of the stories changed to fit the new American surroundings.

The trickster hare of the Housa tribe and the cunning Ashanti spider, Anansi, the leading characters in African animal stories, became the American Br'er Rabbit. The powerful Sky God, Nyame, became the king or plantation owner in the local American stories; the leopard became the buzzard; the zebra the woodpecker. However, the stories themselves continued to be told and retold by the slaves to each other, to their children and, at times, to the children of their white masters.

In the 1860s a young newspaperman named Joel Chandler Harris, working at the Turnwold Plantation in Georgia, listened carefully to the colorful stories told by

249

the elderly slaves on the plantation. He particularly enjoyed the stories of the clever Br'er Rabbit, who by his wits alone outdid stronger animals like Br'er Fox and Br'er Bear. Joel Chandler Harris took these stories, direct descendants of the African folktales, rewrote and refined them, and in 1880 published *Uncle Remus, his Songs and his Sayings*. The Uncle Remus Tales and other black folktales have become an important part of American folklore.

Black authors, however, achieved a measure of fame many years earlier. The years from 1800 to 1859 were important ones for black writers. It was during this period that escaped slaves like Frederick Douglass, William Wells Brown, Moses Roper and many, many more wrote the so-called "slave narratives." These narratives told exactly what it was like and how it felt to be a slave.

Although all along free blacks had been writing essays and articles in opposition to slavery, these firsthand stories of escaped slaves, relating in vivid, authentic detail the inhumanity and countless cruelties of a slave's daily life, were much more effective.

One of the most successful of all the slave narratives, though, was a fictionalized account of a slave's life written not by an escaped slave but a white woman, Harriet Beecher Stowe. Although the book was written in the highly sentimentalized fashion of the day, many of the incidents and characters in the book were taken from actual life.

Mrs. Stowe had lived in Cincinnati, Ohio, for seventeen years. During that time the city, on the border between the slave state of Kentucky and the free state of Ohio, was an active center for runaway slaves. The Stowe home and the Lane Theological Seminary where Mrs. Stowe's husband taught, served as way stations on the Underground Railroad. Mrs. Stowe heard at first-hand from escaping slaves stories about their lives in slavery. In addition, she visited plantations in Kentucky. She was to use this material later when she wrote her book, *Uncle Tom's Cabin.*

Although to be called an "Uncle Tom" today is regarded as an insult, the character of Uncle Tom in Mrs. Stowe's book was a strong, truly religious, compassionate man, bitterly mistreated by his owners. Few slaves, however, accepted their mistreatment with the Christian martyrdom of Uncle Tom. Perhaps a better-drawn character in the book is the escaped slave, George Harris, who was perfectly willing to fight and die to protect his wife, Eliza, and their son during their flight from slavery.

The story of Uncle Tom, and the literally hundreds of other slave stories published during this period, lashed at the conscience of Americans. The books successfully aroused public opinion, making the reader see that slavery, far from being a civilizing influence on the black man and woman, only served to brutalize and degrade the slave and slave owner alike.

Clotelle, the first novel by a black American author, William Wells Brown, was also published during this period. Although oversentimentalized, much in the same fashion as *Uncle Tom's Cabin,* it was also very successful at home and abroad.

After the Civil War, however, former slaves who wanted to become writers found it almost impossible to get their work published. Those few who did manage to be published followed closely the conventional style of the white author, or kept hidden the fact that they were not white. A popular short-story writer, Charles W. Chesnutt, whose best-known story is "The Goo-

251

phered Grapevine," wrote for *The Atlantic* magazine for twelve years before it was revealed to the public that he was a mulatto.

In the years after the war, it was in the field of poetry that the black writer first gained recognition, in the person of a young man named Paul Laurence Dunbar. Born in poverty in Dayton, Ohio, Paul's mother gave him a love of song and poetry, as she told him stories of her past life as a slave. Although he was the only black student in his high school, Paul's talent as a writer was soon recognized and he was made editor of the school paper.

The only job he could get after he graduated was as an elevator operator, but he continued to write, often selling his poetry to the riders on his elevator to earn extra money. Then one day the literary critic William Dean Howells took an interest in his work. From 1893 on, Paul Laurence Dunbar was able to support himself with the money he made writing poetry, short stories and novels.

Paul Laurence Dunbar frequently used dialect in his writings—that is, his characters spoke exactly as an uneducated black person in the rural South would talk. Although he has been criticized for this, Joel Chandler Harris and James Whitcomb Riley, both popular white writers of the same period, also used dialect in their work. Occasionally, Paul Laurence Dunbar wrote poems like "We Wear the Mask" expressing the more bitter side of black life in America, but most of his poems were warm, humorous accounts of black family life. He wrote in the so-called "plantation tradition" of the happy-go-lucky, contented black man, poems that did not offend the white reading public.

By the time of Dunbar's death in 1906, America had

entered a new era of oppression. Jim Crow laws, enacted by many states in the Union, had effectively segregated black Americans from white America. Two famous black writers came out of this period of turmoil. Booker T. Washington, in his book *Up From Slavery*, still believed that the black man could make a success of himself in white America if only he worked hard and knew his place. W. E. B. Du Bois, in his book *Souls of Black Folks,* took the opposite view, that the black person stood little chance to advance in America unless he fought for change.

Both men were undoubtedly sincere in their beliefs, but it took another black writer to bridge the gap between the past, as represented by Mr. Washington, and the future, as seen by Mr. Du Bois.

James Weldon Johnson was not only a writer of poems, short stories and novels, he was a man of many talents: a lawyer, a civil rights leader and a diplomat. In addition, he was a successful songwriter. His popular "Lift Every Voice and Sing," for which his brother wrote the music, became a national anthem for black people. But it was Johnson's novel, *Autobiography of an Ex-Colored Man,* published in 1927, that set the stage for an explosion of black writing in Harlem.

It was a Harlem poet, Claude McKay, who struck the first militant note in the renaissance heralding the arrival of the new black man with his poem that begins:

If we must die, let it not be like hogs
Hunted and penned in an inglorious spot . . .

and ends:

Like men we'll face the murderous, cowardly pack,
Pressed to the wall, dying, but fighting back!

253

Just as works of art of this period reflected a more realistic, if grimly bitter picture of life in black America, so did the flood of writing that came from Harlem begin to show black life in all its facets. Like the artists, some of the writers, such as Arna Bontemps and Helen Johnson, turned to Africa and the African heritage for inspiration. Other authors took renewed pride in their black heritage by writing of the everyday life, dreams and despair of the ordinary black man and woman, struggling to find a foothold in the ghetto life of the city.

Probably the two best-known poets to come out of the Harlem Renaissance are Countee Cullen and Langston Hughes. Cullen's poetry, such as his "What Is Africa to Me?", was written in a traditional lyrical style. Hughes was more interested in constantly experimenting with all forms of poetry, and also tried songs, novels, plays, history and biography.

In his poetry Hughes caught the pulsating, if bleak, Harlem street life in words, as vividly as Archibald Motley, the artist, caught it in paint on a canvas. Later, in his series of short stories called the "Simple" stories, Mr. Hughes' main character, Jesse B. Simple, with shrewd humor exposes the weaknesses of racist arguments, much as Br'er Rabbit inevitably outwitted Br'er Fox.

The writers of the renaissance were forced to ask themselves the same basic question as the artists: Should they write only of the black experience or write on all universal subjects?

Jean Toomer, who during this period wrote *Cane,* one of the most unusual novels ever written, insisted, "I am of no particular race, I am of the human race . . ." Countee Cullen preferred to be known as a poet rather than a black poet, while Langston Hughes said his main purpose in writing "was to explain and illuminate the Negro condition in America."

When the Depression washed over Harlem in the 1930s, writers as well as artists faced lean, hard years. Yet out of the Depression came one of the greatest social-protest novels of all time—*Native Son* by Richard Wright.

Born in Mississippi in abject poverty, as a child Richard Wright was constantly moved from one member of his family to another. He lived in Memphis and Chicago before coming to Harlem, and supported himself with whatever odd jobs he could find, while snatching whatever education he could along the way. But he always knew what he most wanted to do—write.

His first published work, a collection of four short novels called *Uncle Tom's Children,* was based on bitter memories of his Mississippi boyhood. In 1939 the book won the Spingarn medal. Then the next year Wright's novel *Native Son* was published. The book, as well as a stage play based on it, caused a literary sensation.

Many critics found the book shocking in its raw violence. Others disliked the Communist philosophy found in the book. Richard Wright, in revolt against what he considered America's racist society, had joined the Communist Party; but disillusioned, he later left the party in 1944. None of the critics, however, could deny the power of the book or its insight into the ways society can brutally deform and warp a man. For Richard Wright, though, the money and fame came too late. He could never reconcile himself to the life of a black man in the United States. He finally left the country and lived his last years in Paris.

After Wright, the most important black novelist to

255

appear was Ralph Ellison. In 1952 his *Invisible Man,* the search of a black man for identity in white America, established him as a major American writer. A year later a young author named James Baldwin published his novel *Go Tell It on the Mountain,* the story of the coming of age of a fifteen-year-old Harlem boy, and a few years later, a collection of essays called *Notes of a Native Son.* Both Ellison and Baldwin received great critical acclaim, and there was no longer any doubt that the black author had arrived as a major influence on the American literary scene.

Richard Wright, Ralph Ellison and James Baldwin are probably the best-known modern black American novelists. There are many others—Zora Nea Le Hurston, Chester Himes, John A. Williams, John Oliver Killens, Ann Petry, Willard Motley, Frank Yerby—to name only a few. Some have written solely on the problems facing the black man and woman in America; others have touched upon human problems faced by people of all races.

The Renaissance poets Langston Hughes, Arna Bontemps and Sterling Brown continued writing in the 1950s, using the blues, spirituals and folk literature of the black people to give a unique stamp to their poetry. They were not alone. In his *Dark Symphony,* Melvin Tolson told proudly of the black American's history and his contribution to his country. Robert Hayden wrote of the revolt of Gabriel, the courage of Harriet Tubman and other black heroes and heroines.

Gwendolyn Brooks wrote poetry, not only of the black experience, but all human experience. She sometimes used slang and sharp abrupt rhythms to catch the feeling of ghetto life, for example the poem "We Real Cool."

Many of these novelists and poets were still publishing in the 1960s, but in those years the civil rights movement of the 1950s and the big city riots of the 1960s were bringing forth a new black poet. These new voices were more harshly militant, more outspoken than ever before.

Poets like LeRoi Jones, Margaret Danner and Mari E. Evans and prose writers like Eldridge Cleaver and Malcolm X rejected the conventional, the traditional literary tradition. They used words as weapons to fight the white establishment. Poetry was not for entertainment but to serve the cause of revolution. In their prose they spoke with their own voices, searching for new directions, new values for the black man and woman in America. The words they used, the ideas they expressed, were often deliberately shocking.

There were other changes, too, in a lesser-known but important field of literature. For years, history books that included information about black people in America could be counted on the fingers of one hand. There were a few black author-historians before 1900: William Cooper Nell, William Wells Brown and George Washington Williams. But books about black history were seldom published and little read.

Then in 1916 Dr. Carter G. Woodson, who started life as a coal miner and ended his education with a Ph.D. in philosophy from Harvard University, formed the Association for the Study of Negro Life and History. Dr. Woodson, a teacher himself, knew there were many "missing pages" in American history books. Stories of the life of the black man and woman, the role they had played in American culture and history, were either omitted completely or distorted. Few black Americans and fewer white Americans were aware of how much

257

the Afro-American had contributed to the building of the nation.

It was Dr. Woodson's firm belief that if a race has no recorded history, its achievements will be forgotten and finally claimed by other groups. The race then "stands the danger of being exterminated." He was determined that the achievements of the black race would not be forgotten.

In addition to laboring long hours, almost single-handedly, to keep the young historical association from foundering, Dr. Woodson wrote many books on black history, started the scholarly *Journal of Negro History* and was the founder of Negro History Week.

One of the most important results of Dr. Woodson's untiring labor is that today there are hundreds of author-historians researching and writing on the subject of black history. W. E. B. Du Bois was working on an "Encyclopedia of African History" at the time of his death. Some more recent black writer-historians are Alain Locke, Lorenzo Greene, Dr. John Hope Franklin, Benjamin Quarles and Allen Spears.

The association not only encouraged writers of black history, but equally important stimulated collecting and preserving of documents, newspapers, journals, letters and books by and about black Americans. Only through such collections, housed and carefully protected in libraries and universities, can future writers and historians unlock the secrets of the past—and discover the truth about black American history and culture.

One of the most important of these collections was begun in 1926 by Arthur Schomburg, a Puerto Rican of African descent. Angered when a teacher told him that "blacks had no history," he began accumulating everything he could lay his hands on that related to

258

black history. His collection forms the basis for the Schomburg Library, now a branch of the New York Public Library. It is one of the largest sources of material on the history of black Americans, but today there are many more. A selection of such outstanding research libraries is listed below. Because of the value of these collections, they are usually open only to scholars doing research in black history. However, some of these libraries, like the Fisk University Library and the Schomburg Library, also have exhibit areas, containing mementos of famous black writers and artists, that are open to the public.

Unfortunately, there are only a few monuments in America one can visit honoring black authors—but then there aren't too many honoring white authors either! Statues and homes of famous generals and statesmen are more apt to be preserved than those of authors, black or white.

But all authors leave monuments, nevertheless—the poems, stories and other material they have written. And when you read the stories and poetry by black authors about black America, you will be going a long way toward filling in those missing pages in America's history books.

PAUL LAURENCE DUNBAR HOME

In his day Paul Laurence Dunbar was called the "Poet Laureate of his race," though his poetry and novels were read and enjoyed by both black and white readers. Today his poetry may seem old-fashioned. Yet he caught the warmth and love of black family life as few poets ever have. In 1903, at the peak of his success, he returned to the home he had purchased in Dayton, Ohio. Although he was already ill, he continued writing, literally working himself to death in 1906, at the age of thirty-four.

259

The Ohio Historical Society maintains Paul Laurence Dunbar's home, including the study with his desk and books where he did much of his writing. Personal belongings of the poet, as well as many original manuscripts of his poems and stories, may also be seen at the home. The Dunbar home is the only such memorial to a black author in the country.

Location: Paul Laurence Dunbar Home, 219 North Summit Drive, Dayton, Ohio.

Small admission charge. School groups by appointment.

UNCLE REMUS MUSEUM

Two former slave cabins have been made into a log-cabin museum honoring Joel Chandler Harris, who made world-famous the African-American folktale in his Uncle Remus stories. The log cabin is the sort of dwelling in which Uncle Remus might have lived. One end of the cabin contains an old-fashioned fireplace before which Uncle Remus told his humorous animal stories to the Little Boy. All the articles and furnishings in the cabin are authentic to the time Uncle Remus lived and are mentioned in the Uncle Remus stories.

Br'er Rabbit, the most famous of all the characters in the Uncle Remus stories, has a special monument—a statue of himself in front of the courthouse in the center of the town of Eatonton.

Location: Uncle Remus Museum, in Turner Park, one-half mile south on U.S. 129 and 441, Eatonton, Georgia.

Small admission charge.

NATIONAL PORTRAIT GALLERY

The National Portrait Gallery has a special collection of portraits of writers and artists of the Harlem Renaissance period, including such well-known black authors as Countee Cullen, Jean Toomer and Langston Hughes. Also in the collection is a portrait of James Weldon Johnson, painted by black artist Laura Wheeler Waring.

Location: The National Portrait Gallery is located in the south wing of the National Collection of Fine Arts, 8th and G streets, N.W., Washington, D.C. For further information about these museums and their collections, see Chapter Six.

No admission charge.

HARRIET BEECHER STOWE HOUSE

Mrs. Stowe lived in Cincinnati from 1833 to 1850, and it was here that she gained most of the background material on slavery she used in her famous book, *Uncle Tom's Cabin*. Her home in Cincinnati is now a State Memorial dedicated to Mrs. Stowe and to the history of the black American. A portion of the exhibits in the house are devoted to mementos from Mrs. Stowe's life and the rest of the house has displays on the African background of the black American, the life of the Afro-American before and after the Civil War in the United States, and the contributions that black men and women have made to America. In addition, there are fascinating exhibits on slavery and the plantation system, the Underground Railroad and the antislavery movement.

Location: Harriet Beecher Stowe House, 2950 Gilbert Avenue, (U.S. 22 and State 3), Cincinnati, Ohio.

Small admission charge. School groups with teachers free.

SCHOMBURG LIBRARY

One of the most important centers in the world for the study of black people, the Schomburg Library has materials ranging from rare items from the earliest African kingdoms to contemporary materials from Watts in California. The library holdings consist of books, magazines, photographs, original manuscripts, newspapers, playbills, tape recordings, phonograph records and many more materials that document the black experience in every possible way.

The Schomburg Library is not a lending library. All materials must be used within the building. Visitors may see on permanent display a wide variety of African art objects and a collection of African weapons.

Location: Although the Schomburg Library will be moving to a new, larger site in the future, its present location is 103

261

West 135th Street, New York, New York, and may be reached by subway or bus.

UNIVERSITY LIBRARY, FISK UNIVERSITY

On the second floor of the University Library is an extensive collection of materials on the black man in Africa, America and the Caribbean, including books, phonograph records, sheet music, magazines and newspapers.

The manuscripts and literary effects of Charles Waddell Chesnutt and other black authors and leaders, including W. E. B. Du Bois, Jean Toomer and Langston Hughes are preserved in this collection.

Visitors to the library may view original manuscripts of famous black authors, mementos from the Jubilee Singers, and a particularly rare item—the Lincoln Bible. The Bible was given to Abraham Lincoln by a group of ex-slaves. Lincoln's son Robert gave it to Fisk University.

On the third floor of the library are located the MacDonald Collection of African Art and the Alfred Stieglitz Art Collection. The Carl Van Vechten Gallery of Fine Arts is also on the Fisk campus.

Location: Fisk University Library, Fisk University, Nashville, Tennessee.

FOUNDERS LIBRARY, HOWARD UNIVERSITY

The library collection at Howard contains over 100,000 cataloged items on all phases of black life in America. The collection ranges from the papers of abolitionist leaders to a black music and theater collection. The library also has the papers of Mary Church Terrell. Mrs. Terrell fought all her life for women's rights as well as the civil rights of black Americans. At the age of eighty-nine she led an active protest against discrimination in Washington, D.C. restaurants, finally winning her case in court.

The College Museum of Afro-American and African Art and History may also be visited on this campus.

Location: Founders Library, Howard University, 2401 Sixth Street, N.W., Washington, D.C.

THE STORYTELLERS

There are so many outstanding items within this library collection that it is possible to list only a few. The rarest items are autographed copies of poems by Phillis Wheatley. There are also original manuscripts and personal papers from the great black literary figures of the Harlem Renaissance, a large collection of valuable documents on slavery, and a more recent collection of materials on the Black Muslim movement.

On the lower level of the Trevor Arnett Library, visitors may view the permanent collection of paintings and sculpture by black artists, which the university has accumulated over the years. This collection represents the largest assemblage of works by contemporary black artists to be found anywhere in the country.

Location: Trevor Arnett Library, Atlanta University, 273 Chestnut Street, S.W., Atlanta, Georgia.

COLLIS P. HUNTINGTON MEMORIAL LIBRARY,
HAMPTON INSTITUTE

One of the oldest black research libraries in the United States, its collection includes original slave handbills and pamphlets for and against slavery. Other original material includes personal papers of Mary McLeod Bethune, George Washington Carver, Booker T. Washington and Martin Luther King, among many others.

In the library's museum collection, visitors may see an outstanding group of early African masks and sculpture, as well as paintings by Henry Ossawa Tanner and Charles White.

Location: Collis P. Huntington Memorial Library, Hampton Institute, Hampton, Virginia.

LANGSTON HUGHES MEMORIAL LIBRARY, LINCOLN UNIVERSITY

The new Langston Hughes Memorial Library, named for the famous black poet who was a graduate of Lincoln University, contains the personal library of Mr. Hughes, as well as a large collection of literature representing all aspects of the black experience.

263

The library also houses a selection of African art and artifacts on permanent display.

Location: Langston Hughes Memorial Library, Lincoln University, near Oxford, Pennsylvania.

HOLLIS BURKE FRISSELL LIBRARY, TUSKEGEE INSTITUTE

The Hollis Burke Frissell Library is the most important source in the country for the personal correspondence and papers of both Booker T. Washington and George Washington Carver. The library also has many other special collections on black life and history, including an unusual collection of over 3,500 photographs of early and contemporary student life at historic Tuskegee Institute.

The George Washington Carver Museum is also on this campus.

Location: Hollis Burke Frissell Library, Tuskegee Institute, Tuskegee, Alabama.

ASSOCIATION FOR THE STUDY OF NEGRO LIFE AND HISTORY

This is the first association to work for the promotion of black historical research. Its large library contains books, periodicals and manuscripts on black history. The library, however, is restricted to scholarly research and has no exhibit areas open to the public.

Location: Association for the Study of Negro Life and History, 1538 Ninth Street, N.W., Washington, D.C.

CARNEGIE LIBRARY, WILBERFORCE UNIVERSITY

An unusually good collection of source material on early black church leaders may be found at this library, including the Daniel Alexander Payne collection. Daniel Payne was elected a bishop in the A.M.E. Church in 1852 and was the first black president of Wilberforce University. The library also houses artifacts and memorabilia of William Wilberforce, the eighteenth-century British abolitionist leader for whom the college was named.

Location: Wilberforce University, Wilberforce, Ohio.

COUNTEE CULLEN REGIONAL BRANCH, NEW YORK
PUBLIC LIBRARY

Named for the prominent black poet, this branch of the New York Public Library has on display the four murals painted by Aaron Douglas on the history of the black man. In addition, the library has the James Weldon Johnson collection of books for children that gives an accurate, well-rounded picture of black life in all parts of the world.

Location: Countee Cullen Regional Branch Library, 104 West 136th Street, New York, New York.

HOUGHTON LIBRARY, HARVARD UNIVERSITY

Phillis Wheatley died in childbirth at the age of thirty-one. The only mementos of the life of this early black poetess are a few original manuscripts and some pieces of correspondence. On a visit to England, Miss Wheatley was presented with a folio copy of John Milton's *Paradise Lost*. This rare and valuable folio is now in the collection of the Houghton Library.

The library also has an original early manuscript of a poem by Phillis Wheatley in its extensive Afro-American Manuscript Collection, along with personal papers and correspondence of many famous abolitionist leaders.

Location: Houghton Library, Harvard University, 221 Longfellow Hall, Appian Way, Cambridge, Massachusetts.

STERLING MEMORIAL LIBRARY, YALE UNIVERSITY

The James Weldon Johnson Memorial Collection of Negro Arts and Letters, located at Yale University, is one of the most important black research collections in the country.

The collection is so huge it is possible to name only a few of the more important items, such as original manuscripts from authors of the Harlem Renaissance. In the field of music, there is almost a complete collection of spirituals and blues, as well as original musical scores of outstanding black composers like Henry Burleigh.

As with other scholarly collections, the research material is not available to the general public. However, there are constantly changed exhibit areas within the library.

265

Location: Sterling Memorial Library, Yale University, New Haven, Connecticut.

DETROIT PUBLIC LIBRARY

For information on black history collections and exhibits on blacks in music and the performing arts in this library, see Chapter Eight.

The first published American woman poet (London, 1650) was Anne Bradstreet, wife of a Massachusetts Bay Colony governor. The second published American woman poet, however, was the young slave girl pictured above. Her name was Phillis Wheatley and her first book of poetry was published in London in 1733.

PENNSYLVANIA, DELAWARE, MARY-
LAND, AND VIRGINIA

ALMANAC,

FOR THE

YEAR of our LORD 1795;

Being the Third after Leap-Year.

BANNAKER.

An almanac was a very important book for early American farmers. It told them when to plant their crops and forecast the weather, among other things. One of the first almanacs in the United States was published by a black man, Benjamin Banneker (also spelled Bannaker), who was also a scientist. COURTESY THE MARYLAND HISTORICAL SOCIETY, BALTIMORE

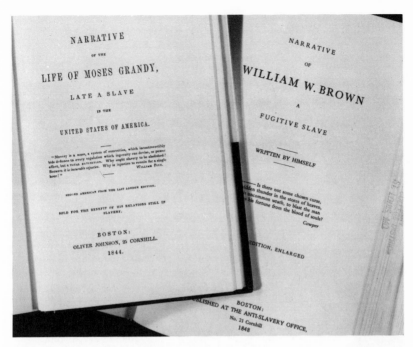

The frontispiece of several books written by fugitive slaves in America before the Civil War. Such books—and there were hundreds published, usually with the aid of abolition societies—stirred the conscience of the nation against slavery. Copies of these slave narratives are a fascinating part of black America's literary history and may be found in many Afro-American and other historical colections in libraries around the country. COURTESY MERAMEC COMMUNITY COLLEGE LIBRARY

It was while living in this home in Cincinnati, Ohio, that authoress Harriet Beecher Stowe learned at firsthand about slavery—experiences she was to use later in her book, *Uncle Tom's Cabin*. Today the Stowe home has been converted into a museum with exhibits on Mrs. Stowe's life and the history of black America before and after the Civil War. COURTESY OF THE ARTIST RALPH FANNING AND THE OHIO HISTORICAL SOCIETY

Paul Laurence Dunbar was the first black poet to win national prominence in the United States. He turned out the majority of his poetry that is remembered today in just ten years and died, tragically young, in 1906 at age thirty-four. COURTESY OHIO HISTORICAL SOCIETY

In his home in Dayton, Ohio, Paul Laurence Dunbar composed many of his popular poems. His home has been restored, including the study shown *below*, where the young poet did much of his work. The Paul Laurence Dunbar home is now operated as a museum by the Ohio Historical Society. COURTESY OHIO HISTORICAL SOCIETY

One of the portraits by Laura Wheeler Waring of black American authors that may be seen at the National Portrait Gallery, Washington, D.C. James Weldon Johnson, shown *above*, was not only an important black poet of the 1920s but also a lawyer, diplomat and one of the founders of the NAACP. COURTESY NATIONAL PORTRAIT GALLERY, THE SMITHSONIAN INSTITUTION, WASHINGTON, D.C.

The Founders Library on the campus of Howard University, Washington, D.C., is one of the oldest black American libraries in the country. Among its extensive archives may be found the manuscripts and papers of famous nineteenth-century black and white antislavery writers, as well as the papers of Oliver Howard, Commissioner of the Freedmen's Bureau and the first president of Howard University. COURTESY HOWARD UNIVERSITY

The Trevor Arnett Library at Atlanta University, Atlanta, Georgia, has rare items in its collection from slave days, including an autographed copy of a poem by Phillis Wheatley. Also in the collection are many of the original manuscripts, correspondence and personal papers of the leading black writers during the Harlem Renaissance, such as Countee Cullen, Claude McKay and Arna Bontemps, among others. A historic and contemporary black art gallery is on the lower level of the library. COURTESY TEXACO, INC.

The E. Azalia Hackley Collection of Music and the Performing Arts, at the Detroit Public Library covers materials, old and new, relating to blacks in music and the performing arts. Over 750 books, 1,400 musical scores, countless photographs, phonograph records and play-bills are contained in this unique collection. COURTESY E. AZALIA HACKLEY COLLECTION, DETROIT PUBLIC LIBRARY

The Will W. Alexander Library at Dillard University,
New Orleans, has an important collection of materials on
black American history, particularly on black people in
New Orleans before the Civil War and black musicians
and composers. The Amistad Research Collection on the
same campus has more than 7 million items on the history of minority groups in America. COURTESY DILLARD
UNIVERSITY, NEW ORLEANS, LOUISIANA

Built in 1972, the Langston Hughes Memorial Library is
the newest building on the campus of Lincoln University,
near Oxford, Pennsylvania. The poet Langston Hughes
was a graduate of Lincoln University, and the library
contains his personal papers, correspondence and library.
There is also on permanent display a collection of African
art and artifacts. COURTESY LINCOLN UNIVERSITY

THE
GIFT OF
SONG

Candlelight gleamed softly in the state ballroom of colonial Williamsburg. Women in silks and brocade, men in powdered wigs, waited for the dance to begin. Then a musician, violin in hand, rose to his feet. His manners were courtly, and he wore a powdered brown wig and was dressed as splendidly as any man in the ballroom in an embroidered silk coat and vest of faded lilac. The only thing different about Sy Gilliat, who was the official fiddler at state balls in this early capital of Virginia, was that he was a black man and a slave.

Black poets and artists may have been considered an oddity in colonial America—but not black musicians. Thomas Jefferson, an accomplished musician himself, writing about the African slave in his *Notes on Virginia*, stated, "In music they are more generally gifted than whites, with accurate ears for tune and time . . . ."

275

During colonial days it was a common sight to see black musicians entertaining at plantation parties. Such musicians were in great demand. A notice in the *Virginia Gazette* of 1753 advertising for "an orderly Negro or mulatto who can play well the violin," or an advertisement offering for sale "A young healthy Negro fellow . . . who plays extremely well on the French horn," were not unusual.

Even along the lowly slave street, plantation owners on Sundays often allowed men, women and children to gather and sing and dance. As one ex-slave remembered, "Both young and old would dress up in hand-me-down finery to do a high-kicking, prancing walk-around."

For the slave, thrust into a new, bewildering culture, music and dance were the only links between his old life and the new. In Africa singing and dancing had been as much a part of his life as eating and sleeping. Professionally trained musicians performed at royal festivals, at funerals and religious rituals and at ceremonies before warriors went into battle. The Africans themselves made their everyday chores lighter by singing as they worked, usually to the call of a leader while the workers kept time and responded in a chorus.

In America it wasn't long before slave owners discovered that their slaves worked harder and faster if they sang while they worked. The most important use of early black music, therefore, was found not in the ballroom but out in the fields and on the levee during the working day. The "call and response" of African music became the "shout and holler" of the plantation. Slaves who were good song leaders often fetched higher prices on the auction block.

In this new world the African worked at new, unfamiliar tasks—husking corn and rice, unloading bales on a levee, picking cotton, cutting cane and tobacco, selling produce on the streets of Charleston and New Orleans. They composed new work songs and street cries to fit their new chores. Sometimes they used melodies they remembered from their African past. Sometimes they borrowed tunes from an Irish jig, Scottish reel or English ballad they had overheard, and then made up their own words as they sang along.

One such work song was sung at rice-husking time on the Sea Islands of Georgia. Two workers faced each other across a wooden mortar. As they pounded at the rice in the mortar with a long pole, the rhythmic pounding provided a percussion background for the chorus:

My old missus promise me,
Hard time in Old Virginie!
When she die she set me free,
Hard time in Old Virginie!
She live so long
Hard time in Old Virginie!
Till her head got bald
Hard time in Old Virginie!

Or a roustabout song would be sung by a black boat crew, perhaps to a borrowed New England sea chantey:

Molly was a good gal and a bad gal too.
Oh Molly, row, gal.
Molly was a good gal and a bad gal too.
Oh Molly, row, gal.
I'll row dis boat and I'll row no more.
Row, Molly, row, gal.
I'll row dis boat and I'll row no more.
Row, Molly, row, gal

Not having any musical instruments, the slaves devised their own. They were forbidden to make drums,

277

the basic African musical instrument, because slave owners were afraid that drums would be used as signals in a slave uprising. Instead, they played their music on kitchen pans and kettles, washboard and washtubs, dried animal bones and hollowed out gourds called calabashes. They even invented a new musical instrument—the banjo. In its original version, the banjo was probably no more than a skin stretched over a cut-down gourd with four strings to pluck on, a throwback to a type of musical instrument commonly used in Africa for centuries. The banjo became—and still is—one of the most popular musical instruments in America.

After 1800 a wave of religious revivalism swept across America. Enormous outdoor camp meetings were held at which loud singing of hymns was combined with highly emotional sermons. Occasionally slaves were allowed to attend these religious camp meetings and hold revival meetings of their own. It was natural, being an enslaved people themselves, that they would be particularly attracted by stories of oppressed people in the Bible —Moses and the Hebrews enslaved in Egypt or Daniel in the lion's den.

From these stories they composed their own hymns:

> *When Israel was in Egypt's land,*
> * Let my people go!*
> *Oppressed so hard they could not stand,*
> * Let my people go!*
> *Go down, Moses, way down in Egypt's land—*
> *Tell old Pharaoh, let my people go.*

For the melodies they used tunes from their own African heritage or from the hymns they heard the white churchgoers sing. They would change the rhythm of the melody here, adding an extra slurred beat there, rewriting the words to fit their own dialect, their own feelings.

Finally they added the clapping hands and stamping feet, the "patting" that was so much a part of their African musical heritage.

What at last evolved was the spiritual. W. E. B. Du Bois called the spirituals "sorrow songs" born out of years of oppression, of a longing of the human heart for freedom. It was only in his music that the enslaved black could express his anguish, his despair of the present and his hope for a better, happier life after death. And not just after death.

When Harriet Tubman sang to her fellow slaves:

> *I'll meet you in the morning,*
> *I'm bound for the promised land,*
> *On the other side of Jordan,*
> *Bound for the promised land.*

they knew she wasn't singing of heaven but of the free states in the North and that she was planning to escape.

The spirituals were the first "protest" songs before the black man was even allowed to protest. A song like the following held a note of militancy despite its hymnlike words:

> *Oh freedom! Oh freedom!*
> *Oh freedom over me!*
> *And before I'd be a slave,*
> *I'll be buried in my grave,*
> *And go home to my Lord and be free.*

Yet, as beautiful and expressive as the spirituals were, and as common as such singing was by slaves on almost every plantation in the South, the spirituals were little written about or noticed before the Civil War.

What the plantation owner did enjoy and encourage was the sort of rollicking music the slaves sang at Jubilee, the time of the year when they were given a day's holiday from work. On that day, dance contests were held. A present, sometimes a cake, was given to the best high-stepping dancer or liveliest, most comical singer. Slave songs like "Uncle Ned," "Zip Coon" and "Juba" were favorites, and the high-kicking, prancing walk-around came to be known as the "cakewalk."

These plantation melodies and dances became so popular that they found their way into the theater, and were known as minstrel shows. The music used in these shows was called "Ethiopian music."

As early as 1830, white entertainers like "Jim Crow" Rice were doing black impersonations and singing slave songs on the stage. It was in February 1843, however, that a white man, Daniel Decatur Emmett, along with three friends, put on the first complete minstrel show. Calling themselves the Virginia Minstrels, they smeared their faces with burnt cork and mimicked expertly the songs and dances of the slaves. The banjo, bone castenets, tambourine and fiddle were used for accompaniment. The show met an enthusiastic reception and many other minstrel groups soon formed. For seventy years the minstrel show was the favorite form of entertainment in America from New England to California.

Songwriters Daniel Emmett and Stephen Foster won their popularity writing for minstrel shows. They used plantation melodies they had overheard slaves singing, reworking the tunes and writing their own lyrics. In a way, they used the black folk song much as Joel Chandler Harris had used the black folktale. In the end, Stephen Foster won everlasting fame for such songs as "Old Folks at Home" and "Camptown Races." Daniel Emmett's most popular song, "Dixie," although it became practically the national anthem of the South, was first introduced at a minstrel show in New York City. It was composed as a minstrel walk-around song, using the familiar "call-and-response" style of African music.

Ironically, although the minstrel shows were based on black music and folkways, almost all the performers were white. It wasn't until the 1870s that a black composer, James Bland, lent his musical genius to the minstrel shows. He toured successfully both Europe and the United States, writing more than 700 compositions, including "Carry Me Back to Old Virginny," "In the Evening by the Moonlight" and many other songs still popular today.

The minstrel show has been called "the only purely native American dramatic entertainment." Although it helped popularize the musical talent of the black man, at the same time it did him a great disservice. While escaped slaves like Frederick Douglass and William Wells Brown were publishing their narratives about how bitter and degrading life really was for the slave on the plantation, the minstrel shows were presenting a stereotype of the black man as a comical, happy-go-lucky buffoon. This stereotype unfortunately lingered on in the American mind long after the minstrel shows had died away.

It was, after all, not contented, shiftless black men who fled slavery, who fought and died in the Union Army, who manned the barricades during the Civil War singing triumphantly to the tune of an African Ashanti war chant:

No more auction block for me, no more, no more
No more auction block for me, many thousand gone . . .
No more driver's lash for me, no more, no more
No more driver's lash for me, many thousand gone . . .

After the war, the minstrel show began to lose in popularity, but another form of black music took its place.

One evening a Northern officer, Major Thomas Wentworth Higginson, overheard a troop of his black soldiers singing around a campfire. The song was plaintively beautiful:

> *I know moon-rise; I know star-rise*
> *Lay this body down*
> *I walk in the moon-light; I walk in the star-light*
> *Lay this body down*
> *I'll walk in the graveyard; I'll walk through the graveyard*
> *Lay this body down*
> *I'll lie in the grave and stretch out my arms*
> *Lay this body down*
> *I go to judgment in the evening of the day*
> *When I lay this body down*
> *And my soul and your soul shall meet in the day*
> *When I lay this body down.*

It was the first time Major Higginson had ever heard a spiritual sung, and the experience, he said later, "sent shivers running down my back."

Other Northern men and women, working in the Freedmen's Schools in the South after the war, also heard for the first time what William Allen has called "these peculiar but haunting slave songs." Impressed by the unusual quality of the music, Major Higginson, William Allen, Lucy Garrison McKim and others began collecting the songs.

Finally, in 1867, a book entitled *Slave Songs in the United States* was published. Although it was not possible to re-create on paper the unique "soul" quality of the songs—spirituals were seldom sung the same way twice by black singers—yet the book did bring the spiritual into world prominence.

Almost immediately after publication of the book, a controversy arose as to whether the slaves themselves had composed the spirituals or had simply borrowed

282

them from the hymnals of their white masters. Perhaps the argument can never be settled to everyone's satisfaction. Yet, borrowed or original—or more than likely a blend of both—the spirituals have been called "the greatest single body of folksong America has produced."

Not all black music, however, consisted of work songs, minstrel songs or religious music. In New Orleans free men of color and slaves had developed their own style of music and dance. Since many of the slaves in New Orleans came from the West Indies, it was natural that their music should have, in addition to African, a heavy French and Caribbean influence not found elsewhere in the United States.

Congo Square, as it was then called (now renamed Beauregard Square), in New Orleans was the center for black music and dancing long before and after the Civil War. There on weekends, black men and women gathered and danced the Juba, Bamboula, Calinda, the Voudou and Congo, dances that may be seen in the West Indies today. Many white visitors to Congo Square watched the dancing, fascinated by the disturbing, exciting rhythms of the music, as well as shocked by the uninhibited style of dancing.

In 1886 the writer George W. Cable, in telling of his visits to Congo Square, wrote, "A sudden frenzy seizes the musicians. The measure quickens, the swaying crowd starts into extra activity, the female voices grow sharp and staccato, and suddenly the dance is the furious Bamboula . . ."

But while George Cable was writing about exotic Congo Square, further north up the Mississippi River a seventeen-year-old black musician came to St. Louis. His name was Scott Joplin. He played the piano in a very special way in honky-tonks and saloons along the riverfront. In 1899 while working in Sedalia, Missouri, his "Maple Leaf Rag" was published. It was an immediate sensation, and a new era in black music began.

Ragtime—a highly syncopated rhythm played over a steady bass—quickly replaced the waltz in popularity. All over the United States people began doing the foxtrot and cakewalk to the rhythm of "rag." It wasn't long before ragtime music was heard in Europe, too. Before it finally faded out in the early 1900s, ragtime had become the first internationally popular American music.

Ragtime, however, brought black music to a new height of popularity at the same time that the black people themselves were suffering new hardships. The boll weevil and the one-crop system brought ruin to Southern planters. Black farmers, already starving under the sharecropping system, and facing new, hostile black laws against them, fled west and north—500,000 black people left the South between 1916 and 1918. Harlem became a natural gathering place for many of these emigrants, the dispossessed farmers as well as black artists, poets and musicians.

Writers and artists have called this period of black history the Harlem Renaissance and the Golden Age. Black musicians, however, with a brand new style of music gave a different name to those years. The music was jazz, and it gave a name to a whole era—the Jazz Age.

How and where did jazz originate? Well, there are as many answers to that question as there are ways of playing jazz. The blues have been called the mother of jazz, but the blues themselves are descended from the work songs and spirituals, the ring shouts and field "hollers" of the slave.

Long before the advent of jazz, black musicians had

been singing and playing the blues in Mississippi River towns, mostly for themselves and their friends, whenever two or three musicians gathered. Then in 1909 a traveling musician in Memphis named W. C. Handy wrote a political campaign song called "Mr. Crump." The song became so popular in Memphis that the composer changed the name of the song to the "Memphis Blues" and tried to sell it to a music publisher.

The "Memphis Blues," using twelve instead of the standard sixteen bars, was too unusual for the publishers of the day. Handy, at last, published the song at his own expense. The "Memphis Blues" made a fortune, but not for Handy, who was defrauded by the man to whom he had sold the rights. Handy had to wait several years before he reaped any profit from his compositions. In 1914 W. C. Handy wrote what was to become an even more famous blues song, the classic "St. Louis Blues." From then on his fame and fortune were assured.

If the blues were born in Memphis, jazz itself started life further south—in New Orleans. The city that had permitted Congo Square to exist had always been a gathering place for musicians, black and white. After the Civil War, band instruments used by Confederate and Union Army military bands could be bought cheaply in New Orleans by ex-slaves who flocked to the city when they were freed.

Marching bands of all sizes became a commonplace sight on the streets of New Orleans. Mostly these were small "Skat" bands using the banjo, guitar, bones and washboard. They played for any and all occasions, from funerals to advertising sales and political speeches.

The black musicians who played in these bands had little formal musical education. Early jazz musicians like Charles "Buddy" Bolden and Freddie Keppard played by ear, improvising as they went along, inventing new techniques, new combinations of tones. They borrowed heavily from the rhythm and harmony of the blues as well as the syncopation of ragtime and the "soul" of the spirituals. In the earliest, purest jazz, these black musicians tried with their instruments to imitate the harsh, guttural throaty sound of the blues singer.

Gradually, in the early 1900s, the black migration started north to Memphis, St. Louis, Chicago, Cleveland and New York. Jazz went along in the person of musicians like Jelly Roll Morton, Charlie Parker, "Hot Lips" Page and, of course, the most famous of them all, Louis Armstrong.

In spite of the Depression of the 1930s, jazz managed to survive. In fact, jazz grew even more popular, as men like Fletcher Henderson, Paul Whiteman and Duke Ellington formed big jazz bands and created sophisticated jazz compositions for orchestras. With the forming of the big bands, though, jazz changed. Jazz notes were no longer improvised but written down and played exactly as written. It even took on a new name—swing. During the height of the Depression, men and women, black and white, filled the dance halls, listening to the sounds of the big bands, dancing to swing music and trying to forget for a time their troubles.

Music, however, like literature and art, is constantly changing. In the 1950s the big bands began to disappear, to be replaced by small jazz ensembles returning to the "pure" jazz, or a combination of rhythm and blues and country and western folk music that was to evolve into rock and roll.

Yet, no matter how modern American music changes, one can still trace the influence of black music and black musicians, from the work songs, spirituals and minstrel songs to ragtime, blues and jazz. For in no other phase of American culture has the black man and woman contributed so much, not just to America, but to the world.

Like authors, musicians in America seldom have monuments or museums dedicated to them, although there are a few scattered throughout the United States. Yet the music they have written, the songs they have composed, are a more enduring monument than bricks and stones can ever be.

When we visit a museum such as the New Orleans Jazz Museum, and listen to the haunting beauty of a spiritual, the earthy sadness of the blues, the mocking sounds of ragtime or the joyousness of jazz, then we begin to understand what W. E. B. Du Bois meant when he spoke of the three gifts the black race brought with it to America: "The gift of sweat and brawn, the gift of the spirit—and a gift of story and song."

NEW ORLEANS JAZZ MUSEUM

One of the most fascinating museums in America, it covers the history of the growth of jazz from its beginnings in Afro-American rhythms, its brass band tradition, ragtime and blues through the popular music of the twentieth century. Photographs and mementos of the great jazz musicians such as William C. Handy, Jelly Roll Morton and Louis Armstrong may be seen—many of the items in the cases were donated by the musicians who used them.

Other displays include the evolution of the banjo and other slave instruments, pictures of early Dixieland jazz bands, jazz sculpture and paintings, and sheet music from the early days of jazz and ragtime. And for the visitors' listening pleasure, there are dial access booths where they may listen to ten half-hour programs of various types of jazz recordings, old and new.

The museum has a collection of over 3,000 jazz phonograph

287

records and tape recordings, including many rare items from the world of jazz.

Location: New Orleans Jazz Museum, 1017 Dumaine Street, New Orleans, Louisiana.

Small admission charge.

PRESERVATION HALL

For those who want to hear Dixieland jazz in its purest form, Preservation Hall offers a different jazz band each night, as five or six bands rotate their appearances. No food or beverages are sold. Limited seating, some standing room.

Location: Preservation Hall, 726 St. Peter Street, New Orleans, Louisiana.

Admission charge.

NEW YORK JAZZ MUSEUM

Founded in 1972, the New York Jazz Museum is located in a converted carriage house in midtown Manhattan. The museum covers the history of jazz by highlighting the lives of famous jazz musicians. Special exhibits, such as recent ones on Benny Goodman and Louis Armstrong, consist of rare photographs, personal memorabilia, original artwork, posters, sheet music and audio material contributed by jazz enthusiasts throughout the world.

In addition to the displays, films on jazz and jazz musicians are shown and visitors may listen to continuous tapes playing music by the great jazz men.

Sunday afternoon jazz concerts are also held at the museum.

Location: New York Jazz Museum, 125 West 55th Street, New York, New York.

Admission by contribution. Charge for film admission.

W. C. HANDY STATUE AND PARK, MEMPHIS, TENNESSEE

Although he was born in Florence, Alabama, William Christopher Handy spent a great deal of his life on Beale Street in Memphis, Tennessee. It was in Memphis that W. C. Handy settled after touring with a music group and teaching school. And it was in Memphis that he formed a band and also set down on paper the first blues song, called "Mr. Crump" but later changed to the "Memphis Blues."

The song helped publicize the city of Memphis throughout the nation and made W. C. Handy one of the town's most popular and best-known citizens. In 1914, while still living in Memphis, Handy wrote the even more popular "St. Louis Blues" and "Beale Street Blues."

Mr. Handy died in 1958, and in 1960 an 8-foot heroic bronze statue of the great jazz composer was placed in the W. C. Handy Park. Horn in hand, W. C. Handy stands overlooking Beale Street, the street he immortalized with his music.

Location: W. C. Handy Statue and Park, Beale Street, Memphis, Tennessee.

HANDY MUSEUM

In 1970 the log cabin in which W. C. Handy was born was moved to a new site in Florence, Alabama, and restored as it might have appeared years ago when Handy lived there as a boy with his mother and minister father.

Behind the restored home is a museum containing many mementos from W. C. Handy's life, including sheet music, photographs, souvenirs and the actual piano on which Handy composed the "St. Louis Blues." His famous golden trumpet may also be seen.

Location: Handy Home and Museum, at the corner of West College Street and Marengo, Florence, Alabama.

Small admission charge.

FISK UNIVERSITY LIBRARY (Jubilee Singers Collection)

Five years after Fisk University opened its doors, the school was almost without funds to operate. A professor of music decided to take a group of students with outstanding voices on a concert tour to raise funds.

The students at first sang the traditional concert songs, barely making enough money to take them from one town to another. Then on November 15, 1871, at a concert they sang the spiritual "Steal away to Jesus," and received a thunderous ovation.

The Jubilee Singers soon realized how anxious their audiences were to hear the beautiful, plaintive spirituals; and once they were added to the program, concert engagements followed all over the United States, including a concert at the White House. There was even travel abroad. At the end of seven years the singers had sent back enough money to enable Fisk to buy a new site for the college and begin construction of their most historic building, Jubilee Hall.

Today the Fisk University Jubilee Singers still tour and sing in America and abroad.

Mementos and photographs from the first group of Jubilee Singers can be seen in exhibit cases on the second floor of the library. A painting of the early group of Jubilee Singers hangs in Jubilee Hall.

Location: Fisk University, Nashville, Tennessee.

MUSEUM OF AFRICAN ART (African Music Collection)

In addition to an outstanding collection of African and Afro-American art, this museum also has an excellent collection of African musical instruments, ranging from the talking drums of Nigeria to reed harps and a thumb piano (a sort of finger xylophone).

In the auditorium of the museum, lecturers tell the history of the various African musical instruments, and young visitors are allowed to try their hand at playing a thumb piano or a talking drum.

Location: Museum of African Art, 316–318 A Street, N.E., Capitol Hill, Washington, D.C.

Admission charge.

METROPOLITAN MUSEUM OF ART (Crosby Brown Collection of Music)

In the Mertens Galleries of this great museum can be found the Crosby Brown Collection of Musical Instruments of all Nations. Included in this collection is one of the most complete collections of African musical instruments in any museum in the world.

Some of the musical instruments are not only centuries old but exceedingly rare—such as the *Kissars,* or lutes, made from

290

the skulls of enemies, and intricately carved ivory elephant tusks used as horns in Zanzibar. There are Congolese drums in the shape of a human body, gourd rattles, thumb pianos, horns made of conch shells and many other fascinating and unusual musical instruments of all sizes and shapes. A modern listening device enables the viewer to hear the instruments as he looks at them.

Location: Metropolitan Museum of Art, the Mertens Galleries, Fifth Avenue and 82nd Street, New York, New York.

Although there is no set admission charge, contributions are solicited at the entrance. There is a small charge for renting earphones that allow the viewer to hear the music as he sees the instruments.

AMERICAN MUSEUM OF NATURAL HISTORY (African Musical Instruments)

The Hall of Man in Africa in this museum covers all phases of the life of African men, women and children. Since music is such an important part of African life, there are six exhibit areas in this hall given over to African musical instruments.

There are four forms of African musical instruments in the exhibit: idiophones, such as clapping sticks and thumb pianos; membranophones, drums of wood, horn and pottery; chordophones, harps, lutes and zithers; and aerophones, flutes, trumpets and horns. Each musical instrument is exactly labeled as to its type and history.

Location: American Museum of Natural History, Central Park West at 79th Street, New York, New York.

Admission by contribution.

MUSEUM OF THE PHILADELPHIA CIVIC CENTER (Musical Instrument Collection)

The African instruments in the music collection of this museum come chiefly from the Senegal region of West Africa. Every major type of African drum is represented, including the most sensational item in the collection—a war drum from the Ivory Coast decorated with the skulls of slain enemies, a sort of mobile (and musical) war museum.

291

All of the instruments are less than 100 years old and are representative of the musical instruments played in Africa today.

Location: Museum of the Philadelphia Civic Center, Philadelphia Civic Center, at 34th Street, Philadelphia, Pennsylvania. No admission charge.

SCHOMBURG COLLECTION (African Music Collection)

The Schomburg Library has one of the best collections in the country of African folk music, completely indexed by tribe, type of song and instruments.

The Schomburg collection also has several thousand phonograph records and tape recordings of musical works by black people, including an exceptional collection of African-American jazz, rhythm and blues recordings.

Location: Schomburg Collection, a branch of the New York Public Library at 103 West 135th Street, New York, New York. No admission charge.

MUSICAL INSTRUMENT MUSEUM

The African musical instruments in this collection are primarily from Nigeria and are of recent origin. The museum is associated with several Minnesota colleges and offers guided tours and lectures. There are also special education programs for children, which allow the children to play the various instruments in the museum.

Location: Musical Instrument Museum, 1124 Dionne Street, St. Paul, Minnesota. Small admission charge.

UNIVERSITY OF SOUTH DAKOTA (Arne B. Larson Collection of Musical Instruments)

The University of South Dakota is a center for the study of historical musical instruments. The "Shrine to Music" Museum includes more than 2,500 antique musical instruments from all over the world, including ancient instruments from Africa. Other exhibits have to do with slave music in America and later forms of Afro-American music such as jazz.

292

Location: University of South Dakota, College of Fine Arts, Vermillion, South Dakota.

No admission charge.

DETROIT PUBLIC LIBRARY (Azalia Hackley Collection of Music and the Performing Arts)

In 1821 the African Grove Theatre opened on Bleecker Street in Greenwich Village, New York. This was the first theater in America organized by a group of free blackmen, where black actors and actresses could perform serious drama. One of the young black actors who played a small role on that stage was Ira Aldridge, who went on to become a world-famous Shakespearean actor. He was particularly known for his interpretation of the lead role in Shakespeare's *Othello*.

The Grove Theater closed in 1830, but blacks continued as entertainers in vaudeville. It wasn't until the black cultural explosion at the turn of the century, though, that black theaters once more opened, this time in Harlem, New York. One of the best known of these was the Lafayette Theater on Seventh Avenue between 131st and 132nd streets. This theater served as a dramatic stock company and proving ground for many fine young black actors and actresses, performing before primarily black audiences.

Then in 1920 black actor Charles Gilpin won an award from the Drama League, as well as the Spingarn Medal, for his role in Eugene O'Neill's *The Emperor Jones*. Many other fine actors and actresses followed him: Paul Robeson, Richard B. Harrison, and later Frank Silvera, Canada Lee and Ethel Waters, to name only a few. Although the struggle to gain a foothold on the American stage was a long, frustrating one for the black actor and actress, today their contributions to the legitimate stage, as well as the motion picture and television industry, are well known.

In the field of serious musical composition, Harry T. Burleigh, singer and composer, arranged spirituals for use on the concert stage, which won him wide acclaim at the turn of the century. In the 1930s William Grant Still became the first black composer-conductor to conduct a major orchestra in the United States, the Los Angeles Philharmonic Orchestra.

293

At the Detroit Public Library there is a special collection and exhibit area honoring the achievements of Afro-Americans in music and the performing arts. The collection was named for Azalia Hackley, a Detroit music teacher who created scholarships for many talented young black musicians, including Nathaniel Dett, who went on to become a highly successful composer.

All types of materials are included in the collection—books, manuscripts, musical scores, photographs, playbills and recordings. Many of the items are irreplaceable: autographed copies of songs by Langston Hughes and W. C. Handy; an original score by Coleridge Taylor, a famous black English composer; a large set of photographs of the most prominent black actors and actresses and musicians of the 1920s and 1930s; and a set of scrapbooks compiled during the Fisk Jubilee Singers' first world tour.

There is a constantly changing display area in the hallway just outside the room that houses the Hackley Collection.

Location: Detroit Public Library, 5201 Woodward Avenue, Detroit, Michigan.

No admission charge.

MUSEUM OF THE CITY OF NEW YORK

There is a gallery in this museum reserved for the use of the Theater and Music Collection. Not always on display is an enormous collection of programs, pictures, playbills, costumes and scene designs of Broadway shows, going back to the nineteenth century. The collection includes material on black performers and musicians.

Recently a bust of Eubie Blake was presented to this collection. Eubie Blake wrote and produced one of the first black musical revues, *Shuffle Along*. It appeared on Broadway in 1921. Some of the songs from this show are still being sung today. Many other top-flight black musical revues followed this show and introduced to Broadway such musical talents as Josephine Baker, Florence Mills, Ethel Waters and Bill Robinson, among others.

Location: Museum of the City of New York, Fifth Avenue

294

between 103rd and 104th streets, New York, New York. Small admission charge.

GRAUMAN'S CHINESE THEATER

Most Hollywood actors and actresses are considered to be "stars" when they have their footprints enshrined in cement in front of this famous theater. In 1967 Sidney Poitier became the first black actor to achieve this mark of respect.

In the early days of Hollywood movies, the roles given to black actors and actresses were usually of the type that maintained the stereotype of the ignorant, shiftless black man or the faithful "Mammy," or—as in the film *The Birth of a Nation*—portrayed the black man as a ravaging beast.

Today the role black actors and actresses play in motion pictures and television have become more realistic and rewarding. It was the role of a proud, competent and compassionate man, which he played in the film *The Lilies of the Field,* that won Sidney Poitier the coveted Oscar as best actor in 1965.

Location: Grauman's Chinese Theater, 6925 Hollywood Boulevard, Hollywood, California.

SCOTT JOPLIN MONUMENT

A marble monument has been placed on the site of the Maple Leaf Club, where Scott Joplin was working as a piano player when his "Maple Leaf Rag" was published. Ragtime, almost overnight, became the rage and the "Maple Leaf Rag" became one of the first pieces of American sheet music to sell over 1 million copies. Ragtime is once again beginning to regain its lost popularity and a Scott Joplin Festival recently held in Sedalia, the town called the cradle of classical ragtime, attracted a capacity crowd.

Location: Intersection of Lamine and Main streets, Sedalia, Missouri.

Music has always been a vital part of the African's everyday life. One of his favorite musical instruments was the xylophone, or "thumb piano," which was brought to the Americas by black musicians. Young visitors to the Museum of African Art, Washington, D.C., enjoy trying their hand at making music on African musical instruments in the collection of the museum. COURTESY RAPHO-GUILLUMETTE PICTURES

One of the famous "talking drums" from the Sudan, Africa, that may be seen at the Metropolitan Museum of Art, New York. The player, in addition to beating the drumhead with a small, curved stick, would hold the drum under his left arm. He would use arm pressure to tighten and relax the leather thongs placed around the sides of the drum, thereby varying the pitch of the drum. A trained player can develop a range of more than two octaves on this instrument. The Metropolitan Museum has an extensive collection of African musical instruments. COURTESY METROPOLITAN MUSEUM OF ART, THE CROSBY BROWN COLLECTION OF INSTRUMENTS, 1889

A portrait of the first group of Jubilee Singers who toured America in the 1870s. It was through their efforts—and the spirituals they helped popularize—that Jubilee Hall was built with money they raised. Their portrait hangs today in Jubilee Hall on the campus of Fisk Universiy, Nashville, Tennessee, and mementos from their tours may be seen in the University Library. COURTESY FISK UNIVERSITY

The marching brass bands are a tradition in New Orleans going back to the days after the Civil War. Originally, the bands would accompany funeral processions, playing very slowly on the way to the cemetery. After the ceremony, the cortege would march to the beat of a snare, then suddenly explode into ragtime. Huge crowds followed, dancing, laughing, pumping parasols up and down to the music in a celebration of life. COURTESY NEW ORLEANS TOURIST AND CONVENTION COMMISSION

The first instruments used by marching bands in New Orleans were the banjo, guitar, bones and washboard, and some of the earliest jazz music was played by these bands. A musical instrument added later to the marching bands was the bazooka, shown *below*. One of these bazookas, now retired, may be seen at the New Orleans Jazz Museum. COURTESY LOUISIANA STATE TOURIST BUREAU

Some of the best traditional jazz is played at Preservation Hall in New Orleans every night. The musicians are jazz veterans who come out of retirement or semi-retirement to play again. Although many styles of music—spirituals, ragtime, blues —have an Afro-American source, jazz is undoubtedly the most popular and has had the greatest influence in the world of of music. COURTESY NEW ORLEANS TOURIST AND CONVENTION COMMISSION

The New Orleans Jazz Museum, begun in 1961, is located on the lower level of the Royal Sonesta Hotel, New Orleans. One of the more popular features of the museum are the dial access phones, on which programs of rare jazz recordings may be dialed by visitors. COURTESY NEW ORLEANS JAZZ MUSEUM

The New Orleans Jazz Museum has the horn on which Louis Armstrong learned to play in 1913, along with photographs of the great "Satchmo" as a young man. Musical instruments and personal mementos that once belonged to other jazz greats also may be seen at the museum. COURTESY NEW ORLEANS JAZZ MUSEUM

THE FIRST HORN ON WHICH LOUIS ARMSTRONG LEARNED TO PLAY IN 1913. USED FOR MANY YEARS AT THE COLORED WAIF'S HOME HERE IN NEW ORLEANS TO SOUND TAPS, MEALS & REVEILLE. PRESENTED TO THE MUSEUM ON NOV. 12, 1962 BY PETER DAVIS - SATCHMO'S FIRST MUSIC TEACHER.

The statue of the "Father of the Blues," W. C. Handy, horn in hand, may be seen at Handy Park, overlooking the famous Beale Street, Memphis, Tennessee. The W. C. Handy Museum is located in Florence, Alabama, where the musician was born. COURTESY MEMPHIS CHAMBER OF COMMERCE

Jazz fans, new and old, wait to enter the New York Jazz Museum for free Sunday concerts. The museum also houses exhibits and recordings of the great jazzmen of the past and present. COURTESY NEW YORK JAZZ MUSEUM. PHOTO BY JACK BRADLEY

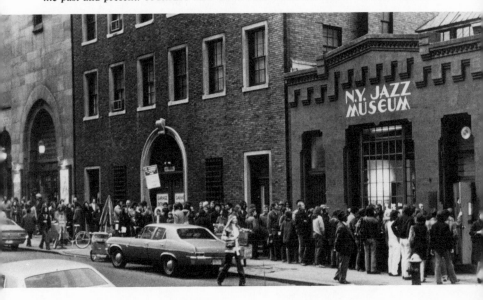

Harry T. Burleigh, whose portrait, painted by Laura Wheeler Waring, hangs in the National Portrait Gallery, Washington, D.C., was a singer, arranger and composer. He was one of the first black singers and composers to win popular acclaim in the early 1900s. One of his greatest accomplishments was his arrangement of spirituals for concert singers. COURTESY NATIONAL PORTRAIT GALLERY

The scrapbooks that were kept by the original Fisk Jubilee Singers are one of the many unusual exhibits on black people in music and the performing arts that may be seen at the E. Azalia Hackley Collection, Detroit Public Library, Michigan. The collection also has photographs of outstanding black actors and actresses of the 1920s and 1930s, as well as modern-day performers. COURTESY E. AZALIA HACKLEY COLLECTION, DETROIT PUBLIC LIBRARY

When world-famous concert and opera singer Marian Anderson was not allowed to sing at Constitution Hall in Washington, D.C., in 1939 because of her color, she gave her concert at the Lincoln Memorial, drawing a crowd of more than 75,000 people. In 1955 she became the first black singer to appear at the Metropolitan Opera House. Her portrait, by Betsy Rayneau, hangs in the National Portrait Gallery, Washington, D.C. COURTESY NATIONAL PORTRAIT GALLERY, THE SMITHSONIAN INSTITUTION, WASHINGTON, D.C.

Paul Robeson worked his way through law school playing professional football. However, it is as an actor and concert singer that he won world-wide acclaim. In this portrait, by Betsy Rayneau, which hangs in the National Portrait Gallery, Washington, D.C., he is shown in one of his leading roles, Shakespeare's *Othello.* COURTESY NATIONAL PORTRAIT GALLERY, THE SMITHSONIAN INSTITUTION, WASHINGTON, D.C.

SCHOLARS,
SCIENTISTS—
AND THE
TALENTED TENTH

By the turn of the century, Henry O. Tanner had painted his masterpiece, *The Resurrection of Lazarus,* Paul Dunbar had written his first volume of poetry and Scott Joplin had composed "The Maple Leaf Rag." But if a survey had been made in 1900 asking the name of the most famous black American, almost every American, white or black, would have given the name of just one man—Booker T. Washington.

From 1885 until his death in 1915, Booker T. Washington was the leading, if unofficial, spokesman for black America. He so completely dominated this period of black history that it has been called the Age of Booker T. Washington. His far-reaching organization, with headquarters at Tuskegee Institute, Alabama, was powerful enough to be dubbed the "Tuskegee machine."

Yet strangely enough, Mr. Washington won his fame

as an educator during an era when most black children in the South attended school in a crude, wooden shack open eight to ten weeks a year, if they attended school at all. Schools in the North were not much better. As inadequate as these educational facilities were, however, they were, at least, a vast improvement over the slave years.

Before the Civil War, few Southern states had any public schools, even for white students. It was difficult for the poor white Southern child to get an education; for the slave child, it was not only difficult, it was illegal. As early as 1819, Missouri passed a law forbidding slaves to be taught to read. And by the time the Civil War began, every Southern state except Maryland and Kentucky had passed laws providing severe penalties for anyone caught teaching a slave (and in some states, free blacks were included) to read or write. The penalties for teaching slaves ranged from imprisonment to death.

The reasoning behind the law was obvious. The slave who could read and write might become discontented with his lot and promote insurrection and rebellion among his fellow slaves. After the Nat Turner Rebellion of 1831—Nat Turner had been taught to read by his master's son—slave owners were even more convinced that it was dangerous to educate slaves.

In spite of the law, there were slaves who did manage to secure an education of sorts. Some attended underground schools taught by free blacks or sympathetic white teachers. One such school in Savannah was taught by a black woman known as "Miss Deaveaux," who managed for twenty-five years to elude what she called the "lynx-eyed vigilance of slaveholders."

Some slaves received secret instruction from their

masters or their master's children. In South Carolina Sarah and Angelina Grimke, young daughters of plantation owner Judge John Grimke, gathered slave children into their room at night. Then, as Sarah reported gleefully in later years, "The light was put out, the keyhole secured and flat on our stomachs before the fire, with spelling books in our hands, we defied the laws of South Carolina."

Free black parents who could afford the tuition often sent their children north to school, usually to the District of Columbia, where there were several private schools for black students. Some mulatto children of white slaveholders were sent as far west as the Wilberforce School in Ohio, which had been opened to take care of the education of such children. In New Orleans the nuns at the Ursuline Convent provided schooling for slave and free black children.

If a slave child or free black lived in the Northern states, the possibility of receiving some schooling was a little greater. The Quakers were the first group to offer education to slaves and free blacks. In 1750 Anthony Benezet started a school in his home, and in 1770 opened a free school for black children in Philadelphia. By 1797 there were seven such schools.

In Boston in 1787 Prince Hall petitioned the city to establish a school for black children equal to the one for whites. When the city fathers refused, the free blacks in Boston employed two Harvard College men and set up their own school. By 1820 Boston had a public school for black children, and by 1855 segregation in Massachusetts schools was prohibited by law.

New Jersey educated some of her slaves and free blacks as early as 1770, and New York City started the first African Free School in 1786 at 245 William Street.

Even in the North, though, there was resistance to the idea of education for free blacks. In Canterbury, Connecticut, in 1832, when a Quaker schoolteacher, Prudence Crandall, admitted a black girl, Sarah Harris, to her school, the parents of the white students immediately withdrew their children. Refusing to give up, Miss Crandall opened a school entirely for black students. Her school was destroyed by vandals, and Miss Crandall herself imprisoned for breaking a law that made it illegal to operate a school for black students without the permission of the city fathers.

Before the Civil War, a few colleges in the North had begun opening their doors, at least partly, to black male students. Edward Jones graduated from Amherst and John Russworm from Bowdoin College in 1826, the first two black college graduates in the United States. Lafayette College in Pennsylvania was fully integrated from its beginning in 1832; but no woman, black or white, was allowed to attend any college in the United States at that time. Oberlin College in Ohio, founded in 1833, was the first American college to admit black and white students, both male and female, to its classes.

The first all-black institutions for college students were also established before the Civil War: Cheyney State College in Philadelphia in 1837; Avery College in Allegheny City, Pennsylvania, in 1849; Lincoln University near Oxford, Pennsylvania, in 1854; and Wilberforce College in Wilberforce, Ohio, in 1856.

For every slave or free black who managed somehow to surmount the almost impossible obstacles and secure an education, there were thousands more who were forced to remain in ignorance. A few slaves were given what might be called a vocational education on the plantation, learning a skill like blacksmithing, brickmaking or carpentry. The majority of plantation slaves, though, were unskilled field hands.

Perhaps most damaging of all, every slave was carefully "educated" by his master in the values and attitudes that the slave owner deemed necessary. Each slave was subtly but firmly taught not to display too much initiative or self-confidence. And what was important, he was also given a feeling of childish dependency and inferiority to the white man. It was this type of education, or rather miseducation, that was to prove the most damaging to the black American in his later strivings for equality.

If asked, most slave owners would have said that it was a waste of time to educate slaves. Slaves not only couldn't learn, they didn't want to learn. Then in 1865, at the end of the Civil War, the Freedmen's Bureau was set up by the United States government to provide clothing, food, medical care—and schools for the "destitute and suffering refugees and freedmen" throughout the war-ravaged South. And freed slaves by the thousands flocked to the schools.

As Booker T. Washington, who was himself educated at a Freedmen's School, later said, "It was a whole race trying to go to school. Few were too young and none too old to make the attempt to learn. As fast as any kind of teachers could be secured, not only were day schools filled but night schools as well."

The Freedmen's Bureau did not work alone. Even before the end of the war, the American Missionary Association (which had begun in 1846 with funds left over from the money gathered for the *Amistad* mutineers defense fund) had begun to provide schools among the freed slaves. Teachers of all faiths—Methodists, Baptists, Presbyterians—young and old, men and women, almost 1,000 strong, headed South. They arrived with spelling books, readers, blackboards and chalk in hand, a sort of early American Peace Corps.

Free blacks also established and taught in their own schools wherever they could. One of the very first schools set up after the war was at Ft. Monroe, Virginia, and was run by a free black woman, Mary Peake.

By 1869 there were almost 10,000 teachers in Freedmen's Schools in the South. Not only were elementary and vocational schools set up by the Bureau and the American Missionary Association, but colleges as well. Schools like Howard, Hampton, Atlanta, Fisk, Talladega, Virginia Union, Tougaloo, to name only a few, were started during this period. Many of these colleges are still in existence today.

The Northern teachers not only had to teach students —some of whom had never even seen a book before— but often faced the open hostility of white Southerners still embittered by the war. Schools were burned, teachers attacked, and black pupils physically threatened if they dared to attend the Freedmen's Schools.

One result of the Freedmen's Schools was that slowly, after the war, Southern states began to set up public-school systems of their own. It was, of course, a segregated system. To make sure that black students did not attend white schools, state laws were passed. Then in 1896, in the *Plessy v. Ferguson* decision, the United States Supreme Court made segregation for the black American the law of the land. In this decision the Court decided that the creation of "separate but equal" accommodations (which included schools as well as public transportation, railroad stations, restaurants, theaters, hotels, even drinking fountains) was a "reasonable" use of state police power. Only one justice, John Marshall Harlen, dissented, stating in part that "The thin disguise of equal accommodations . . . will not mislead anyone nor atone for the wrong this day done."

Of course, even if the South had been willing to provide separate but equal schools for black children, it was difficult enough for most Southern states to raise taxes to support schools for its white students, much less support an expensive, separate system of education for black students. Whatever tax money was available was channeled first to white schools. What little was left over went to black schools. In many cases the poorly paid and trained black teachers were not much better educated than the students they taught.

In the South for every seven dollars spent for a white student, two dollars was spent for a black student. By 1920 one out of every four black persons in the South still could not read or write, compared with one out of every twenty Southern whites. And few black students who did attend school went any further than the fourth grade.

The situation was a little better in the Northern and Western states. Although several Northern states had integrated public-school systems, a de facto type of segregation still existed. That is, schools built in black neighborhoods automatically became all-black schools. These were often in the poorest "ghetto" type of neighborhood and the schools reflected their poverty-stricken surroundings.

The Freedmen's Bureau—the one modest attempt by the federal government to make up for the wrongs suffered for 200 years by enslaved blacks—was discontinued in 1870. With the inability or refusal of whites to support black education, many Southern black schools would have disappeared completely if it had not been for the financial support given them by several wealthy philanthropists. Millionaires like George Peabody, John F. Slater, John D. Rockefeller, Anna T. Jeanes, Caroline Phelps-Stokes and Julius Rosenwald gave money to build schools for black students and to pay the salaries of teachers. Although the funds were never enough to equalize the educational opportunity of the black child, at least it kept the dream of education alive for the black family.

By the turn of the century, the question was no longer, Should the black child receive an education, but What kind of an education?

There were those who felt that all the education a black child needed was to say "Yes, sir" and "No, sir" to a white man and "Gee" and "Haw" to a mule. To some Americans, the idea that a black man might be as intelligent as a white man was disturbing. These same people were just as disturbed at the idea of equal education for women, white and black, or education for other minority groups like Indians and Spanish-Americans.

Other Americans thought a vocational education was all a black student needed. After all, what sort of a job, except a semiskilled job, could a black man find after he graduated from school? There were a few, however, a small group, who argued that a black student should be educated exactly as a white student—to the very best of his capability.

Then on a hot September afternoon in 1895 at the Atlanta Exposition, a black educator arose to give a talk. His speech would decide once and for all the course black education would take for several generations of black students. The speaker was Booker T. Washington.

312

He was already well known among educators for his remarkable accomplishment in changing two rickety buildings and thirty students in a small town in Alabama into a thriving, successful college called Tuskegee Institute.

Described as a "tall, bony man, straight as a Sioux chief . . . with piercing eyes and a commanding manner," Mr. Washington's speech catapulted him into national prominence. He became the confidant of industrialists and statesmen and the first black man to be invited by a President of the United States to have dinner at the White House. What he said that September day in Atlanta was exactly what the majority of white men present in the audience wanted to hear: that the black man should be content with a vocational education and the common occupations of life; that any question of social equality was folly—that, in effect, the black man was and should remain a second-class citizen.

Although most of white America was pleased by his words, there were those black Americans who called Mr. Washington's speech the "Atlanta Compromise." John Hope, the black educator who was later to head Atlanta University, complained, "If we are not striving for equality, in heaven's name for what are we living?"

Washington's most annoying gadfly, though, was another educator named William E. B. Du Bois. Du Bois' philosophy of education for the black person was almost exactly opposite from Washington's. In his book *Souls of Black Folks,* Du Bois dared to challenge Washington.

The two men could not have been more different. Washington was the son of slaves. He had known crippling poverty as a child and had walked 200 miles, arriving with only fifty cents in his pocket, to enroll at Hampton Institute. He had all the instincts of a New

313

England Yankee. He was prudent, sober, thrifty, and believed that hard work was next to godliness.

Du Bois came from an established free black family in Great Barrington, Massachusetts. His ancestors had fought in the Revolutionary War. He attended an integrated school and received a scholarship to Fisk University, studied for two years in Germany, and received his Ph.D. at Harvard University. Brilliant, egotistical, proudly independent, he believed that blacks should be educated beyond vocational subjects. He was convinced that by educating black students to their fullest capability, the "talented tenth" of the black population could serve as leaders for all other black Americans.

There is no doubt that of the two men Washington had the most power and influence until his death in 1915. He was a leader. He knew how to organize, and he had the support of the white establishment. Du Bois, like many brilliant men before him, was not a leader. He was more at ease with members of his intellectual group than with the uneducated masses, and the "talented tenth" upon which he placed his faith were often too busy nourishing their talents to have the time to lead the great mass of black people to social and civil equality.

Looking back, it is easy to say that Du Bois' philosophy was right and Washington's wrong. Many of the vocational skills Washington was teaching at Tuskegee were already being made obsolete by the Industrial Revolution. But the sad truth was that no matter how hard a black man worked, he would invariably come up against a wall of white prejudice that would allow him to advance so far and no further.

There are those historians who say that Washington was, in fact, secretly more liberal than he has been shown to be. In any case, in starting a black college like Tuskegee in the midst of a rural, predominantly white and suspicious community, Washington had had to learn to walk a dangerous tightrope. It was essential that he win the support of the community if he and the college were to survive. And the only way he could win that support was to make sure that he and his students did not pose a threat to white supremacy, that the school with its work-study students provided an essential service to the white community.

The one thing the whole rural South desperately needed was a way to move out of a one-crop agriculture. Cotton had leached the soil until much of the land was useless. With only one crop, the destruction of that crop by the boll weevil or the drought could and did plunge the South into one economic depression after another. If Booker T. Washington had accomplished nothing else in his lifetime, his bringing a black scientist who changed all this to Tuskegee to work would have given him a place in history books.

The scientist Washington brought to Tuskegee was George Washington Carver. Born a slave at Diamond Grove, Missouri, young George and his mother were stolen from their owner, Moses Carver, when George was a baby. Mr. Carver paid the ransom of a horse for the return of the child, who was near death from exposure, but never managed to regain the mother. A frail, quiet boy, George and his brother were treated more as sons by the Carver family than slaves, and after the Civil War, they took the Carver name. Even as a child, George had been interested in growing things and very early gained a reputation as a plant doctor among the Carver neighbors.

He was thirty years old before he finally managed

315

to work his way through various schools and graduate from agriculture school at Iowa State College. He was on the faculty of Iowa State when Mr. Washington in 1896 asked him to come to Tuskegee and start an agriculture department.

But George Washington Carver did more than teach students at Tuskegee. He worked miracles in rejuvenating Southern agriculture. He provided black and white farmers in Alabama with practical ways they could improve their soil and their income by switching from cotton to other crops like soybeans, sweet potatoes and peanuts. He invented an amazing number of new products that could be made from these crops. His experiments were performed with the simplest of equipment, and he turned down the great financial rewards that would have been his if he had patented his products. As his fame increased, he could have worked at the finest laboratories in the country, but he preferred to work among his own people, where he stayed till his death in 1943.

Perhaps the only drawback to Carver's work was that he became so well known that many people thought he was the *only* scientist and inventor black America had produced. This was, of course, not true.

During the colonial years, Benjamin Banneker was as famous a black scientist as Carver. An unschooled Maryland farmer, he made the first striking clock of wood in America. He studied mathematics and astronomy on his own and assisted in the surveying and planning of the new city of Washington, D.C. When Pierre L'Enfant, the chief designer, returned to Paris in a huff, taking the plans for the yet unbuilt city with him, it was Banneker who had memorized the plans well enough to be able to duplicate them, and the building could continue. Returning in triumph to his simple farm cabin, he published in 1792 an almanac that was so useful he became known as the "Afro-American Astronomer."

In New Orleans in 1846, Norbert Rillieux, the mulatto son of a wealthy planter, invented a more efficient system of obtaining sugar crystals from sugarcane. The invention was as important to America's agricultural economy as the McCormick reaper, yet Rillieux's name is seldom, if ever, mentioned in books about America's great inventors.

Between 1863 and 1913, 1,200 inventions were patented by black inventors. Many more hid their race to avoid discrimination or sold their inventions to white men to patent.

Elijah McCoy was one black inventor who patented his own inventions. In 1872 he discovered a process for lubricating railroad and other engines. His invention was so useful that it was quickly copied by others. The copies, however, were inferior and the saying "Is this the real McCoy?" began when purchasers insisted upon buying McCoy's original lubricator.

Although Thomas Edison's name is known by every student, few know of the black inventor Granville Woods, who had more than sixty patents to his credit. Called the "Black Edison" in his day, he improved Alexander Graham Bell's telegraphing system, and, among other inventions, devised an electrical motor that made the underground subway possible and greatly improved the air brake.

Jan Ernst Matzeliger revolutionized the shoe industry by inventing a lasting machine that increased production from 50 to as many as 700 shoes a day. Lewis Latimer worked with Edison and patented a filament used in the first electric light bulb. Garrett Morgan invented a safety hood for firefighters. Ironically, when some Southern cities discovered the inventor was a black man, they canceled their orders! Morgan's best-known invention, the traffic signal, saved thousands of lives when the motorcar became popular in America.

Despite the evidence that black Americans did have the intelligence and ability to contribute important gifts to the country, the costly dual segregated system of education continued in its separate but unequal fashion. The enrollment of black students in school, however, increased steadily. By 1950 almost 95 percent of all blacks over twenty-five years of age had had some schooling, although only 8.6 percent had completed high school. By 1955 there were more than 100 institutions of higher education for blacks.

Unfortunately, many black institutions calling themselves colleges were understaffed and underfinanced, actually little more than high schools. Black students who left these colleges to go on to graduate study ran into difficulties. At the graduate and undergraduate level, black students found themselves competing with white students who had received a much superior basic education.

The black Southern college graduate who wanted to pursue his studies further in law, medicine and science ran into even more problems. He was often forbidden by law to attend graduate schools in the South, even though these universities were supported by both black and white tax dollars.

Then in 1954 the U.S. Supreme Court came to a unanimous decision in *Brown v. the Board of Education of Topeka*. The decision caused a giant upheaval in the world of education. The Court agreed with the

NAACP lawyers that "separate educational facilities are inherently unequal." Chief Justice Earl Warren stated further in his opinion that separating pupils "solely because of their race generates feelings of inferiority as to their status in the community that may affect their hearts and minds in a way unlikely ever to be undone." Integration of the American school system was to be "carried out with all deliberate speed."

As it turned out, the integration was carried out with more deliberation than speed. There were people, both in the North and the South, who reacted with outraged anger and indignation to the Court's decision. Some communities decided to close their public schools rather than allow black students to enter. White citizen councils, reminiscent of the days of the Ku Klux Klan, were formed to fight the decision. The more radical believers in white supremacy bombed black schools and harassed and threatened black students attempting to attend white schools.

In 1957 President Eisenhower had to call out federal troops to protect nine black students from mob violence when they registered at the all-white Central High School in Little Rock, Arkansas. President Kennedy again had to use federal troops to protect James Meredith when he enrolled at the University of Mississippi in 1962. Fifteen years after the Supreme Court decision, almost eighty percent of the black children in the United States were still attending all-black schools.

Yet slowly but surely, at times against almost overwhelming opposition, gains were made. One of the most important has been in the field of medical education. When Dr. Daniel Hale Williams, the first doctor to perform open-heart surgery, started practice in Chicago, few white hospitals would admit blacks, except in some cases as charity patients. A black doctor, no matter how skillful, could not treat his patients in a white hospital.

With the help of the black community, Dr. Williams started the Provident Hospital in Chicago in 1891, which was open to both black and white patients. In addition, he started the first training school for black nurses. Later he set up a similar internship and nursing program at Freedmen's Hospital in Washington, D.C.

In 1928 when Charles Drew, an outstanding black athlete, wanted to go to medical school, there were only two accredited medical schools for black students in the country. They could handle only a fraction of the black students wanting to become doctors. Dr. Drew finally attended medical school in Canada and went on to invent a process for storing blood plasma that saved thousands of lives in World War II.

Although discrimination against minority groups and women has been accepted in United States medicine up to the present time, today, at least, almost every white medical school accepts qualified black students. Black doctors still comprise only two percent of the total number of doctors in the country, but their number is steadily increasing.

Perhaps the most interesting result of the integration of black and white students in the last years has been the introduction of "black studies" courses into a previously all-white curriculum. Until recently a white student—not to mention the black student—could go through his whole school life without ever being aware of black history, literature, art or any other contribution the Afro-American has made to American life. Centuries of oppressive slavery were passed over in history books as a benevolent if peculiar institution.

A student, black or white, might know about Booker

T. Washington or George Washington Carver but never hear of Frederick Douglass or W. E. B. Du Bois. A black student might be taught of the bravery of John Paul Jones but not Joseph Cinqué, or the selfless devotion of a Clara Barton but not the equally selfless devotion of a Sojourner Truth. Certainly almost all students have heard of Yale and Harvard University, but how many know of historic Hampton Institute or Howard University?

The number of monuments to black scientists and educators is unhappily small, the most impressive being the several museums and monuments dedicated to George Washington Carver and Booker T. Washington.

BOOKER T. WASHINGTON

No other black American, with the possible exception of Frederick Douglass, has as many monuments in his honor as Booker T. Washington, the spokesman for black America at the turn of the century. His most outstanding memorial, of course, is the college he founded in 1881 at Tuskegee, Alabama.

TUSKEGEE INSTITUTE

On July 4, 1881, twenty-five-year-old Booker T. Washington and thirty young men and women gathered in a one-room shanty to open Alabama's first normal school for the training of black teachers. Washington was a strong believer in learning by doing and vocational education—beliefs that were to be the center of controversy in black education for years.

Nevertheless, under this leadership and by the time of his death in 1915, Tuskegee Institute was one of the outstanding black colleges in the country.

Today Tuskegee has changed from a trade school to a college offering thirty-three different degrees. There are many interesting sites to visit on Tuskegee's campus, from Washington's study in his home "The Oaks" (restored as it was when Mr. Washington lived there) to the Carver Museum and Art Center,

321

which houses many mementos of Booker T. Washington's life and work.

Location: Tuskegee Institute, Tuskegee, Alabama.

Free guided tours of the Tuskegee campus are available.

BOOKER T. WASHINGTON NATIONAL MONUMENT (The Burroughs Plantation)

The man who was to become the best-known black educator in America was born a slave in 1856 in a cabin on the Burroughs Plantation. Today the National Park Service has restored the birthplace of Washington, as well as a portion of the Burroughs farm, as a National Monument to Booker T. Washington.

During the summer, visitors to the farm can see it much as it appeared and was operated during the years Washington lived there as a boy. On summer Sundays and other special days, visitors may see lye soap being made, tobacco worked, butter churned, all the chores done on a nineteenth-century farm.

Facilities available include a visitors center, museum, movie of Washington's life, picnic area and self-guiding trails through the plantation.

Location: Booker T. Washington National Monument is 16 miles east of Rocky Mount, Virginia, via Virginia 122, and 20 miles south of Roanoke, Virginia, via Virginia 116 or County Road 634.

No admission charge.

THE HALL OF FAME FOR GREAT AMERICANS

For many years Booker T. Washington was the only black American honored by a bronze bust in the Hall of Fame for Great Americans. His statue was executed by black sculptor Richmond Barthé in 1946. Then in 1973 the black scientist George Washington Carver was elected to the Hall of Fame, and he eventually will join those distinguished American men and women whose lives reflect the highest ideals of American culture.

Location: Hall of Fame for Great Americans, on the University Heights Campus of New York University, 181st Street and University Avenue, Bronx, New York.

No admission charge.

322

GEORGE WASHINGTON CARVER MUSEUM

George Washington Carver, the brilliant black scientist, worked at Tuskegee for more than sixty years, improving the living conditions of rural and farm people, black and white. A museum was dedicted to him in 1941 by the late Henry Ford, who was a friend of the scientist.

The museum has a replica of Carver's early laboratory with its primitive equipment, personal mementos of his life, his unusual hobbies and art work, and exhibits of the results of Mr. Carver's research with the peanut, sweet potato and Alabama clay.

The museum also houses twenty dioramas covering the contributions the black race has made to civilization from early times to the present. There is an art gallery on the lower level of the museum and examples of African art and sculpture on the first floor.

Location: George Washington Carver Museum, Tuskegee Institute, Tuskegee, Alabama.

No admission charge. Guided tours may be arranged.

CARVER BURIAL SITE

George Washington Carver, who died in 1943, is buried next to Booker T. Washington on the grounds of the Tuskegee Institute, near the George Washington Carver Museum and the Chapel.

GEORGE WASHINGTON CARVER NATIONAL MONUMENT

The George Washington Carver National Monument is located at the site where the young Carver spent his childhood on the Carver farm. Although he was born a slave, young George and his brother were treated more as members of the family than servants.

The trails young George enjoyed walking have been preserved, along with his own private garden area. In the midst of this garden is a statute of the "boy Carver" with a plant in his hand, and visitors may listen to a tape recording of Carver's last public speech.

There is also a demonstration garden, containing the major

crops the scientist used in developing hundreds of products. A visitor center displays exhibits of Carver's early life and work and the honors showered upon him.

Location: George Washington Carver National Monument, U.S. 71 alternate to Diamond, Missouri, then west for 2 miles on County Highway V and south for almost a mile on county road to the monument entrance.

No admission charge.

GREENFIELD VILLAGE

The pioneer automobile manufacturer Henry Ford was a close friend of George Washington Carver. When Henry Ford established Greenfield Village (a collection of historic homes moved to the village of Greenfield from all over America), one of the homes he had built was a replica of the three-room log cabin in which Carver was born.

Visitors to Greenfield Village may stroll through the town visiting the Henry Ford Museum, the old homes and shops, historic automobiles and trains, or take a horse-drawn carriage with driver guide from the Village Green.

Location: Greenfield Village, Village Road and Oakwood Boulevard in Dearborn, Michigan.

Admission charge.

THE SMITHSONIAN INSTITUTION

The Smithsonian has several exhibits featuring contributions made by black scientists to America.

The Hall of Medical Sciences has a special panel exhibit, "Pioneering Heart Surgery." The exhibit shows the early life of Dr. Daniel Hale Williams, a record of his accomplishments, and other mementos of his life and work. Dr. Williams was the black doctor who pioneered open-heart surgery.

"Laying out the Nation's Capital" is a diorama in the Hall of Physical Sciences. The scene shows Benjamin Banneker, an assistant surveyor, with Andrew Ellicott, the surveyor in charge. Banneker is shown seated so he could make calculations on the slate in his left hand, since he was known as a mathematician and not as an observer.

Location: The Smithsonian Institution, on the Mall, Washington, D.C.

No admission charge.

PROVIDENT HOSPITAL AND TRAINING SCHOOL

In addition to performing the first successful operation on the human heart in 1893, Dr. Daniel Hale Williams also founded the Provident Hospital and Training School in 1891, the first hospital in America created for the use of all physicians and patients without regard to color.

Location: Provident Hospital, 51st Street and Vincennes Avenue, Chicago, Illinois.

FREEDMEN'S HOSPITAL

In 1894 Dr. Williams was called to Washington to head the Freedmen's Hospital, which at the time had only primitive medical facilities for black people. Under Dr. Williams, Freedmen's Hospital was reorganized and modernized and the first nursing school in America for black women was started. A portrait of Dr. Williams hangs in the main hall of the hospital.

Location: Freedmen's Hospital, Washington, D.C.

JOHN CHAVIS MEMORIAL PARK

John Chavis, a free black teacher and Presbyterian minister, was educated at Princeton University. He taught and preached to both blacks and whites in Raleigh, North Carolina, in the early 1800s. After the Nat Turner Rebellion, John Chavis was forced to give up the ministry and stop teaching black students. So brilliant was John Chavis as a teacher that one of his white students went on to become a senator and another a governor.

A plaque in the John Chavis Memorial Park honors this black educator and minister.

Location: John Chavis Memorial Park, East Lenoir and Worth streets, Raleigh, North Carolina.

THE BERKSHIRE MUSEUM (Matthew Henson)

The Berkshire Museum has several rare mementos of the Peary expedition to the North Pole in 1909, including one of the sledges that made the trip and the polar suit worn by Matthew Henson on the expedition. Henson was a black man, and the only man to accompany Admiral Peary on all of his polar expeditions.

Although six men started on the expedition to the North Pole, only Peary and Henson survived the hardships of the trip. On April 7 Peary carefully calculated the precise point of the Pole and Matthew Henson placed the American flag on the spot.

Location: The Berkshire Museum is located in the center of Pittsfield, Massachusetts, on U.S. Route 7.

No admission charge.

MATTHEW HENSON PLAQUE

A plaque honoring Matthew Henson, the black explorer, who was born in Charles County, Maryland, may be seen at the State Capitol Building in Annapolis, Maryland.

BENJAMIN BANNEKER PARK

The Benjamin Banneker Park was dedicated on November 9, 1971, on the 235th anniversary of Banneker's birthday. The park consists of 4 acres of land and is on the Mall end of L'Enfant Plaza promenade and Maine Avenue, Washington, D.C.

Benjamin Banneker was appointed by President George Washington to the commission that laid out plans for the city of Washington, and surveyed the site. Banneker, a brilliant, self-taught mathematician, astronomer and inventor, published the first almanac in America and was the first black American to be granted a federal appointment.

LOUISIANA STATE MUSEUM

This museum has a tablet dedicated to the memory of Norbert Rillieux, the black scientist whose invention of a more efficient process for obtaining sugar crystals from sugarcane, revolutionized the sugar industry in Louisiana. While he was alive, Rillieux received little gratitude from the sugar planters for his invention and finally he left America to live the remainder of his life in Paris.

Location: Louisiana State Museum, 751 Charles Street, New Orleans, Louisiana.

Small admission charge.

JAN ERNST MATZELIGER MARKER

It was in Lynn, Massachusetts, that Jan Ernst Matzeliger developed the shoe-lasting machine that greatly increased the production of shoes. Many inventors before Matzeliger had tried and failed to invent such a machine, and it took this young black inventor ten years of tireless work to perfect his machine.

A small monument in the inventor's memory has been placed on his grave in the Pine Grove Cemetery, 25 Gentian Path, Lynn. A portrait of the inventor hangs in the First Church on Lynnfield Street, Lynn, Massachusetts.

TIDAL BASIN BRIDGE

Archie Alexander was discouraged from entering the field of engineering because of the difficulties he would face as a black man in that field. Mr. Alexander persisted, however, and finally headed his own construction firm. One of his most outstanding achievements—and a monument that many might envy—is the Tidal Basin Bridge in Washington, D.C. From this bridge one can look out in the spring over a mass of cherry blossoms blooming beside the Tidal Basin.

Location: Tidal Basin Bridge, Washington, D.C.

MARY MC LEOD BETHUNE STATUE AND BETHUNE COLLEGE

One of seventeen children, Mary Bethune spent her childhood picking cotton. She attended school only a few months of the year. After struggling to achieve an education and become a teacher, she was determined to start a school for the black railroad laborers' children in Florida, who were without schools.

With only her "faith and a dollar and half" she rang doorbells, made speeches, wrote and distributed leaflets. Her school grew from a shack near the city dump to one of the outstanding black teacher-training colleges in the country. Mrs. Bethune

327

was not only a teacher but became a highly respected adviser to presidents Roosevelt and Truman.

In 1960 Congress authorized a statue of Mrs. Bethune to be placed in Lincoln Park, Washington, D.C.

Location: Mary McLeod Bethune Statue, Lincoln Park, Washington, D.C.

Location: Bethune College, Daytona Beach, Florida.

The colleges that follow—with points of interest on the campuses that may be visited—do not make up a complete list of all the predominantly black colleges in the country. It is a select list of historic black schools that were started, in some form, before 1870.

CHEYNEY STATE COLLEGE

In 1829 Cheyney's founder, Quaker Richard Humphreys of Philadelphia, willed $10,000 for "an institution to instruct the descendants of the African race." The first school took shape in 1837, a farm school that failed. But as a school for the training of teachers, it was successful.

The school prospered even further under the leadership of Fanny Jackson Coppin, the first black woman college graduate in America. By 1920 the operation of the school had been transferred to the Commonwealth of Pennsylvania. The transfer was agreed to only when the Cheyney board was assured that Cheyney graduates would be allowed to teach in either white or black schools in Pennsylvania, a promise that was not fulfilled until the 1950s.

There are few historic buildings still standing on this campus of 275 acres, but there are many interesting new buildings, including the George Washington Carver Science Center, which houses a planetarium and a rooftop weather station.

Location: Route 926, off the West Chester Pike, 8 miles southeast of West Chester, Pennsylvania.

LINCOLN UNIVERSITY

The oldest college in America established specifically to provide higher education for black students—and still very much in

328

existence today—is Lincoln University. The school was founded as Ashmun Institute by an abolitionist, Reverend John Miller Dickey, in 1854. When Mr. Dickey was unable to gain admission to white colleges for young freemen, he decided to establish a school himself. In 1866 the name of the school was changed to Lincoln, and gradually students of "every clime and complexion" were encouraged to enroll.

The oldest building on campus, Lincoln Hall, was built in 1866; the newest building, the Langston Hughes Memorial Library, in 1972. The library has a special exhibit area of African art and artifacts. Another new building, the Alumni Memorial Gymnasium, has an Olympic-size swimming pool.

Location: On U.S. 131, 45 miles southwest of Philadelphia, between Oxford and West Grove, Pennsylvania.

WILBERFORCE UNIVERSITY

The first institution of higher education in the United States to be owned and operated by blacks was Wilberforce University, founded in 1856. Its first students were freedmen or escaped slaves, and sometimes the mulatto children of Southern planters.

The school was named for William Wilberforce, an early British abolitionist who helped bring the English slave trade to a close in 1807. Memorabilia of William Wilberforce, as well as historical items that relate to black history and culture, may be seen in the Wilberforce library.

The school has an excellent Cooperative Education Program and was one of the first to pioneer a work-study program.

Location: Adjacent to U.S. 42 South, Wilberforce, Ohio (near Dayton).

SHAW UNIVERSITY

Shaw University was founded in 1864 by a Civil War veteran who saved his army pay, a woolen goods manufacturer, and the Freedmen's Bureau.

One of the first schools to train black lawyers and doctors, today, Shaw University specializes in a broad liberal arts education. The buildings on the campus are a mixture of historic and modern, including a learning resource center with its own radio station.

Location: Raleigh, North Carolina.

ATLANTA UNIVERSITY

One of the schools begun by the Freedmen's Bureau was Atlanta University, established in 1865. In 1929, under the brilliant leadership of John Hope, Atlanta combined with Morehouse and Spelman College. Later Clark College, Morris Brown College and the Interdenominational Theological Center joined the Atlanta University complex.

Today the Atlanta University campus, spread over 145 acres, is one of the loveliest college campuses in the South. In addition to many beautiful buildings, there is an outstanding black art collection in the lower level of the Trevor Arnett Library.

Location: Atlanta, Georgia.

VIRGINIA UNION COLLEGE

Virginia Union, founded in 1865, is one of the many church-related colleges established after the Civil War for black students. The college has had many distinguished graduates, including the first black admiral in the U.S. Navy.

The beautiful 55-acre campus contains historic buildings of granite, hand-hewn by newly freed black men following the Civil War, as well as modern buildings like the Belgium Friendship Building, gift of the Belgium government. The Vann Memorial Tower of this building has been designated a Virginia Historical Landmark.

Location: 1500 North Lombardy Street, Richmond, Virginia.

FISK UNIVERSITY

In 1866 the American Missionary Association, the Freedmen's Bureau and General Clinton B. Fisk decided to found a school "equal to the best in the country" primarily for the newly freed slaves.

The many interesting buildings on the campus include Jubilee Hall, erected in 1876 with funds raised by the Jubilee Singers,

330

and the Little Theater, the oldest building on campus. It was used as a hospital during the Civil War.

The third floor of the new library has a museum of African sculpture, and contemporary black American art may be seen at the Carl Van Vechten Gallery of Fine Arts on the campus.

Location: About 2 miles northwest of downtown Nashville, Tennessee.

LINCOLN UNIVERSITY

Lincoln University was founded on the dreams of uneducated ex-slaves, the men of the 62nd Missouri Colored Volunteers, who served during the Civil War. The money for the school was raised from the men in the regiment, with enlisted men who drew only $13 a month in pay giving as much as $100. Although the school opened in 1866, it wasn't until 1871 that the Lincoln Institute was able to erect its first permanent building, and on that day the men of the 62nd and 65th Missouri Colored Volunteers held a happy reunion on the campus.

The painter Thomas Hart Benton has done a mural for the school that shows its development from the battlefields of the Civil War to the present time. The Art Department at Lincoln also has a small collection of paintings by well-known black artists, such as Hale Woodruff, Aaron Douglas and James Porter.

Location: Jefferson City, Missouri.

RUST COLLEGE

Rust College was begun in 1869 on land that had once been slave auction grounds, with financial help from Northern Methodist churches. As with other black colleges of the time, not only college students but students of all ages were given an education at Rust College.

One of the oldest buildings on campus is the Oakview Mansion, built in 1866; and one of the newest is the beautiful Leontyne Price Library, named in honor of the world-famous black opera star.

Location: Rust Avenue, Holly Springs, Mississippi.

331

ST. AUGUSTINE'S COLLEGE

Another church-related college founded after the Civil War for black students was St. Augustine's, chartered in 1867 by the Episcopal Church. Some of the buildings on the tree-shaded 110-acre campus have been named historical landmarks, including the college chapel and Taylor Hall.

Location: Raleigh, North Carolina.

TALLADEGA COLLEGE

Founded in 1867, Talladega was the first college in Alabama to grant college degrees to black students, and today is rated as one of the outstanding predominantly black colleges in the United States.

One of the oldest and most historic buildings on the campus is Swayne Hall, built in 1853 as an academy for white students and used during the Civil War as a prison for Union troops. The Savery Library at Talladega has three panels of frescoes by Hale Woodruff depicting the famous *Amistad* slave mutiny.

Location: Talladega, Alabama.

MORGAN STATE COLLEGE

Originally begun in 1867 for the training of black Methodist ministers, today Morgan State College is a state-supported institution on a 130-acre wooded tract of land in suburban Baltimore. There is an undergraduate and graduate school of arts and sciences, a Center for Continuing Education and a Center for Urban Affairs.

In the new Sopher Library can be found rare artifacts belonging to the black explorer Matthew Henson and an exhibit area for black American art. There is also a statue of the abolitionist leader Frederick Douglass on the campus.

Location: Baltimore, Maryland.

BOWIE STATE COLLEGE

Bowie State College has had several names since it was established by the Freedmen's Bureau for the training of black

332

teachers in 1867. The campus has both historic and modern structures, is state-supported and fully integrated.

Location: 1 mile north of Bowie, Maryland, off Maryland Route 197.

HOWARD UNIVERSITY

The largest college for black students established by the Freedmen's Bureau was Howard University, begun in 1867. Started as a school for ministers, today the university offers studies leading to twenty-one different degrees and enrolls the largest percentage of foreign students of any university in the nation.

Of particular interest to visitors is the Gallery of Art with its collection of African and Afro-American art.

Location: 2400 Sixth Avenue, N., Washington, D.C.

HAMPTON INSTITUTE

In 1868 Hampton Institute was begun by General Samuel Armstrong and the Freedmen's Bureau on a 120-acre waterfront estate known as Little Scotland. For the first three years male students lived in old army tents and the women in barracks. Many of the beautiful buildings on the campus were built by students learning a trade. Virginia Hall was "sung up" in 1874 by the Hampton Singers, who toured the country much like the Jubilee Singers.

Although there are many new buildings on the Hampton campus today, some of the most interesting buildings are the historic structures: the magnificent Mansion House, built prior to 1868; the Wigwam, constructed in 1878 as a dormitory for Indians who were sent to Hampton to be educated; Memorial Church, built in 1886; and a still flourishing oak tree called the Emancipation Oak. It was under this tree that Mary Peake, a free black woman, first taught children of former slaves in 1861.

The College Museum and Art Center includes unusual relics and artifacts from Indian reservations in the West, as well as art objects and artifacts from all over the world. Contemporary art shows are a regular feature of the museum program.

Guided tours of the museum and other areas on campus are offered to visitors by the staff of the museum.

Location: Hampton, Virginia.

333

TOUGALOO COLLEGE

Built on the grounds of a former plantation in 1869 by the American Missionary Association, the first years of Tougaloo were unsettled and financially difficult. Because the educational philosophy at Tougaloo was that black students should be educated not to "know" their place but to "find" it, there were those who considered the college a "hotbed of impudent blacks." During the late 1950s and early 1960s, Tougaloo became the cornerstone of the Mississippi civil rights movement, with many Tougaloo students leading demonstrations and sit-ins.

Tougaloo has preserved some of its finest historic buildings, including a mansion built in the 1850s. Recently the Tougaloo Permanent Art Collection was started by a group of prominent New York artists and housed in Warren Hall.

Location: Interstate Highway 55, Tougaloo, Mississippi.

DILLARD UNIVERSITY

Dillard University's roots go back to 1869 and the Congregational and Methodist Episcopal Church. Today Dillard is still a privately owned, church-related liberal arts college. Located in a residential section of New Orleans, Dillard has one of the most beautiful campuses in the country, with oak-shaded walkways, handsome white buildings and lovely landscaped lawns.

The Amistad Research Center is located on the campus.

Location: 2601 Gentilly Boulevard, New Orleans, Louisiana.

A portrait by R. Woodward of Booker T. Washington, the founder of Tuskegee Institute, Tuskegee, Alabama. Until his death in 1915, the noted educator was considered by many as the unofficial spokesman for black America. COURTESY HARMON FOUNDATION COLLECTION, NATIONAL ARCHIVES

The reconstructed log cabin on the James Burroughs farm in which Booker T. Washington was born a slave in 1856. Today the cabin and farm are part of the Booker T. Washington National Monument, near Rocky Mount, Virginia. COURTESY NATIONAL PARK SERVICE, U.S. DEPARTMENT OF THE INTERIOR. PHOTO BY M. WOODBRIDGE WILLIAMS

The room Booker T. Washington used as a study in his home, "The Oaks," located on the campus of Tuskegee Institute, Alabama, is now a National Historic Landmark and has been restored to look much as it did when Washington was alive. COURTESY TUSKEGEE INSTITUTE

Tuskegee Institute, Alabama, under the energetic leadership of Booker T. Washington, grew from a one-room shanty in 1881 to become one of the outstanding black colleges in the country. Many of the older buildings still standing on the campus were constructed by the students from bricks they made themselves. COURTESY TEXACO, INC.

One of the best-known artworks by black sculptor Richmond Barthé is his statue of the scientist George Washington Carver studying a handful of peanuts. It was from the lowly peanut—as well as the soybean and sweet potato—that the scientist developed many valuable products that helped revolutionize agriculture in the South. The statue is at Fisk University Art Gallery, Memphis, and a copy at the Carver Museum, Tuskegee, Alabama. COURTESY FISK UNIVERSITY ART GALLERY, PHOTO BY MAX FEAMAN

A view of a portion of the Carver Museum on the campus of Tuskegee Institute. Alabama. The museum contains many interesting exhibits and mementos from the life of George Washington Carver and Booker T. Washington, as well as an African and black American art collection. COURTESY TUSKEGEE INSTITUTE

The first national monument in America to a black man is the George Washington Carver National Monument near Diamond, Missouri. The Visitor Center and park contains a museum and walking trails, with many exhibits on the scientist's life as a young boy in Missouri and later as a scientist-teacher at Tuskegee Institute, Alabama. COURTESY NATIONAL PARK SERVICE, U.S. DEPARTMENT OF THE INTERIOR

Since there were no schools for black students near the Carver farm, young George attended school in nearby Neosho, Missouri. The personal effects from Carver's stay in Neosho—his bed, wardrobe and the family Bible—may be seen at the Visitor Center Museum at the Carver Monument, Diamond, Missouri. COURTESY NATIONAL PARK SERVICE, U.S. DEPARTMENT OF THE INTERIOR, AND WALKER, MISSOURI. TOURISM

A bronze statue by Robert Amendola of the boy Carver has been placed in the midst of a garden area that was a favorite spot of the young George Washington Carver. The Moses Carver farm is now part of the Carver National Monument, Diamond, Missouri. COURTESY NATIONAL PARK SERVICE, U.S. DEPARTMENT OF THE INTERIOR

A diorama in the Hall of Physical Sciences of The Smithsonian Institution, Washington, D.C., shows Benjamin Banneker, the black mathematician, assisting Andrew Ellicott, the surveyor in charge, in laying out the city plan for the nation's capital, Washington, D.C. COURTESY THE SMITHSONIAN INSTITUTION, WASHINGTON, D.C.

A plaque honoring the black scientist Norbert Rillieux may be seen at the Louisiana State Museum, New Orleans. Rillieux's invention in 1846 of a new sugar-refining process greatly helped the sugarcane industry in Louisiana. COURTESY LOUISIANA STATE MUSEUM

A portrait of Dr. Daniel Hale Williams, who performed the first open-heart surgery in America in 1893. This portrait hangs in the Freedmen's Hospital, Washington, D.C. A special exhibit on "Pioneering Heart Surgery," honoring Dr. Williams, may also be seen at the Hall of Medical Sciences, The Smithsonian Institution. COURTESY THE SMITHSONIAN INSTITUTION, WASHINGTON, D.C.

The fur suit Matthew Henson, the explorer, wore on his trip to the North Pole with Admiral Peary, as well as one of the sledges he used on the trip and other personal mementos, may be seen at a special exhibit at the Berkshire Museum, Pittsfield, Massachusetts. COURTESY THE BERKSHIRE MUSEUM

A picture of one of the newly opened Freedmen's Schools in the South that appeared in *Harper's Weekly*, a popular magazine of the nineteenth century. The Freedmen's Bureau was set up to assist white as well as black refugees after the Civil War and worked closely with church groups, such as the American Missionary Society. Although the Bureau lasted only a few short years, the schools educated thousands of ex-slaves, young and old. Some of the historic primarily black colleges still in existence today were begun by the Freedmen's Bureau.

From simple one-room schoolhouses begun after the Civil War by the Freedmen's Bureau and various church groups developed great colleges like Howard University, Washington, D.C. This is a picture of the Chemical Building on the campus of Howard University today. COURTESY HOWARD UNIVERSITY

In 1867 Hampton Institute, Virginia, was begun on a 120-acre waterfront estate known as Little Scotland under the sponsorship of the Freedmen's Bureau. Historic buildings on the campus include the Mansion House, the Wigwam and Memorial Church. The College Museum on the campus, begun by General Armstrong, includes many unusual items from Indians of the early West. COURTESY HAMPTON INSTITUTE PHOTOGRAPH BY REUBEN V. BURRELL

Atlanta University, with one of the most beautiful campuses in the South, was another school established by the Freedmen's Bureau in 1865. The university came into national prominence under the brilliant leadership of Dr. John Hope, who consolidated Atlanta University with several other colleges. Harkness Hall, shown *at right*, was the first building on the present site of Atlanta University. COURTESY ATLANTA UNIVERSITY

The oldest college in America established for the purpose of providing higher education for black students is Lincoln University, near Oxford, Pennsylvania. The college was begun in 1854 and has been interracial ever since 1866. One of the newest buildings on the campus, the Alumni Memorial Gymnasium, finished in 1972, has an Olympic-size swimming pool. COURTESY LINCOLN UNIVERSITY

The Emancipation Oak, named by the National Geographic Society as one of the Great Trees of the World, may be seen on the campus of Hampton Institute, Hampton, Virginia. It was under this oak that Mary Peake, a free black woman, began teaching former slaves in 1861. The tree's limb-spread makes an umbrella of 100 yards in circumference. COURTESY HAMPTON INSTITUTE, PHOTOGRAPH BY REUBEN V. BURRELL

FROM
CHURCHS TO
CIVIL RIGHTS

On December 1, 1955, Mrs. Rosa Parks, a neatly dressed black seamstress, boarded the Cleveland Avenue bus in Montgomery, Alabama. She was tired after a hard day's work, and when the bus driver ordered her to give up her seat to a white man and stand in the crowded, segregated rear of the bus, she refused. She was promptly hauled off the bus by the police, arrested, and taken to jail. Rosa Parks' arrest was to spark off a black revolution in America in much the same way as the death of Crispus Attucks at the Boston Massacre had helped spark the American Revolution against the British.

The two revolutions, though almost two centuries apart, had a great deal in common. Both were fought against overwhelming, numerically superior forces and both were fought for the same basic belief: that all men

345

are created equal with the right to life, liberty and the pursuit of happiness.

Unlike the Revolutionary War, however, the first battle of the black revolution was not fought with muskets and rifles. It was fought with feet—thousands of aching, tired feet that belonged to black men and women who ordinarily rode in the rear, segregated sections of the city buses because they were required to by law. Instead, the black residents of Montgomery—75 percent of bus riders were blacks—pledged themselves not to ride the city buses at all.

The night after Mrs. Parks' arrest, a protest meeting was held at the Dexter Avenue Baptist Church, not far from the State Capitol building of Alabama. The group of ministers and black leaders who called the meeting selected an unknown man, the newly arrived twenty-six-year-old minister of the Dexter Church, to lead a boycott against the city bus system. The young minister's name was Martin Luther King, Jr.

The boycott, or "act of massive noncooperation" as the Reverend King called it, lasted for 381 days. Despite harassment of the black men and women who refused to ride the buses, mass arrests of the leaders of the boycott, and the bombing of their homes, the Montgomery buses remained almost completely empty of black riders. As one old woman said who had to walk many weary miles to work each day, "My feet are tired but my soul is at rest."

To many white Americans, who for the first time saw a black community banding effectively together to fight back against a white community, what was perhaps most startling about the event was that it was led by the black church and black ministers. Yet, from the very beginning, the church has played a crucial role in the history of black Americans.

Christianity came to west Africa in the sixteenth century with the Spanish and Portuguese, but the labors of the missionaries brought few conversions to the Christian faith. The African kingdoms already had strong religious traditions of their own that included the concept of one God, a respect for priests and ancestors, and a strong feeling of unity between man and nature. In any case, since the slave traders followed closely on the heels of the missionaries, the African might well have wondered about converting to a religion that saved his soul while imprisoning his body!

When the Africans were brought to America as slaves, they were completely cut off from the tribal religion they had known. On some early plantations, a "conjure man," often a former tribal priest, could be found, conjuring or "goophering" among the slaves, dispensing potions of roots and herbs to ease their burdens and sorrows. Recent research has shown that there were in the early days instances of slaves being buried with African funeral rites. But it was in and around New Orleans that remnants of an African religion managed to survive the longest, in the form of Dahomean voodoo worship of the snake god Damballa.

One such voodoo priestess was Marie Laveau, born in 1794, a free woman of color. With the power from her voodoo rites, Marie Laveau became an unofficial boss of New Orleans. Blacks and whites beat a path to her door to buy from Marie the *gris-gris* or magic potions that would solve their problems. Although she died in 1881, staunch believers today still visit her grave, make a mark, and hope that Marie will grant their wishes.

Most plantation owners discouraged what they called "heathen worship" by their slaves. Yet there were those white Christian slave owners who pondered long and hard about the souls of their black servants. If a supposedly pagan slave had a soul, and he was converted and baptized, did that make him a free man?

By 1700 most Protestant and Catholic slave owners had concluded, to their own satisfaction at least, that even if a slave had a soul, his conversion to Christianity had no effect on his condition of slavery. Some slave owners found passages in the Bible that made it sound as if the Bible itself sanctioned enslavement of the black man.

The slaveholder who was concerned for the soul of his slaves encouraged them to attend church services on Sunday. Even before the Revolutionary War, there were a few churches for black worshipers. As early as 1773 black minister George Liele had organized a Baptist church in Silver Bluff, Georgia. There were other Baptist churches in Savannah, Petersburg, Williamsburg, Lexington and Richmond. In the Northern colonies there were black ministers like Lemuel Haynes, Samuel Ward and Henry Highland Garnet who preached to all-white congregations, as did John Chavis, an outstanding black Presbyterian minister-teacher in North Carolina.

After the slave revolts of Denmark Vesey and Nat Turner, however, and the rise of the abolition movement, slave owners became concerned about allowing black churches in their midst. They feared revolt and insurrection was being preached from the pulpit. Black ministers were outlawed after 1830 in the majority of Southern states, and the religious activity of both slaves and free blacks was strictly controlled. They were forced to attend and sit in segregated sections of white churches

348

or have a white person present at all their meetings. The only preaching allowed had to be in favor of a meek, obedient submission to slavery.

In the North, although the black man and woman had more religious freedom, after the Revolutionary War the white churches became more and more segregated. When Richard Allen, Absalom Jones and their friends in Philadelphia attempted to worship in the white pews of the St. George Methodist Episcopal Church in 1787, they were dragged to their feet. Leaving the church in disgust, Richard Allen founded the first American Methodist Episcopal church in 1794, while a few years earlier, in 1791, Absalom Jones had founded the first African Episcopal church.

Other all-black churches soon followed. Thomas Paul organized the Abyssinian Baptist Church in New York in 1809. Several years earlier the first African Baptist church, called the Old African Meeting House, was built in Boston. James Varick of North Carolina started the A.M.E. Zion Church, and later John Chavis brought the Presbyterian Church to black people in the South.

After the Civil War, many former slaves and free blacks withdrew from white churches completely and formed their own independent churches. Church membership in the independent churches increased rapidly. The African Methodist Episcopal Church alone grew from 20,000 members in 1856 to 200,000 in 1876. The Baptists, too, formed their own churches, although, like the black Episcopalians, they remained more closely tied to white churches than did the Methodists.

By 1854 the first black American Catholic priest, James Augustine Healy, the mulatto son of a Georgia planter, was ordained in Paris; and in 1891 Charles

349

Uncles became the first black priest to be ordained in America.

Black ministers played an active role in the Reconstruction days following the Civil War. It was a black A.M.E. minister, Hiram Revels, who was elected to the U.S. Senate in 1870, and another Methodist minister, Richard Cain, served two terms in Congress.

Other black ministers were delegates to the conventions held after the war to draw up new constitutions for the former Confederate States. Although the myth has arisen that these state conventions were run by scalawags and "ignorant and deprived" blacks, in point of fact, many of the new state constitutions written at that time were progressive documents. They provided for free public education, court reforms, women's rights, voting suffrage and reduced taxes for the poor.

By 1877, however, the more liberal Reconstruction period had ended, and the restrictive Jim Crow era had begun. The Civil Rights Act passed in 1875 (never in any case enforced) was declared unconstitutional in 1883. The Thirteenth Amendment to the Constitution had freed the slaves, but the Fourteenth Amendment (1868), promising "equal protection" for all citizens under the law, and the Fifteenth Amendment (1870), guaranteeing the right of the citizens of the United States to vote, were just hollow words on paper. The Fourteenth and Fifteenth amendments did not apply to black or white women and the civil rights of the black man were seldom recognized.

White supremacists were once again in control of the South, and Northern liberals, with economic problems of their own, had grown tired of dealing with the "Negro problem." The black man in the South was no longer physically bought and sold on the auction block, but he was still bound to the plantation owner by the share-cropping system. The "equal protection" under the law was destroyed by specially written local laws discriminating against the black man—and by lynch mobs that made sure a black man never received a fair trial in court. The right to vote was denied by literacy tests, poll taxes and grandfather clauses written into state constitutions. Those black citizens who attempted to exercise their right to vote found themselves receiving midnight visits from the local Ku Klux Klan or facing eviction from their homes and dismissal from their jobs.

In 1896 the Plessy decision by the U.S. Supreme Court, which made separate "accommodations" legal, put the last nail in the coffin of civil rights for the black man and woman. Black Americans now had to ride on separate trains, sit in separate sections of the buses, attend segregated theaters and restaurants, use segregated public accommodations, train and bus stations, lavatories and drinking fountains. One state even required separate phone booths!

The blacks who moved north found conditions little better. They had to live in crowded ghettos, and they faced the antagonism of the white laboring man, who felt the black man was being used as a strikebreaker and a threat to his own job. In times of economic depression, the black worker soon discovered he was "last hired, first fired."

Under these conditions, there was very little the black minister could do to help his parishioners. Yet, as the black church had been the one place under slavery where black people could congregate and find some measure of relief from oppression, the black church, during the Jim Crow era, was the one place where black men and women could meet safely with-

351

out being accused and arrested for "unlawful assembly." The black church was the organization that could work for civil rights with the least fear of harassment from the white community.

Perhaps, most importantly, the church pulpit offered the aspiring black man, who was deprived of political or economic leadership, an outlet for his abilities.

By the early 1900s, however, some of the more educated black Americans felt that the church had become too passive and conservative. They felt that the church, like Booker T. Washington's organization, was more interested in keeping on good terms with the white establishment than in fighting for the civil and social rights of the black American. They could point bitterly to the fact that between 1900 and 1915, 1,100 black men and women in America had been lynched, shot or burned alive. At a meeting in Boston where Washington spoke, William Trotter, a militant black publisher, broke up the meeting by demanding of Washington: "Is the rope and torch all the race is to get under your leadership?"

Gradually the black church began to lose its effectiveness as a leader in the civil rights movement. When in 1905 a small group of black professional men met at Niagara Falls, Canada—they had been refused hotel accommodations on the American side—the meeting was not led by a clergyman but by a professor-historian and a journalist—W. E. B. Du Bois and William Trotter. The platform of the Niagara Movement listed the grievances blacks had suffered at the hands of white America and demanded bluntly that the black man be granted the rights that belonged to all American men. The Niagara Movement was considered too radical by Booker T. Washington. Without his powerful support, the movement dwindled and finally died.

Then in August 1908, in a small Midwest city a mob gathered to lynch two black prisoners held in the city jail. When the prisoners were secretly removed to safety, the frustrated mob turned in savage fury on the black community, plundering, murdering and looting. What shocked many people was not just that respectable members of the white community sat and indifferently watched the mob, but that the riot took place in the home city of Abraham Lincoln—Springfield, Illinois.

To fight this rising tide of terrorism, white liberals like Walter Walling, Mary White Ovington and Oswald Garrison Villard (grandson of the famous abolitionist) joined with black leaders to form a new national organization. In 1909 the National Association for the Advancement of Colored People (NAACP) was formed. Some of the more militant blacks, like William Trotter, refused to join, calling the organization "too little, too late, too white," but James Weldon Johnson, the author, became Executive Secretary of the NAACP. W. E. B. Du Bois, although often at odds with the leaders of the organization, resigned his teaching job at Atlanta University to edit the NAACP's monthly magazine, *The Crisis.*

The purpose of the NAACP was to improve the life of the black American through "litigation, legislation and education." But the organization proved most effective in fighting in the courts for justice for black men and women. One of its earliest, most important successes was convincing the Supreme Court in 1915

353

that the grandfather clause in state constitutions was unconstitutional.

In 1911 a second national organization was formed to help black people. Called the National Urban League, its goal was to find employment for the thousands of unemployed black men and women from the rural South crowding into the ghettos of the North.

The membership of both the NAACP and the Urban League was mostly white liberals and middle-class black families. In the early 1920s, however, a movement arose in Harlem, led by a dynamic, flamboyant black man, that appealed directly to the great mass of unemployed and low-income black people. The name of the man was Marcus Garvey, and his organization was called the UNIA—United Negro Improvement Association.

Born in Jamaica, Garvey traveled widely before coming to the United States in 1916 and settling in Harlem. His organization, the UNIA, which he had started in Jamaica, was originally founded as a "back to Africa" movement. His most important contribution, though, was convincing black Americans, after generations of being taught they were inferior to the white race, to take pride in being black. Garvey was a segregationist, opposing all integration with the white race, saying, "I believe in racial purity . . . I am proud I am a Negro." The UNIA supported black-owned businesses, formed its own African Orthodox Church, which celebrated a black Holy Trinity, started its own newspaper, *The Black World,* and the Black Star Steamship Line, to be used to transport black Americans to a new life in Africa.

The UNIA's flag—a crimson, green and black standard—hung over the lecture platform where Garvey, a spellbinding orator, would exhort his audience to remember, "Black men, you were once great; you shall be great again." Poverty-stricken, downtrodden black men and women, with only a bleak past and no hope for the future, listened eagerly to his words, caught up in the emotion and pageantry with which Marcus Garvey surrounded himself. By the mid-twenties the UNIA had more than a million members, with chapters in every major American city with a large black population.

Although the UNIA lasted only a few short years, in its time it was called the first and only real mass movement among Negroes in the history of the United States. Even for some of the more radical black leaders, however, Garvey's ideas were too extreme. Du Bois questioned whether Garvey was a lunatic or a traitor. By 1923 the UNIA was in serious financial trouble, and Garvey himself was sent to jail for mail fraud.

By 1940 Marcus Garvey was almost a forgotten man, and Du Bois, partly because of his Communist leanings (although he actually did not join the Communist Party until 1961), had been ousted from the NAACP and had lost his influence as a black leader. The world was about to erupt into World War II, and a new breed of religious leader and black spokesman was coming to the fore.

In 1941 the prominent black labor leader Asa Philip Randolph, who had succeeded in unionizing the black Sleeping Car Porters, threatened President Franklin D. Roosevelt with a mass march of blacks on Washington, D.C., if black people weren't allowed the right to work in the new war industries. Executive Order 8802, giving equal employment opportunities in these industries, opened thousands of jobs that had been closed to black workers.

Also in 1941, in Harlem, the Reverend Adam Clayton Powell, Jr., pastor of the world's largest black church, the Abyssinian Baptist Church, was elected to the U.S. Congress, and in Chicago, in 1942, James Farmer, a Methodist clergyman, helped organize a new civil rights group, the Congress of Racial Equality (CORE). Operating on the principle of nonviolent self-sacrifice, which had been used successfully by Mahatma Gandhi against the British in India, CORE conducted the first successful sit-in in a Chicago restaurant in 1943.

It was this principle of massive nonviolent resistance that Martin Luther King was to use successfully in Montgomery in the 1955 bus boycott. The same principle was used later by two new black national organizations, the Southern Christian Leadership Conference (SCLC), formed in 1957, and its offshoot, the Student Nonviolent Coordinating Committee (SNCC), formed in 1960.

The principle of nonviolent resistance against injustice was not the coward's way. It required, as Dr. King said, its followers to "return love for hate, patience for anger, to accept blows without striking back." In 1960, when black college students began deliberately sitting at Southern segregated white lunch counters, they followed the principle of peaceful resistance, although there were cases of students being pistol-whipped, gassed and even shot. Yet as soon as one group of students was dragged off to jail, many more students, both black and white, took their place. Students all across the South took up the crusade, conducting sit-ins at segregated restaurants, movies, churches and libraries.

Freedom riders, sponsored by CORE, rode buses through the South to see if bus terminals had really been desegregated in accord with the Supreme Court decision that had made separate but equal accommodations illegal. Black and white riders were pulled off the buses and attacked by mobs waiting at the bus stations while the local police looked the other way.

In an attempt to encourage black voters, student civil rights workers from all the national black organizations were sent south to set up "Freedom Schools." (In one county in Alabama that was 81 percent black, no black voters at all were registered.) The civil rights workers trying to register black voters were often beaten, arrested and tortured while in jail. Two of the workers were shot, and in 1964 three more were killed. More than sixty black homes, churches and schools were bombed. The men brought to trial for the charges of committing murder and arson were tried by all-white juries and given light sentences or released.

In the summer of 1963 the black revolution reached its peak. Protesting against segregation and the harassment of black voters, Dr. King led street demonstrations in Birmingham, Alabama. Shocked television viewers saw the unarmed protestors attacked by the police with guns, dogs and fire hoses. In outrage, thousands of Americans, black and white, streamed south to join the protestors. Demonstrations sprang up all across the country. And on August 28, a quarter of a million black and white Americans marched to Washington, D.C.—the largest protest group in the history of the country—demanding equality and justice for the black American.

Then on July 2, 1964, President Johnson signed the first enforceable Civil Rights Act, and in 1965 the Voting Rights Act was passed protecting the black citizen's right to vote by federal legal action, if necessary.

Despite the passage of these laws, there were still angry pockets of resistance to full civil rights for black Americans. Voters were still turned away from polls, and there was a mass arrest of workers in the voter registration campaign in Selma, Alabama. To protest these arrests, Dr. King led a group in a march from Selma to Montgomery. The marchers were turned back by state troopers with tear gas, clubs and whips, and the National Guard had to be called out to protect the participants before the march could be completed.

The cost of nonviolent resistance was high. Many of the younger black militants in the movement were beginning to wonder if the cost was not too high. In 1963 NAACP leader Medgar Evers was shot to death outside his home; four black children were killed when a bomb was thrown into a black church in Birmingham. In 1968 Dr. Martin Luther King was murdered. By the time of Dr. King's death, the swing from a nonviolent to a violent revolution had already begun.

The fight for civil rights had moved from the rural South to the ghettos of the Northern cities. By 1960 more than half of the nation's black citizens lived outside the Deep South, and 96 percent of the blacks living in the North lived in the big cities. Most of them lived a substandard existence, lagging far behind white Americans in income, housing, education and employment opportunities.

358

The new, more militant black leaders like Floyd Mc-Kissick, Roy Innis and Stokely Carmichael began to feel the only way to achieve equality in America was through "black power." It was a phrase that sounded new and frightening to many Americans.

However, as early as 1826 David Walker had written, "We must and shall be free—and woe, woe, will be to you, if we have to obtain our freedom by fighting." Frederick Douglass, an early advocate of black power, stated that "those who profess to favor freedom and yet deprecate agitation, are men who want crops without plowing up the ground . . . power concedes nothing without demand."

To most black Americans, black power simply meant economic and political power. But to many white Americans, especially after the explosion of racial riots in 1965 and 1966 in Los Angeles, Detroit, Newark, Cleveland and Dayton that left parts of these cities in smoldering ruins, black power meant violence. And the new Black Panther Party, breathing open defiance of the white establishment, seemed to symbolize what many white Americans most feared.

The church, which had been a strong leader in the civil rights movement, was unable to halt the swing toward violence or control the young black militants. For a while a new religious sect, the Black Muslims, led by Elijah Muhammad and incorporating some of Marcus Garvey's ideas on black nationalism and black pride, seemed destined to become a new leader in the movement.

Malcolm X (who renamed himself Al Hajj Malik al-Shabazz after making a holy pilgrimage to Mecca) was a brilliant organizer and publicist for the Black Muslims. His rapid rise to fame brought him enemies, however, and he was killed shortly after he started his own Organization for Afro-American Unity. His writings and philosophy are still studied by many young black Americans.

In his early career Malcolm X believed in segregation of the races and the inherent evil of all white men. By the time of his death, however, he had begun to modify his views, believing that integration was not completely impossible and that not all white men were evil.

For the black American, as with Malcolm X, the question has always been: Should black men and women make their own way, form their own distinctive channel, or should they join with the mainstream of American history and culture? As early as 1897 Du Bois saw the problem and wrote: "Here, then, is the dilemma—am I an American or am I a Negro? Can I be both?" This "twoness" has had to be faced by artists, authors, scientists, black men and women in all fields of endeavor. Are they black artists first or simply American artists? Should the black author write only on black subjects or on subjects of interest to all Americans?

Today it is difficult to tell which direction the civil rights movement will take and who will be the new leaders—politicians, labor leaders, professors or clergymen? Whether or not the black church regains its leadership in the movement, a visit to the historic black churches still in existence throughout the country will show that the black American has a proud, religious tradition.

And no matter which direction the black revolution takes, the revolution in one form or another, violent or nonviolent, will continue. There can be no turning back. Too many Americans, black and white, have suffered and died, as bravely as any soldier in battle, in the cause of the revolution. Although there are few monuments to these martyred dead, as long as black and white Americans struggle and work together for equal justice and liberty for all, then they have not died in vain.

GRAVE OF MARIE LAVEAU, VOODOO QUEEN

Although discouraged by slaveholders, African religious rituals persisted in the New Orleans of the 1800s. A black woman by the name of Marie Laveau was well known throughout the city for her "voodoo powers." The actual voodoo rites were kept secret, and the worshipers would meet far back in a swamp near the lake end of Bayou St. John. By allowing slaves to hold their dances at Congo Square, the authorities hoped to discourage the secret rites of voodoo, but Marie Laveau lived only a half-block from Congo Square. Voodoo meetings, with their wild, uninhibited dancing, were often held in her own backyard.

In her old age, Marie Laveau returned to the Catholic Church. She gave her money to the poor and brought what comfort she could to men and women in the prisons of New Orleans.

Today so-called voodoo powders may still be bought in shops in the old quarters of New Orleans. Devotees still bring gifts of food and money, especially on St. John's Eve, June 23rd, to Marie Laveau's grave and scrawl red cross marks across the concrete slab grave marker.

Location: Marie Laveau's grave is in St. Louis Cemetery No. 2, North Claiborne Avenue and Bienville Street, New Orleans, Louisiana.

MUSEE CONTI MUSEUM OF WAX

This fascinating museum recreates in wax figures the exciting history and legends of New Orleans. One scene shows Marie Laveau, the Voodoo Queen, in her cottage receiving a "client"

361

who needs assistance in solving a problem. Another scene shows the voodoo dancers performing. Still other scenes show a slave auction and the infamous home of Madame Lalaurie, who treated her slaves so cruelly that she was run out of New Orleans. Her house at 1140 Royal Street is still known today as the Haunted House. The museum also has scenes from the jazz days of New Orleans.

Location: Musee Conti Museum of Wax, 917 Conti Street, New Orleans, Louisiana.

Admission charge.

AMERICAN MUSEUM OF NATURAL HISTORY

Many museums with African collections have exhibits that interpret the various African tribal religions. One with a particularly interesting display on the religions of Africa is the American Museum of Natural History in New York City. For more information on this museum—and other museums with outstanding African collections—see Chapter One.

It is difficult to determine the exact age of many black churches in America. The records have often been lost or destroyed and a church may have moved several times before locating in its permanent building. The following, therefore, is a select list of historic black churches or congregations still in existence today.

MOTHER BETHEL A.M.E. CHURCH

One of the oldest black churches in America, Mother Bethel A.M.E. Church was founded by Richard Allen, who opened the church doors in 1794. The land on which the church stands is the oldest parcel of real estate owned continuously by black people in the United States.

The first Mother Bethel A.M.E. church was a blacksmith shop, but the third and present church, built in 1841, is of brick and stone. Richard Allen became the first bishop of the African Methodist Episcopal Church in 1816.

From the pulpit of the Mother Bethel A.M.E. Church many prominent abolitionists spoke out against slavery, among them Lucretia Mott, Frederick Douglass and William Still. Escaped slaves were sheltered, fed and clothed in the basement of the church.

Today the lower level of the present church, completely renovated in 1890, contains the tomb of Bishop Richard Allen and a museum where the pulpit built by Richard Allen, his Bible, prayer stool chair and other historical articles are on display.

Location: 419 South 6th Street, Philadelphia, Pennsylvania.

MT. PISGAH A.M.E. CHURCH

In 1792 black and white worshipers held their church services together in homes and outdoors under trees in the small town of Lawnside, New Jersey. A Methodist church was built about 1800, and after 1815, when the white members withdrew, the Mount Pisgah Church still continued to grow, with only black members.

The church cemetery contains the graves of black veterans of many of the nation's wars, including a Navy veteran of the War of 1812 who served on the *U.S.S. Constitution.*

Location: Warwick and Mouldy Roads, Lawnside, New Jersey.

ST. ANDREW'S AFRICAN METHODIST EPISCOPAL CHURCH

The first A.M.E. church on the Pacific Coast was organized in 1850 and called St. Andrew's. The first public school for blacks, Indians and Orientals was held in the basement of the church. The present attractive church was built in 1951 at a cost of over $65,000.

In 1852 the second oldest A.M.E. church west of the Mississippi was located at 916 Laguna Street, San Francisco, California.

Location: 2131 Eighth Street, Sacramento, California.

MOTHER A.M.E. ZION CHURCH

The first church built in New York City by and for black Americans was the Mother A.M.E. Zion Church built in 1800 at 156 Church Street. The money for the land was do-

363

nated by Peter Williams, a slave whose Tory owner left America rather than support the Revolution. The church moved several times before coming to its present location.

A famous worshiper at the church, before the Civil War, was a woman known simply as Isabella. One day she stood up in the middle of a service and said that henceforth she would be known as Sojourner Truth. "Sojourner," she explained, "because I am a wanderer, Truth because God is Truth."

Location: 146 West 137th Street, New York, New York.

SPRINGFIELD BAPTIST CHURCH

The oldest black Baptist church still surviving today is the Springfield Baptist Church, formed by the Reverend Jessie Peters and George Liele in 1793. Because of his work with the church, George Liele was finally forced to leave the country. He settled in Jamaica.

An even earlier black Baptist church, the Silver Bluff Baptist Church of South Carolina, founded in 1783, is no longer in existence today.

Location: 114 12th Street, Augusta, Georgia.

FIRST BRYAN BAPTIST CHURCH

When George Liele was forced to leave the country, his work was continued by Andrew Bryan. At the end of the Revolutionary War, however, opposition rose in the South to black churches, and Bryan was imprisoned. After his release, he continued his missionary work, and the history of the First Bryan Baptist Church can be traced back to Bryan and the congregations he formed in Savannah.

There is a monument to Reverend George Liele at the church, and the church itself is dedicated to Andrew Bryan.

Location: 559 West Bryan Street, Savannah, Georgia.

OLD AFRICAN MEETING HOUSE

The Old African Meeting House was originally built in 1804 as a Baptist church. However, the church soon became a meeting house for the black community settling the North

Slope of Beacon Hill. When William Lloyd Garrison was refused the use of Faneuil Hall for meetings of his abolitionist group, the meetings were held at the Old African Meeting House. Soon the building began to be called "The Abolitionist Church." The building remained an active Baptist church until the early 1900s, when it was sold to a Jewish congregation as a synagogue.

In 1971 the Museum of Afro-American History acquired the Meeting House as a permanent home for its exhibits relating to Afro-American history and art. The Black Heritage Tour sponsored by the museum begins at the Old African Meeting House. Arrangements for visits to the museum and guided walking tours must be made in advance with the curator of the museum. For more information about the Black Heritage Trail, see Chapter One.

Location: Smith Court, Boston, Massachusetts.

DEXTER AVENUE BAPTIST CHURCH

It was from the pulpit of this church that Dr. Martin Luther King, Jr., a very new pastor of the church, preached his philosophy of passive resistance and nonviolence in the Montgomery bus boycott of 1954. However, the Dexter church and its leaders had been in the forefront of the civil rights movement even before the arrival of Dr. King.

The original Dexter Avenue Church, organized in 1878, held its meetings in a building once used as a slave-trading pen. It was known as the slave pen church. Carpenters in the congregation built the frame structure of the first church on the present site on Dexter Avenue. From the horror of the slave pen has risen a church that became a beacon light in the struggle of the black race against oppression.

Location: Dexter Avenue, Montgomery, Alabama

ABYSSINIAN BAPTIST CHURCH

Thomas Paul began the movement toward establishing independent black Baptist churches in the United States. He first organized a congregation of free blacks in Boston, then in 1808 he formed a separate black Baptist congregation in New

365

York, which became known as the Abyssinian Baptist Church. One of the well-known leaders of this church was Adam Clayton Powell, Sr., who became pastor in 1908. Today the church has the largest black congregation of any church in the world. In 1921 the church moved to its present location and built a magnificent Gothic structure of New York bluestone. Reverend Powell's son, Adam Clayton Powell, Jr., became pastor of the church after his father's retirement. During his controversial career, he became a member of the United States Congress, in addition to being pastor of the Abyssinian Baptist Church.

Location: 138 West 138th Street, New York, New York.

SECOND BAPTIST CHURCH

One of the oldest Baptist churches in the North is the Second Baptist Church in Detroit. Although organized in 1836, the congregation could not afford to build a permanent building until 1857. There is a marker in front of the present church commemorating the first celebration of the Emancipation Proclamation in Detroit, which was held at this church on January 6, 1863.

Location: 441 Monroe, corner of Beaubien, Detroit, Michigan.

ST. THOMAS EPISCOPAL CHURCH

When Richard Allen withdrew from St. George's Methodist Church rather than sit in segregated pews, Absalom Jones was among those who left with him. While Richard Allen formed the Mother Bethel A.M.E. Church, Absalom Jones formed the African Episcopal Church of St. Thomas. The congregation was formed in 1791, and St. Thomas formally opened its doors in 1794, receiving a charter from the State of Pennsylvania in 1796. Thus St. Thomas Church became the first and oldest incorporated body of blacks in the United States.

Like Richard Allen, Absalom Jones had been born a slave, and through hard work purchased his wife's freedom and later his own. With Richard Allen, they formed the Free African So-

366

ciety and helped raise a company of militia to defend Philadelphia against the British in the War of 1812.

The church has moved several times in its long history. It has faced many problems, including a disastrous fire; but St. Thomas Church is still very much in existence today, almost 200 years after it was first established.

Location: 52nd and Parrish streets, Philadelphia, Pennsylvania.

ST. PHILIP'S EPISCOPAL CHURCH

After the Revolutionary War, the original members of St. Philip's worshipped in primarily white Trinity Parish. Then, refusing to be segregated, they secured their own separate place of worship in 1810, and in 1818 built the first St. Philip's Episcopal Church on Centre Street in New York.

The congregation moved into its present building in 1911, and today St. Philip's is one of the leading Episcopal congregations in the United States.

Location: 134th Street, west of Seventh Avenue, New York, New York.

FIRST PRESBYTERIAN CHURCH

One of the earliest black Presbyterian churches in America, the original building of the First Presbyterian Church was dedicated in 1822. The second, and present, church was dedicated in 1860. Names of all the ministers who have served this church are recorded on plaques in the sanctuary. The marker was erected on the 150th anniversary of the church.

Location: Huntsville, Alabama.

15TH STREET PRESBYTERIAN CHURCH

The 15th Street Presbyterian Church was launched in 1841 by an ex-slave schoolmaster in Washington, D.C., John F. Cook. The church has had many outstanding leaders, including the Reverend Henry Highland Garnet, an abolitionist and powerful antislavery speaker. One of his most famous sermons was "Let Your Motto Be Resistance." Another well-known minis-

367

ter was the Reverend Francis J. Grimke, who was active in forming the NAACP.

The present church building was erected in 1917; the church is still very active in the community.

Location: 15th and R streets, N.W., Washington, D.C.

ST. FRANCIS XAVIER'S CATHOLIC CHURCH

As early as 1798 Reverend Louis W. DuBourg was giving instruction in the Catholic faith to black men and women in Baltimore, Maryland; but it wasn't until 1863 that the first church for primarily black Catholics in America was founded —St. Francis Xavier. From this parish of the Josephite Missions, priests were sent to establish black missions in other cities.

The first black priest to be ordained in the United States, Father Charles Randolph Uncles, was a member of this parish. After he became a priest, he celebrated his first solemn high mass at St. Francis Xavier on Christmas Day, 1891.

Location: 1007 North Caroline Street, Baltimore, Maryland.

FATHER PATRICK FRANCIS HEALY AND GEORGETOWN UNIVERSITY

The son of a slave mother and a wealthy Irish father, Father Healy became the first black president of an American Catholic University when he became rector of Georgetown University in 1874. Under his leadership, this historic university was greatly expanded. The building which today houses the administration offices of the college is named in honor of Father Healy, who is buried in the Jesuit campus cemetery.

Father Healy's brother, James Augustus Healy, was the first Catholic bishop of African descent in the United States.

Location: 37th and O streets, N.W., Washington, D.C.

WYANDOT MISSION

Among the early religious missionaries who wanted to convert the Indians of America to Christianity was a black missionary, John Stewart. Although poor and uneducated, he had a fine singing voice. After his own conversion to Christianity at a Methodist prayer meeting, he made his way north to

368

Ohio in 1816, working among the Wyandot Indians at Upper Sandusky. So successful was John Stewart's mission that a church was built among the Wyandots as a result of his labors. The church, restored in 1889, is today a Methodist Historical Shrine. John Stewart's grave is on the mission grounds.

Location: East Church Street, Upper Sandusky, Ohio.

MUHAMMAD'S TEMPLES OF ISLAM

One of the newest—and most controversial—religions on the black American scene was begun in the 1930s by Elijah Poole of Georgia, who claimed to have met "Allah on earth" and later renamed himself Elijah Muhammad. As much a political and social movement as a religious one, the religion stresses the Mohammadan belief in Allah as the true God and the separation of the black and white races.

Temple No. 1 was created in Detroit in 1931, and today there are temples and mosques in every major city in the country. An offshoot of the Muslim religion are the more than fifty schools where black Muslim children and adults receive instruction.

Location: The Headquarters for the Universities of Islam, as they are called, is Chicago's Temple No. 2, 7351 South Stony Island, Chicago, Illinois. Visitors to the temples and schools of the Black Muslim must follow the strict dress codes of the Temples of Islam.

MARTIN LUTHER KING, JR., MEMORIAL SITES

Dr. King was assassinated in Memphis, Tennessee, on April 4, 1968, and his funeral was held at Atlanta, Georgia. Thousands of mourners followed the simple mule-drawn wagon that carried Dr. King's coffin from Ebenezer Church through the streets of Atlanta. Originally laid to rest in South View Cemetery, Dr. King's grave was later moved to a site adjacent to the Ebenezer Baptist Church, in the area of Atlanta where Dr. King was born and reared. His marble crypt is inscribed with words from an old slave spiritual: "Free at last, free at last, thank God Almighty, I'm free at last."

The Martin Luther King, Jr., Center for Social Change in

Atlanta has been entrusted with building a permanent memorial to Dr. King and continuing the work for nonviolent social change and justice that Dr. King had begun.

The memorial plans include a four-block area which will enclose the modest wooden house in which Dr. King was born, the Ebenezer Baptist Church, the landscaped crypt next to the church, a community center and memorial park, as well as the offices of the Center itself.

At present the crypt area is open to the public, as is Dr. King's home at 501 Auburn Avenue. Visitors on Sunday are welcome to attend services at Ebenezer Baptist Church, 413 Auburn Avenue, N.E. The Center for Social Change is presently located at 671 Beckwith Street, S.W., Atlanta, near Atlanta University, and may be visited by the public. It is hoped the complete memorial to Dr. King will be finished by 1976, the 200th anniversary of America.

Location: The Memorial Site will be bound by Edgewood Avenue, Boulevard, Irwin and Jackson Streets, in Atlanta, Georgia.

W. E. B. DU BOIS MEMORIAL PARK

W. E. B. Du Bois was born on Church Street in Great Barrington, Massachusetts, on February 23, 1868. One of the most influential and profound thinkers and authors of twentieth-century America, the views of Du Bois were often too controversial and far-reaching to be accepted in the time he was most active. In 1961, at the age of ninety-three, Du Bois moved to Ghana, Africa.

In 1969 a five-acre park in Great Barrington, supposedly on the site where his grandparents once lived, was dedicated and named in honor of W. E. B. Du Bois. Within the wooded park area there is a ten-ton boulder upon which a bronze plaque has been placed.

Location: Great Barrington, Massachusetts.

MEDGAR EVERS GRAVESITE

Medgar Evers, a leader in the civil rights movement in Mississippi, was slain outside his home in Jackson, Mississippi, on June 12, 1963. He is buried at Arlington National Cemetery among the graves of many other Americans who fought and died to preserve the highest ideals of this country.

Three of the best-known grave sites in this cemetery are the Tomb of the Unknown Soldier and the graves of President John F. Kennedy and his brother Robert. On the day that Medgar Evers was buried, President Kennedy forwarded to Congress a bill guaranteeing equal rights in public accommodations and giving the Attorney General the power to sue for enforcement of the Fourteenth and Fifteenth amendments. The Attorney General at the time was Robert Kennedy.

Location: Arlington National Cemetery, Arlington, Virginia, directly across the Potomac River from Washington, D.C.

Visitors must obtain a temporary pass to drive into the cemetery at the Visitors Center.

MALCOLM X COLLEGE

Malcolm X, before and after his death in 1965, had become the greatest hero of modern times for many black youths. Militant in his approach toward gaining political, economic and social freedom for black Americans, he gave them hope for the future and pride in their race.

In 1969 a junior college in Chicago was renamed Malcolm X College, in his honor. The Carter G. Woodson Library in the college, with a collection of 50,000 volumes, has given special emphasis to books by and about black people. The Art Gallery displays works of professional artists and students. In addition to regular college courses, the college has an outstanding black studies program.

Location: Malcolm X College, 1900 West Van Buren Street, Chicago, Illinois.

DETROIT HISTORICAL MUSEUM

The "Detroit Story" exhibit in this museum includes much material on the growth and development of Detroit's black community. One of the important black personages shown in the exhibit is Fannie M. Richards, the city's first black schoolteacher and a fighter for equal rights in the 1870s and 1880s.

371

The museum also has an exhibit about local black sports heroes who have gone on to national fame, people like Joe Louis, Thomas Tolan, Willis Ward and others.

Location: Detroit Historical Museum, 5401 Woodward Avenue, Detroit, Michigan.

No admission charge.

NATIONAL BASEBALL HALL OF FAME AND MUSEUM, INC.

A new type of civil right was won by a black man in 1947 when Jackie Robinson became the first black player in major-league baseball. Before his acceptance by the Brooklyn Dodgers, black baseball players played on all-black teams. For many sports fans, the admittance of a black baseball player into the batter's box of a national team was as important as admittance of ballots into the voting box.

After Jackie Robinson broke the color barrier, black athletes came quickly to the fore in other major sports, although they had been breaking records even before that time in college track and field events, basketball and football.

The National Baseball Museum exhibits memorabilia of famous baseball players, and the Hall of Fame wing features outstanding baseball players who, over the years, have become the "great" players in baseball. There is also a section in the museum devoted to the old Negro Leagues.

Black ballplayers featured in the museum are Jackie Robinson, Monte Irvin, Josh Gibson, Satchel Paige, and others.

Location: National Baseball Hall of Fame and Museum, Inc., Cooperstown, New York.

Admission charge.

ST. LOUIS SPORTS HALL OF FAME

This live-action museum of St. Louis sports history includes all sports, but in large part tells the story of baseball in St. Louis. The room honoring players of the St. Louis Cardinal team has larger than life-size pictures of famous black Cardinal baseball players.

Location: St. Louis Sports Hall of Fame, Busch Memorial Stadium, between gates 5 and 6, St. Louis, Missouri.

Admission charge.

372

NATIONAL PRO FOOTBALL HALL OF FAME

Dedicated in 1963, and expanded in 1970, the Pro Football Hall of Fame offers something of interest for every football fan of every team and every age. The Hall of Fame area includes both black and white football "greats," as well as a dramatic exhibit area. The visitor can also listen to sound recordings and watch motion pictures of outstanding pro football events.

Location: 2121 Harrison Street, N.W., next to Fawcett Stadium, Canton, Ohio.

Admission charge.

The African people had strong tribal religions before the arrival of Christianity in the sixteenth century. They believed in one major god, as well as lesser gods. A guide at the American Museum of Natural History, New York, is explaining to a group of young students the religious cult that fosters the Leopard Man, lurking high in a tree in the Hall of Man in Africa. The Leopard Man is called upon to serve the tribe in times of crisis. COURTESY AMERICAN MUSEUM OF NATURAL HISTORY, NEW YORK

African artists, just like European artists, were involved in creating religious works of art to decorate their altars, sacred temples and ancestral shrines. A young visitor to the Anacostia Museum, Washington, D.C., studies a Yoruba altarpiece (from Nigeria). COURTESY ANACOSTIA NEIGHBORHOOD MUSEUM

In some areas of America, remnants of the African religion lingered among the black people. In New Orleans in the early 1800s, voodoo priestess Marie Laveau, whose grave is shown *above*, was well known for her powers to heal the sick, cure the lovelorn, and put a hex or *gris-gris* on one's enemies. Believers still visit her grave in New Orleans today. PHOTO COURTESY PIERRE LEPRE.

After the Nat Turner and other slave revolts in the South in the 1830s, slave owners discouraged church services for black people unless there were white people present. In the picture above, a plantation owner and his family attend a local religious service to make sure no "insurrection" is taught from the pulpit. ILLUSTRATED LONDON NEWS, DECEMBER 5, 1863

In New England the fear of black ministers teaching revolt was not as strong as in the South because there were fewer black people and slaves in the North. In Vermont one black minister, Lemuel Haynes, preached to white congregations as well as black. This painting of Reverend Haynes preaching in the Old First Church may be seen in the Bennington Museum, Bennington, Vermont. PAINTING COURTESY OF THE BENNINGTON MUSEUM, INC., BENNINGTON, VERMONT

Not all Northern churches welcomed black ministers or members. In most churches, black members of the congregation were segregated in the rear of the church. In 1794, refusing to worship in white, segregated churches, Richard Allen and his friends started the Mother Bethel A.M.E. Church in Philadelphia. COURTESY MOTHER BETHEL A.M.E. CHURCH

Most early black congregations began their churches in whatever makeshift building they could find, above stables or in stores. The first home of the Mother Bethel A.M.E. Church, begun by Bishop Richard Allen, was in a blacksmith shop. Its second home, seen *above*, was built in 1805 of roughcast stone. COURTESY MOTHER BETHEL A.M.E. CHURCH

Absalom Jones, like Richard Allen, refused to worship in a segregated church. In 1791 he founded the first African Episcopal church in America, called the St. Thomas African Episcopal Church, still located in Philadelphia. This portrait of Reverend Absalom Jones by Raphaelle Peale hangs in the National Portrait Gallery, Washington, D.C. COURTESY NATIONAL PORTRAIT GALLERY, THE SMITHSONIAN INSTITUTION, WASHINGTON, D.C.

The present Mother Bethel A.M.E. Church, *at left*, was dedicated in Philadelphia in 1890. Although there have been four Mother Bethel A.M.E. church buildings, since 1794, they have all been built on the same site, making this parcel of land the oldest piece of real estate in America owned continuously by black people. COURTESY MOTHER BETHEL A.M.E. CHURCH

In the nineteenth century missionaries tried to convert Indian tribes to Christianity. One of these early and most successful missionaries was John Stewart, a black man, who worked among the Wyandot Indians in northern Ohio. The Wyandot Mission he founded is today a Methodist Shrine. COURTESY WYANDOT METHODIST MISSIONARY SHRINE

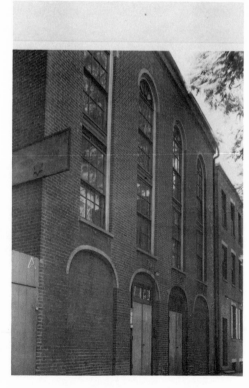

Black Baptist churches had begun in the South as early as 1773. In the North the first black Baptist church was built in Boston in 1804 and called the African Meeting House. In the 1900s the church became a Jewish synagogue, and today the old African Meeting House, shown *at right*, is being restored at the Museum of Afro-American History. COURTESY MUSEUM OF AFRO-AMERICAN HISTORY, BOSTON

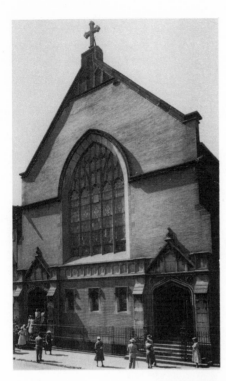

The first black Episcopal church was the St. Thomas Episcopal in Philadelphia, built in 1791. In New York in 1810, refusing to worship in segregated Trinity Parish, a black Episcopal congregation founded St. Philip's Episcopal Church. The present church, seen *above*, was built in 1911. COURTESY ST. PHILIP'S CHURCH

It was at the Dexter Avenue Baptist Church, shown *above*, that the first meetings were called by black citizens of Montgomery, Alabama, on December 2, 1955, to organize the bus boycott. The boycott was, in effect, the opening shot of the great Civil Rights Revolution of the 1950s and 1960s. COURTESY DEXTER AVENUE BAPTIST CHURCH

Dr. Martin Luther King, Jr., was the very new pastor of the Dexter Avenue Baptist Church at the time of the Montgomery bus boycott. By the time of his assassination in 1968, he had become one of the best-known civil rights leaders in the country. Eventually his grave site in Atlanta, Georgia, will be part of a permanent memorial area, including his family home, church, and the Martin Luther King, Jr., Center for Social Change. PHOTO BY BUD SKINNER

Shown *below* is the unveiling of the Dr. Martin Luther King, Jr., portrait, which will hang in the Georgia State Capitol Building in Atlanta. It is the first time a portrait of a black American leader has been hung in the Georgia State Capital. With Mrs. Coretta King at the unveiling is Governor Jimmy Carter of Georgia. PHOTO BY BUD SKINNER

This portrait by Laura Wheeler Waring of W. E. B. DuBois, one of the great black historians, authors and civil rights leaders, hangs in the National Portrait Gallery, The Smithsonian Institution, Washington, D.C. COURTESY NATIONAL PORTRAIT GALLERY, THE SMITHSONIAN INSTITUTION, WASHINGTON, D.C.

In honor of Malcolm X, the young black leader who symbolized for many black people their never-ending quest for political, economic and social equality, a junior college in Chigago was renamed the Malcolm X College. COURTESY CITY COLLEGES OF CHICAGO

Black athletes won a civil right of a different sort when baseball player Jackie Robinson was accepted as a player by the Brooklyn Dodgers in 1947. Robinson broke ground for other black baseball players who followed him into the major leagues. Shown is Bob Gibson, a member of the St. Louis Cardinals, whose portrait may be seen in the St. Louis Sports Hall Museum, St. Louis, Missouri. PHOTO FROM RICHARD J. LYNCH

Although black football players were on the professional sports scene from 1919 to 1933, they did not enter professional football again until 1946. Marion Motley was one of the first black football players to enter the ranks of professional football in that year with the Cleveland Browns. The drawing of Marion Motley, *above,* appears in his niche at the Pro Football Hall of Fame, Canton, Ohio. COURTESY PRO FOOTBALL HALL OF FAME, CANTON, OHIO

Geographical
Index

385

388

390

391

Index

393

398

400

402